Banking Regulation and the Financial Crisis

This book is a review on the economic theories of systemic risks in the financial market and the topics in constructing the macroprudential framework for banking regulation in the future. It explains the reasons why the traditional microprudential regulatory framework missed its target in stabilizing the market and preventing the crisis, and discusses the principles and instruments for designing macroprudential rules.

The first part of this book is dedicated to the analysis of systemic risks, which were largely missing in the design of traditional banking regulation. It shows how financial instability emerges from the changing intermediation structure and increasing product complexities, and how systemic risks arise from the banks' endogenous collective risk taking. It explains how market stress is amplified through the damaging leverage cycle, the network effects, and the feedback with the real economy. The book argues that the future banking regulation should be based on the macroprudential approach that takes into account the systemic risks as well as the feedback mechanism between the regulated institutions and the regulatory policies, and provides a framework for efficiency analysis.

This book takes the endogenous approach to better understanding the sources of the systemic risks in the financial market, the origin of the financial crisis, and the failure of traditional framework of banking regulation in maintaining financial stability. It emphasizes the strategic responses of the financial institutions to regulatory policies, and contributes to the construction of macroprudential rules for managing systemic risks.

Jin Cao is an Advisor of the Research Department, Financial Stability Wing of Norges Bank, Oslo.

Routledge international studies in money and banking

Banking Regulation and the Financial Crisis

Jin Cao

Routledge
Taylor & Francis Group

LONDON AND NEW YORK

First published 2012
by Routledge
2 Park Square, Milton Park, Abingdon, Oxfordshire OX14 4RN

Simultaneously published in the USA and Canada
by Routledge
711 Third Avenue, New York, NY 10017

First issued in paperback 2014

Routledge is an imprint of the Taylor & Francis Group, an informa business

British Library Cataloguing in Publication Data
A catalogue record for this book is available from the British Library

Library of Congress Cataloging in Publication Data
Cao, Jin, 1977–
Banking regulation and the financial crisis / Jin Cao.
    p. cm.
    1. Banks and banking. 2. Financial services industry–Risk management.
    3. Banking law. 4. Global Financial Crisis, 2008–2009. I. Title.
    HG1615.C36 2011
    332.1–dc23   2011034938

ISBN 978-0-415-60780-3 (hbk)
ISBN 978-1-138-79867-0 (pbk)
ISBN 978-0-203-12698-1 (ebk)

Typeset in Times New Roman
by Wearset Ltd, Boldon, Tyne and Wear

Contents

Preface

This book is a review on the economic theories of systemic risks in the financial market, and topics in constructing the macroprudential framework for banking regulation. I hope this book can shed some light on the recent debates of reconstructing finance, but I am also fully aware of my limit: there are fast increasing theoretical findings on the legacy of the recent global financial crisis, and the effort in building up the new global standard in banking regulation just took off. Therefore, I am very looking forward to the constructive critiques from the readers.

In writing this book, I owe much debt to my advisor and co-author, Professor Gerhard Illing, for his enormous effort in teaching, guidance, and discussions. I thank my co-advisor, Professor Ted Temzelides, who made many insightful comments on the early drafts of several chapters. I owe many thanks to Douglas Gale, Antoine Martin, Tommaso Monacelli, Lars Norden, Rafael Repullo, Jean-Charles Rochet, Marti G. Subrahmanyam, and Uwe Vollmer, among many others, for very useful comments on some chapters in various seminars and conferences. I thank my former colleagues in the Department of Economics, University of Munich, and my colleagues in Norges Bank, for their numerous very helpful discussions and suggestions during writing this book. I gratefully acknowledge financial support at the Munich Graduate School of Economics (MGSE) from the German Research Foundation (DFG) through GRK 801. The views expressed in this book are completely from myself, and should not be interpreted as reflecting those of Norges Bank.

Special thanks go to editors Thomas Sutton and Louisa Earls at Routledge. Without their strong support and generous help, writing this book is hardly possible.

Jin Cao
Oslo, Norway

Abbreviations

ABS	asset-backed securities
AIG	American International Group
CDO	collateralized debt obligations
CDS	credit default swaps
CoCo	contingent convertible debt
CoVaR	Conditional/Contributing Value-at-Risk
DSGE	dynamic stochastic general equilibrium
ECB	European Central Bank
ES	expected shortfall
FDA	Food and Drug Administration
MBS	mortgage-backed securities
MES	marginal expected shortfall
SES	systemic expected shortfall
SPV	special purpose vehicle
VaR	Value-at-Risk

Introduction

In 2007–2009 the world has seen the severest financial crisis since the Great Depression. The crisis erupted after years of lax monetary policy, financial deregulation, global imbalance, and financial innovation, which made more households and entrepreneurs accessible to cheap credit and share the prosperity of the Great Moderation, while the financial institutions more exposed to each other and vulnerable to aggregate shocks. The crisis started from the bursting of housing bubbles, liquidity dried up nearly completely as a response to doubts about the quality of subprime mortgage-backed securities. Despite massive central bank interventions, the liquidity freeze did not melt away, but rather spread slowly to other markets such as those for auction rate bonds, commercial paper, and money market mutual funds. At its peak, the collapse of big financial giants such as Lehman Brothers and American International Group (AIG) brought the global financial market into a systemic meltdown, and the bailout effort cost the taxpayers hundreds of billions of dollars. In the beginning of 2010, when the world economy just started to see some signs of recovery, several European economies slipped into another quagmire of public debt crisis. From the numerous US foreclosed homes to the nearly bankrupted arctic Norwegian towns, the mess left by the crisis needs to be cleaned up for many years to come.

Although history repeats, it is much too simple to conclude that the financial practitioners, regulators, and researchers were completely unconscious about the risks in the market and the crisis just happened to everyone's surprise. The fragility of the financial system, the principle–agent problems inherent in the market structure, the regulatory arbitrage that helps the banks get rid of the restrictions, had been intensively studied, and rich lessons had been taught by the previous crises. As early as the virtues of financial deregulation and innovation got their momentum and started to be triumphed all over the world, Minsky (1986) already warned of the devastating instabilities the Wall Street revolution brought. Many episodes in the classic on financial crash and failure, Kindleberger and Aliber (2005), much resemble the stories in the current world crisis. Taleb (2004, 2007) argued that the seemingly highly improbable disasters may actually easily arise in the contemporary financial system. Goodhart and Illing (2002) selected the studies on the sources of systemic risk and the central bank's role in mitigating the market stress. Allen and Gale (2007) is an excellent survey on how far researchers have understood the cause of financial crises; Rochet (2008) is a collection of the author's comprehensive studies on market failure, showing why the market discipline is not sufficient to maintain the financial stability and the system needs better regulation in an era of global deregulation. Had these voices been carefully listened to, the system stability could have been well maintained and the financial turbulence could have been controlled at a much lower cost.

Since the eruption of the crisis, there has been a wide variety of literature on the origin of the crisis and the lessons people can learn. Reinhart and Rogoff (2009) present the regularities of financial crises in the history: crises are usually companied by soaring pre-crisis credit expansion, government default, currency crises, and so on. Akerlof and Shiller (2009) tries to understand the origin of financial crisis from human behavior, a field that has been long neglected in financial economics. Brunnermeier (2009) shows how the "originate and distribute" banking model led to the explosion of credit, followed by the implosion of the banking system. Cooper (2008) argues that the financial bubbles before the crisis were much fueled by the central bank's too loose interest rate policy and light-touch regulation based on the belief of efficient market. Duffie (2011) presents the key role the big dealer banks played in the crisis and calls for better regulation on these systemically important institutions. Gorton (2008, 2009) rebuild the timeline of the crisis, showing how subprime lending changed the entire financial system and sowed the seeds of the Great Recession. Gorton (2010) explains what makes the current crisis different: the market turbulence and lending freeze much happened in the rather invisible shadow banking system which has gained the pivotal role in financial firms' funding in the past decade. A case study on the failure of Northern Rock, Shin (2009) unveiled the cause that is different from the media coverage: instead of being too much involved in securitization, the bank's difficulty much came from its strong reliance on short-term borrowing. Tirole (2009) examines all the myths of liquidity – the origin, the demand and supply of liquidity, and liquidity in the crisis – and provides the reasons why liquidity disappeared suddenly when the panic started. Besides studying any specific institutional failure, a lot of recent work also questions the entire financial system at work, such as Krugman (2009), Lewis (2010), Posner (2009), Rajan (2010), Roubini and Mihm (2010), Sinn (2010), Stiglitz (2010), just name a few.

The crisis also stimulated the fast growing literature on rebuilding the financial system out of the debris. Wolf (2008), the Geneva Report (Brunnermeier *et al.*, 2009), the NYU Reports (Acharya and Richardson, 2009, Acharya *et al.*, 2010a, 2011), the LSE Report (Turner *et al.*, 2010), the Squam Lake Report (French *et al.*, 2010), Blinder (2010), among the others, already build comprehensive frameworks and key principles for restructuring the financial system and regulating the financial market. Shin and Morris (2008) shows how regulatory rules can serve as equilibrium selection devices for the desirable outcomes. Rochet (2010) suggests that the current crisis implies both philosophical and methodological changes, from a microprudential toward a more macroprudential perspective in the future regulation. Bank of England (2009) poses the thoughts of using capital or taxation surcharges to tame the systemically important institutions. Tirole *et al.* (2010) investigate the incentive problems in the financial sector, raising proposals for better capital structure and corporate governance in the banks.

This book is not written as a complete review on the origin of financial crises and the tools for banking regulation. Rather, the author attempts to summarize the new developments in economic theories for better understanding the new concerns on financial stability, and the lessons the regulators can learn from the current crisis. In the first part of this book, we present the systemic risks arising from the fast changing financial market structure and examine to what extent the existing economic theories explain the new features in the recent crisis. Especially, we focus on the externalities, network effects, procyclical leverage fluctuations, etc. – the flaws that the financial market fails to correct by itself and need to be fixed by external disciplines and rules. Based on these findings, the second part of this book is dedicated to the discussions on the new challenges for better banking regulation.

Compared with the idiosyncratic risk in an individual financial firm, that is often easily identified and managed, the systemic risk – which is somewhat hidden but brings out devastating consequence when it gets revealed – has become a major concern for both practitioners and regulators in the past decade, and the recent crisis just demonstrated how poorly the policy maker knew about it. Although the term "systemic risk" now frequently appears in mass media, policy debates, as well as academic research, there is still no widely accepted definition for it. Various working definitions are listed in Dwyer (2009): although these definitions describe the phenomenon from different angles, they all point to some unique features of such risk; the risk inherent in the entire financial system is related to some common factor of the financial institutions, which is hardly identified merely on the micro level of the firms, while the co-movement of the financial market after some trigger event causes the disruption and dysfunction of the system. As is perceived by the practitioners as well as documented both by researchers and by supervisory authorities, the structural changes in the modern financial system have been raising the systemic risks; however, the fact was largely neglected by the regulatory agencies before the crisis. Since the identification of such risk relies on the systematic analysis and the market discipline based solution to minimize such risk is hardly available, there is a challenge for the regulators to switch their focus, from only monitoring the individual financial firm's health to having more weight on the stability of the entire financial system.

Systemic risk is more easily recognized at the time when it gets revealed than at the stage when it has been built up. Probably the best known revelation of the coordinated systemic disruption is the bank run phenomenon, which has existed throughout the entire history of banking. Chapter 1 reviews the classical textbook theory of bank run, but points out that in modern finance the run happens in a quite different manner. First, the phenomenon becomes universal to financial intermediaries of all categories, as long as the potential liquidity problem lives on the maturity mismatch – a fact that financial intermediaries finance their risky long-term assets by short-term borrowing. In this book, financial intermediaries are sometimes referred to as "banks" for simplicity. Second, the fact that modern banks rely more on the extremely short-term funding from the interbank market, an institution designed to avoid individual liquidity shortage, in fact increases the likelihood of a systemic liquidity dry-up, putting the entire financial system to a halt. The liquidity dry-up causes the fire sale of assets across the market, and to avoid such costly liquidation is therefore one of the key values of maintaining financial stability.

The systemic risk in the financial market is built up through the externalities, the network effects, etc., which are imposed on the system from the financial firms' behavior and not internalized in any individual financial institution's profit maximization calculus. Modern banks are highly interconnected through the financial network, making it much easier for a small ripple to propagate into a financial tsunami. Chapter 2 investigates several channels through which financial interconnectedness increases systemic risk. Local liquidity stress can spread through the market via lifting the overall borrowing cost in the interbank market or through the web of claims such that the counter parties in the network have to restructure their balance sheets which increases the probability of bank failure in the other part of the network. The chapter also addresses the increasing concern on the banks' "too-interconnected-to-fail" problem, where the banks *ex ante* intentionally build up connections as a bargaining chip against supervisory and regulatory authorities in the crisis – the moral hazard endogenously arising from the banking network.

A big part of bank run and banking network literature focuses on the evolution of bank failure; therefore, it is sufficient to model the financial intermediaries in a partial equilibrium framework where the banks' exposure to liquidity risks is taken as given. However, the partial equilibrium approach is much silent about the source of financial instability, since systemic risk arises as a result of the banks' coordinative failure to hedge against the aggregate shocks. Therefore, one can only uncover the root of systemic risk by endogenizing the banks' exposure in a general equilibrium framework. Only in the case where the market discipline and market mechanism fail to incentivize the banks to internalize the cost of maintaining the system stability, is there a role for the regulator to step in and intervene. A theory of the banks' endogenous exposure to systemic liquidity risk is presented in Chapter 3. The banking competition forces the banks to chase for yields, generating the incentive for some banks to free-ride on the other banks' provision of liquidity. The excessive risk taking raises the expected return for the banks in the orderly time, while leads to a complete liquidity dry-out in the downturn.

The modern financial system is also blamed as too complicated to penetrate. In the past decade, the growing complexity in the intermediation chain as well as the financial products substantially improved the market efficiency, made the assets more liquid, and significantly reduced the financing costs. Chapter 4 shows the caveats of increasing financial complexity. A simple securitization model demonstrates how computational complexity explodes as the financial products get complicated; the consequence is that the financial institutions have to rely on some assumptions that are abstract from the true risks, which leads to the loss in tracking the risks, raising the aggregate risk in the financial system. In addition, such complexity complicates the identification of the assets' quality and illiquidity, making the asset price more volatile when the signal of the assets' yields get revealed. Furthermore, the products' complexity in the financial market is also a strategic instrument of the financial firms to increase their monopolistic power – hence profit – which infringes the social welfare.

The systemic risk in the financial sector is amplified through the leverage–deleverage cycle in the banks' balance sheets, making the market even more vulnerable to the business cycles. The chase for yield incentive drives the banks fully leveraged up in the boom, which yields too much risk taking and leaves too thin capital buffers in the banks' balance sheets. This exacerbates the market stress in the bad time. Chapter 5 offers two reasons why such damaging leverage cycle comes into being. The first reason stems from the banks' risk management practice. In order to survive a reasonable worst possible scenario, a bank needs to hold an equity buffer in order to cushion against the potential loss. However, given that the bank's balance sheet is continuously market to market, its net worth – approximately equivalent to its equity value – varies with asset prices, too. This gives the bank a strong incentive to expand its balance sheet for higher profit when the asset price is high, which further increases the demand for assets, leading to an even higher asset price. Such self-fulfilling positive feedback also implies a vicious cycle in the bust. The second reason is due to the general equilibrium effect in the asset market. Because of the heterogeneous belief in the risky asset's return, the optimistic investors in the market become the borrowers, borrowing from the pessimistic ones using leverage. However, the business cycle alters the threshold separating these two groups of agents, hence the leverage and equilibrium asset price. In the downturn, the most optimistic agents get bankrupted, and the risky assets are owned by the investors with less willingness to pay and lower borrowing capacity, leading to an even lower equilibrium asset price. The leverage cycle and business cycle reinforce each other, making the economic slumps more damaging.

The financial turbulence is hardly separable from the macroeconomic fluctuations, and this is proved once again in the current crisis. The crisis triggered the Great Recession in the real economy, while output decline and soaring unemployment soon put the viability of the entire financial system under question. However, macroeconomics and finance have been for long time two rather isolated fields in economic research. Finance models usually have no concern about the aggregate outcome and the impact on real economy, and as for the macroeconomics workhorse, there is seldom a role for financial sector in the dynamic stochastic general equilibrium (DSGE) framework. Chapter 6 tries to bridge the gap. We show how financial frictions affect the real economy, and how the feedback from the business cycles exacerbates the financial stress. Although the research on financial applications in macroeconomic models is still in its infant stage, several channels have been successfully established for such macro-finance transmission mechanism. One of them is the financial accelerator effect: the financial friction in the economy arises from the costly state verification problem where the borrowers may lie on the return. To equilibrium is therefore associated with a probabilistic monitoring scheme that amplifies the credit constraints in the downturn. Another channel goes through the financial intermediaries' balance sheets. Because of the borrowing constraints out of the agency problem, the banks have to "skin in the game," combining the outside equity with inside equity for funding. The business cycle changes the banks' profit, making the borrowing constraints looser or tighter, and this further affects the investment as well as output in the real economy.

Financial stability is public good, and is hardly to be achieved solely by the market mechanism. This is the reason why regulation is crucial for a well functioning financial market, and is also a distinguished feature that makes financial regulation differ from the other regulatory policies. Taming the market power for consumer protection is only one aim of financial regulation; the even more important goal is to maintain financial stability. Since the cost of financial crises for the economy as a whole usually far outweighs the cost that financial sector takes to meet the regulatory rules, the regulator needs to have a systemic perspective when some bold and necessary measures need to be adopted.

The changing nature of financial intermediation and the associated systemic risk imply that the regulator must have more emphasis on macroprudential policies. Traditionally, the effort of financial supervisor and regulator was mostly exerted on the microprudential issues, i.e., the aims of the supervision and regulation were mainly restricting the market power of individual firms, monitoring the managerial practice through establishing better governance of each financial institution, improving every bank's likelihood of survival and protect the creditors via regulating the bank's capital buffer, and so on. The idea was that macro stability could be automatically achieved if micro fragilities were minimized. However, the crisis perfectly showed the fallacy in such approach. Before the crisis, the giant banks held much higher capital buffer than they were required, but this didn't avoid the entire banking sector going to the brink of bankruptcy; the financial institutions were supposed to keep their credit risks under control and remain liquid, but this didn't prevent the liquidity in the market from suddenly draining up completely. The key problem is, as has been presented in the first part of the book, that in a highly interconnected system each individual bank's behavior may impose externalities on the rest of the sector. Such externalities are not taken into account by any single bank's profit calculus and excessive risks thus are being built up when the market is in its upswing, while in the downside the entire market fails systemically. Therefore, beyond the concern of idiosyncratic risks in each financial institution, the financial regulator and supervisor now need to spend much effort on maintaining the stability of the system.

Both in research and practice establishing a macroprudential regulatory framework is still in progress; by the time the book is written many questions still lack answers and the details in regulatory design are still unclear. Instead of joining the policy debate, the second part of this book is rather dedicated to the discussions on the systemic risk indicators, macroprudential instruments, as well as the transmission mechanism of the regulatory rules, which may help researcher and regulators understand the micro incentives as responses to macroprudential policies and the macro effectiveness of various regulatory tools.

Chapter 7 presents the indictors that regulatory and supervisory authorities may use to measure the systemic risks, and the instruments targeting at maintaining financial stability. Since systemic risks arise with externalities and network effect in the financial market, the crucial indicator therefore turns out to be the systemic importance of the financial institutions. The direct policy response is to curb the risk taking incentives of the systemically important financial institutions. In addition, the damaging leverage cycle and the risk ridden financial complexities need to be managed as well. The regulators have to at least understand the banks' business before any regulatory policy is designed to tackle these problems.

However, inefficiency rises as more regulation is diverted toward directly supervising the banks' daily operation, since the regulators have less information and expertise than the banks in financial intermediation and the banks can always undo the policies by regulatory arbitrage. Just as in any nuclear power plant, a robust reactor pressure vessel alone does not guarantee the systemic stability, one also needs a companion mechanism for the defense in depth when the reactor failure cannot be completely insulated. In banking regulation, such mechanism works mostly through liquidity buffers and capital cushions. When one financial firm is under stress, such buffers and cushions make sure that the trouble will not spill over its counter parties and insulate the problem from the rest of the system. In addition, since the banks are required to hold the buffers *ex ante*, in the crisis they get "bailed in" by the resources they hold, avoiding the costly bailout bill paid by the taxpayers.

The regulatory liquidity buffers and capital cushions will be discussed in Chapters 8 and 9. The advantage of such rules and the components of the buffers have been relatively well understood so that this book will not cover these issues. Instead, this monograph will try to deal with the incentive problems associated with these policies, i.e., the feedback mechanism between the banks' risk taking and financial regulation.

The biggest trouble in banking regulation is the time inconsistency problem. Since the cost of a systemic collapse is too high, the regulator always has the incentive to step in and bail out the systemically important banks when they are in trouble. With such implicit guarantee, the banks have a strong incentive to engage in excess risk taking *ex ante*. In addition, the regulatory authority, usually the central bank, can only ease the liquidity stress via nominal tools instead of raising real resources. This implies an implicit real transfer to the troubled banks, which in fact penalizes those prudent ones who sat out of the gambling, encouraging moral hazard. As a result, the prudent banks are driven out of the market. The excessively risk taking banks thus choose to be "too-big-to-fail" or "too-interconnected-to-fail," holding the entire economy for ransom. Similar risk taking channels also put many recent regulatory proposals under question and suggests that much research still needs to be done before these new tools are really adopted in practice. Regulators have to understand the banks' incentives in order to make sure that the regulatory rules are indeed moral hazard proof. Regulators must look beyond current crisis in designing policies so that they will not simply be fighting the last war, but addressing market incentives to circumvent latest regulation.

Besides the effectiveness issue, another practical question is to evaluate the efficiency of various regulatory policies. There is inefficiency in all regulatory practice, companioned by the regulatory cost. Based on the models in the previous chapters, Chapter 9 establishes a quantitative framework so that one can see the benefit and cost of different regulatory regimes. The chapter also discusses the possibility of combining several rules for better efficiency.

The crisis in the past years left a rich legacy both for researchers and for regulators; research on many issues just starts to take off for better understanding the mechanisms, incentives, and finding the solution to preventing the next crisis. This book is a product of the author, during the long march exploring the unknowns. I sincerely wish it can shed some light on the current regulatory debates.

Part I

Externalities, network effects, and systemic risks

1 Unstable banking

There are many theories that justify the banks' role as financial intermediaries. In the typical stylized banking relationship, by intermediating the "investors," who have abundant financial resources but lack of the expertise of value producing, with the "entrepreneurs," who have the expertise of generating higher value added goods and service, the banks allocate the scarce resources to the sectors where such resources are best used, improving the social welfare. Here "investors" and "entrepreneurs" have wider meanings than the words themselves. The "investors" are owner of the resources, which can be depositors, pension funds, and so on; the "entrepreneurs" can be the entrepreneurs in the manufacturing firms, but can also be house owners who generate a steady cash flow from their mortgage repayments. Finally, "banks" in modern finance have many faces as well. A "bank" can be a traditional saving bank which takes deposits from individuals and issues loans to the firms, but it can also be an investment bank, a broker–dealer institution trading securities for its customers. There are more "shadow banks" such as money market funds, hedge funds, etc. Although they are not subject to the traditional banking regulatory rules, their role as financial intermediaries is much the same as that of the conventional banks. In the rest of this book, we take the wider view on the parties in the banking relationship. To simplify the discussions, most of the time we use the terms "investors," "entrepreneurs," and "bank" as the abstracts of these parties in the banking sector.

The banking system is unstable because of the bank runs. The high yield projects from the entrepreneur side are often long term; however, the investors' time preference of getting cash is not necessarily long term: they may want their cash back before the projects return, for example, when they want to consume early or redirect their money to some better investment opportunities. This creates a maturity mismatch: the banks' long assets have to be financed by the short borrowing, and the liquidity problem arises once the banks have difficulties in getting cash. When some of the investors – call them "early investors" – demand their money before the projects mature, the banks need to raise cash to meet the demand. Quite often, this means that the banks need to sell part of the long, illiquid assets, or to terminate the premature long-term projects. But such early liquidation usually does not return as much as the value if the projects mature: this reduces the expected return of the other investors (or, the "late investors") who would otherwise like to wait and encourages them to demand liquidity as well, leading to the bank run. We will start the chapter by briefly presenting the classical bank run model in Diamond and Dybvig (1983), which is the foundation of many models in this book.

However, "this time is different." The current crisis, the worst one since the Great Depression, though, is not featured by the long queues in front of the banks – there are only a few of them, Northern Rock being one of the most infamous (Shin (2009) provides an excellent survey of Northern Rock's failure) – but rather, is a "slap by the invisible hand" (Gorton, 2010), and the failure in the banking system this time is almost invisible to the outsiders. In modern finance, the sheer size repo market serves as the main financing resource for the banks, where the banks roll over their long-term debt by the very short-term repurchase agreements, subject to some haircuts. In the good time the repo market is fairly liquid and the haircut is next to nil. However, in the bad time, the banks cease to lend to each other and the haircuts get skyrocketed. The financing conduits are clogged and the entire financial system gets to halt. Instead of explicitly withdrawing deposits from the banks like in the traditional bank runs, the modern version of bank failure starts from the dysfunction of interbank market, or, the "run on the repos." This will be discussed in Section 1.2.

A bank run can be triggered by the fundamentals, i.e., it happens once the late investors figure out that they will not get the return as high as the early investors if they wait till the long projects mature, so that they will join the early investors and run on the bank. However, a bank run can also be triggered by the "sunspot," the bank run becomes a self-fulfilling equilibrium if the investors start running on an otherwise solvent bank. In Section 1.5 we further explore when and how such non-fundamental bank runs happen. Since bank run is a coordinated action of the investors, the questions turn out to be what is the device that coordinates the investors and how they respond together. The global game approach by Goldstein and Pauzner (2005) implies that the investors may coordinate on their private but imperfect signals about the bank's fundamentals. One individual late investor may want to demand liquidity early if her signal is poor, but whether she really does that depends on her inference on how likely the other late investors withdraw. The coordinative withdrawal, or the bank run, only happens when the private signal is lower than some threshold, or, when everyone believes that everyone else is going to run on the bank.

In such run-like phenomena much comes from the fact that financial contracts are often inflexible. For example, the typical deposit contracts are fixed demand contract, which allows the depositors to demand the full repayment at any time. Because of the first-come-first-served rule, the depositors will coordinate to run on the bank whenever they are suspicious about the bank's health. Should the contracts be renegotiatable or made contingent on the states of the world, or suspended when a bank run starts to happen, or should the deposit be fully insured, the costly bank runs could be completely avoided. Therefore, it is seemingly a puzzle why such inflexible contracts are still widely adopted. However, such fragile structure in banking is actually desirable for monitoring the banks' behavior. The reason why the banks are justified as financial intermediaries is that they have better expertise on collecting the returns of the projects from the entrepreneurs' side; however, such expertise opens the opportunity for the banks to abuse their special skills. Suppose that the financial contracts are flexible in the sense that the banks are allowed to renegotiate *ex post* with the investors on the repayments, the banks will always have the incentive to capture some private rent and the investors are made worse off. On the other hand, knowing that the banks won't keep their promises, the investors will decline to accept the banks' long assets for collateral; therefore, it is hardly possible for the banks to raise liquidity, using their illiquid assets as collateral. To make the contracts inflexible, the potential bank run is a credible threat as well as a disciplinary device for the banks, preventing the inefficient renegotiation and making the banks' long assets acceptable collaterals. The fragile structure is thus not a defect in the banking system, but rather a desirable design to make both the banks and investors better off, as Section 1.3 shows.

Another associated question is why early liquidation is so costly. The traditional answer is that the assets' value can only be poorly recovered from the "fire sale," that is, a project isn't worth much if it is terminated prematurely. However, this does not completely explain why the long assets have to be sold at a price below its fundamental value, because as long as there are other investors or banks whose time preference for cash is longer, they can purchase the assets at a better price and hold them till they fully mature. The reason why such occasion fails to take place is that in the crisis such potential buyers are capital constraint as well, and this limits their capability of arbitrage (Shleifer and Vishny, 1997). In the end, the assets on the sale can only end up in the hands of those investors whose willingness to pay is low. As is observed in the current financial crisis, the typical business model adopted by most modern financial institutions makes such "limit of arbitrage" problem even worse. Via securitization, the banks expand their balance sheets via "originating and distributing" their loans, and get short term financing from the repo market. This increases the banks' profit in the good time, but leads to more liquidation in the downturn. In Section 1.4, we show that the fire sale arising from the "limit of arbitrage" is aggravated by the feedback between two cycles: the leverage cycle and the asset price cycle. In the boom the banks leverage up for profit, driving up the asset prices; but when the economy gets into the bust, the banks have to deleverage and liquidate their long assets. Since all the banks are now trapped by liquidity shortage, the assets can only be sold to the noise investors who have low willingness to pay. This depresses the asset prices even further and leads to more liquidation.

1.1 Bank runs

The structure of financial intermediation is fragile in the sense that banks are subject to bank runs. The fact that banks finance their risky, high yield, long assets by short-term borrowing creates a maturity mismatch, or liquidity problem. Once the liquidity demand from the investors exceeds the liquid assets held by the bank, it has to liquidate the long assets for cash. However, such early liquidation reduces the payoff of the "patient" investors – who otherwise prefer to withdraw later – encouraging them to demand liquidity together with the impatient ones: the typical scenario of a bank run. In this section, we present the mechanism of such classical version of bank run, following Diamond and Dybvig (1983).

1.1.1 Model setup

As Diamond and Dybvig (1983), in this economy, there are two groups of agents: investors and banks. The economy extends over three periods, $t=0, 1, 2$ (the details of timing will be explained later). It is assumed that

1   There is a continuum of *ex ante* identical investors, each of which is endowed with one unit of consumption good at $t=0$. *Ex post*, each investor learns her true time preference at $t=1$.

   a   With probability $p \in (0, 1)$ one investor is early investor so that she only values consumption at $t=1$, i.e., $U=u(c_1)$. Assume that the utility function $u(\cdot)$ is neoclassical, twice differentiable, and with the relative risk aversion greater than one.
   b   With probability $1-p$ one investor is late investor so that she only values consumption at $t=2$, i.e., $U=u(c_2)$.

2   The banks offer demand deposit contracts to the investors. By pooling the deposits from the investors and investing the funds on different types of assets, the bank is able to provide optimal consumption plans to investors of both types. In the demand deposit contract issued at $t=0$, the bank promises a fixed return profile (c_1, c_2) for each unit of deposit, in which c_1 (c_2) denotes the payment when a investor withdraws at $t=1$ ($t=2$). There is a perfect competition among the banks in the deposit market.

There are two linear technologies:

1   Storage technology. This technology is shared by both investors and banks, transferring one unit input at t into one unit output at $t+1$. The projects using such technology are *short assets*, or *liquid assets*.
2   Investment technology. This technology transfers one unit input at $t=0$ into $R>1$ units output at $t=2$. The projects using such technology are *long assets*, or *illiquid assets*. If the project is terminated at $t=1$ before it gets matured, it only gives a poor return $c \in (0, 1)$, which is the recovered value from the prematurely terminated project.

1.1.2 The baseline results

Planner's problem

As a reference for welfare criterion, we start from the planner's problem which defines the first best allocation. Suppose that the planner chooses the share of the banks' funds invested on the liquid assets, denoted by α, along with (c_1, c_2) to maximize a representative investor's expected utility

$$\max_{\{\alpha, c_1, c_2\}} pu(c_1) + (1-p)u(c_2), \tag{1.1}$$

$$s.t. \ pc_1 = \alpha, \tag{1.2}$$

$$(1-p)c_2 = R(1-\alpha). \tag{1.3}$$

The early investors are paid by the return from the short assets, and the late investors are paid by the return from the long assets. The optimal solution is featured by the first order condition, $u'(c_1) = Ru'(c_2)$, which implies that $c_1 < c_2$ since $R > 1$. Furthermore, $c_1 < c_2$ means that a late investor doesn't have the incentive to mimic the early ones, i.e., she will wait till $t = 2$ to withdraw.

Note that the relative risk aversion is assumed to be greater than one, i.e.,

$$-\frac{cu''(c)}{u'(c)} > 1,$$

which implies that $cu'(c)$ is decreasing in c,

$$\frac{d[cu'(c)]}{dc} < 0.$$

Therefore, we have

$$1 \cdot u'(1) > Ru'(R) \tag{1.4}$$

as long as $R > 1$. To have (1.4) along with the budget constraints (1.2) and (1.3) hold simultaneously, the first order condition $u'(c_1) = Ru'(c_2)$ implies that $1 < c_1 < c_2 < R$.

Market equilibrium without intermediation

The representative investor's problem is to choose α to maximize her expected utility at $t = 0$

$$\max_{\{\alpha\}} pu(c_1) + (1-p)u(c_2), \tag{1.5}$$

$$s.t. \ c_1 = \alpha + P(1-\alpha), \tag{1.6}$$

Table 1.1 Timing of the model (planner's solution)

$t=0$	$t=1$	$t=2$
Investors Deposit	Time preferences get revealed: Early investors: withdraw c_1 Late investors: wait	Withdraw c_2
Planner Decide α	Get returns from short assets Repay early investors	Get returns from long assets Repay late investors

$$c_2 = \frac{\alpha}{p}R + R(1-\alpha),\tag{1.7}$$

$$P = \frac{\alpha(1-p)}{p(1-\alpha)}.\tag{1.8}$$

Budget constraint (1.6) says that an early investor consumes the proceeds both from her liquid assets and selling her illiquid assets, and (1.7) says that a late investor consumes the proceeds both from her own illiquid assets and the ones purchased from the early investors. The market clearing condition (1.8) says that the price for illiquid assets at $t=1$ is determined by the demand and supply rule.

The optimal solution to the investors problem is $\alpha^* = p$, with $P=1$. To see the intuition, note that in a symmetric equilibrium, the representative investor should choose a proper α which at $t=1$ (1) maximizes her revenue in selling long assets if she turns out to be an early investor, and (2) minimizes her cost in purchasing the long assets if she turns out to be a late investor. The only factor that determines such revenue and cost is the asset price P; therefore, the only P that meets the investor's trade-off at $t=0$ is $P=1$, which implies that $c_1^* = 1$ and $c_2^* = R$.

Comparing with the first best solution, the early investors get less consumption in the market equilibrium without intermediation, and the late investors get more. The representative investor's expected utility at $t=0$ is thus lower. Therefore, the planner improves social welfare by better hedging against the uncertainty on the investor's time preference.

On the other hand, even in the first best solution $c_1 < c_2$ as long as $R>1$, implying that the investors are not perfectly insured as long as it is impossible to freely reshuffle resources between period 1 and 2. Therefore, with the presence of different time preferences, the first best solution is actually *constrained efficient*.

Market equilibrium with intermediation

Instead of having a central planner, introducing banks as intermediaries of the market may help improve efficiency as well. The intermediation allows the investors to insure against the liquidity shocks, and it also allows the early investors to share the high yields from the long assets. In this model, the banking solution is likely to replicate the first best allocation.

Table 1.2 Timing of the model (no-run equilibrium)

$t=0$	$t=1$	$t=2$
Investors	Time preferences get revealed:	
Deposit	Early investors: withdraw c_1	
	Late investors: wait	Withdraw c_2
Banks	Get returns from short assets	Get returns from long assets
Offer deposit contract	Repay early investors	Repay late investors
(c_1, c_2) along with α		

Since the banks engage in a perfect competition in the deposit market, every bank offers the optimal deposit contract (c_1, c_2) to maximize the representative investor's expected utility

$$\max_{\{c_1,c_2\}} pu(c_1)+(1-p)u(c_2). \tag{1.9}$$

The banks then pool all the deposits, invest a share $\alpha(1-\alpha)$ of the funds on short (long) assets. The early (late) investors are paid by the return from the short (long) assets, i.e., $pc_1=\alpha$, and $(1-p)c_2=R(1-\alpha)$. It is easily seen that the banks' problem is no different from the planner's, therefore it is not surprising that the market equilibrium outcome under intermediation is exactly the same as the first best allocation.

1.1.3 Bank run and financial fragility

However, the market equilibrium described above is not the only equilibrium. There is another equilibrium in which the investors run on the banks at $t=1$. This happens when all the investors, both the early and the late ones, panic and attempt to withdraw their money at $t=1$. According to the demand deposit contract, an early withdrawal request has to be met by a payment of c_1. When the investors line up in front of a bank, they are paid by the "first come, first served" rule. However, after the investors of measure p get paid, the bank's liquid assets are exhausted so that it has to liquidate the illiquid assets. But even the bank liquidate all the illiquid assets, it is not able to meet the demand of all the investors since $\alpha+r(1-\alpha)<1<c_1$, and the bank gets bankrupted at $t=1$.

Under such situation, every investor has the incentive to stand in the front of the queue because those who come late will not be served. In the end, the expected return of each investor is $\alpha+r(1-\alpha)$, making everyone strictly worse off than if the late investors coordinate to wait.

The bank run is an equilibrium outcome, since no one has the incentive to deviate. To see this, suppose that a late investor does not join the queue at $t=1$. The bank gets bankrupted at $t=1$, leaving her expected consumption $\tilde{c}_2=0<\alpha+r(1-\alpha)$. This is why the late investors choose to mimic the early ones, withdraw their deposit at $t=1$ – as long as each one of them believe that everyone else will do so, too. The bank run equilibrium is summarized as Table 1.3.

Table 1.3 Timing of the model (bank run equilibrium)

$t=0$	$t=1$	$t=2$
Investors	Time preferences get revealed:	
Deposit	Early investors: withdraw c_1	
	Late investors: withdraw c_1 if in the front of the queue, 0 otherwise	
Banks	Get returns from short assets and liquidated	Bankrupted
Offer deposit contract	value from long assets to meet the demand	
(c_1, c_2) along with α		

1.2 Run on the repos

The evolution of the recent crisis is a presentation of a bank run in its modern version. What made this crisis different, as observed in Gorton (2010), is the silent and rather invisible run on the banks by the other financial institutions instead of the run by the depositors. The reason behind such scenario comes from the fact that in the past decade large financial institutions have been relying heavily on the repurchase agreement, or repo, market as their main funding resource. In a stylized repo relation, the banks finance their investments on securities by borrowing from the other financial institutions (such as banks, institutional investors) for very short term (usually, overnight), using the securities as collateral. The borrowing is generally over-collateralized, i.e., the market value of collateral is higher than the borrowing. The difference, or "haircut," reflects the risk premium. In the orderly time, the risk in short-term borrowing is low and the haircut is thin, so that the banks easily get financed in the repo market. The mechanism makes the banks' assets much more liquid. However, when the market faces a stress, the haircut asked by the counter parties rises and it becomes difficult for the banks to roll over the debt. In contrast to the traditional bank runs where the investors rush to withdraw their deposits, such "run on the repo" is more like a refusal for refinancing. The borrower banks then quickly run out of liquidity, and the banking crisis starts.

To understand the impact of repo on financial stability, in the following, we introduce repurchase agreement in a dynamic overlapping generation model with liquidity shock, which is based on Martin, Skeie, and von Thadden (2010).

1.2.1 Model setup

Agents, technologies, and time preferences

Consider an infinitely lived economy in discrete time populated by overlapping generations. In the beginning of each period t, a continuum young generation of *ex ante* identical investors with measure N, called generation t, are born with one unit of endowment for each one of them. Each generation lives for three periods, and, similar to Diamond and Dybvig (1983), the investors of generation t become heterogeneous in their time preferences at $t+1$ such that

1   with probability p, one becomes an early investor who only values her consumption at $t+1$, denoted by $c_{1,t}$, and
2   with probability $1-p$, one becomes a late investor who only values her consumption at $t+2$, denoted by $c_{2,t}$.

The investors' preference on consumption is captured by a neoclassical utility function $u(c)$, which is increasing in consumption c, strictly concave, and twice differentiable. Although by the Law of Large Numbers it is easily inferred that the population of early investors for the entire generation t is pN, the type of an individual investor is her private information and cannot be observed.

There are also a finite number of M infinitely lived, risk-neutral banks indexed by $i \in \{1, \ldots, M\}$. The banks don't have any endowment so that they need to borrow from the investors. There are two technologies in the economy:

1   Storage technology, which is available for both investors and banks, returns zero net profit for the storage made one period before. Similar to Diamond and Dybvig (1983), if necessary the late investors can mimic the early ones by withdrawing early and consuming later.
2   Investment technology, which is exclusively owned by the banks. This creates the role as intermediaries for the banks. By investing $I_{i,t}$ at t on some projects, one bank i gets $R_i I_{i,t}$ at $t+2$ as long as $I_{i,t}$ doesn't exceed some threshold, denoted by $\bar{I}_i$, as one bank's maximum investment capacity. The investment above $\bar{I}_i$ generates zero return, i.e., the expected return for bank i's investment at t is

$$\begin{cases} R_i I_{i,t} & \text{if } I_{i,t} \leq \bar{I}_i, \\ R_i \bar{I}_t & \text{if } I_{i,t} > \bar{I}_i \end{cases}.$$

However, the investment at t returns zero if it is terminated prematurely at $t+1$.

There are further restrictions regarding the investment technology. First, the return to the banks' investment is not verifiable so that one bank may claim that the return is not sufficient to repay the investors. As a result, the lender i.e., an

Table 1.4 Timing of the model

t	$t+1$	$t+2$
Investors of generation t Lends to banks	Time preferences get revealed: Early investors: withdraw $c_{1,t}$ Late investors: wait	Withdraw $c_{2,t}$
Bank i $B_{i,t}$ borrowing $S_{i,t}$ on short assets $I_{i,t}$ on long assets	Get returns from short assets Repay early investors	Get returns from long assets Repay late investors

investor in this model, needs to take the borrowers, i.e., the bank's assets, as collateral. As is seen later, this is the key assumption to motivate the prototype repo relationship between the banks and the investors. Second, one bank has the expertise in running its own projects due to inalienable human capital (see Hart and Moore, 1994) so that its projects achieve full return only if they are operated by the bank itself. Otherwise, the projects return γR_i if they are taken over by the investors, or $\hat{\gamma} R_i$ if by the other banks, and $0 < \gamma \leq \hat{\gamma} \leq 1$. In addition, assume that $\Sigma_{j \neq i} \bar{I}_j > N$, $\forall i \in \{1, \ldots, M\}$, which implies that the endowment from the investors is the limiting factor for the banks so that they have to compete for funding, even after any one of the banks fails.

Timing of the model

At the beginning of any arbitrary period t of the infinite time horizon, the representative bank i aims to maximize its life time profit

$$\max{}_{\{c_1,\tau, c_{2,\tau}, B_{i,\tau}, S_{i,\tau}, I_{i,\tau}\}_{\tau=t}^{+\infty}} \Pi_i = \sum_{\tau=t}^{+\infty} \beta^\tau \pi_{i,t},$$

in which $\beta \in (0, 1)$ is the discounting factor, and $\pi_{i,t}$ is the profit in period t such that

$$\pi_{i,t} = R_i I_{i,t-2} + S_{i,t-1} + B_{i,t} - pc_{1,t-1}B_{i,t-1} - (1-p)c_{2,t-2}B_{i,t-2} - I_{i,t} - S_{i,t},$$

which says, if the bank still survives, it collects the return $R_i I_{i,t-2}$ from the long assets invested at $t-2$, and the return $S_{i,t-1}$ from the short assets invested at $t-1$, along with the fresh debts from the generation t investors, $B_{i,t}$. At the same time, it has to repay the early investors from the generation $t-1$ by $pc_{1,t-1}B_{i,t-1}$ and the late investors from the generation $t-2$ by $(1-p)c_{2,t-2}B_{i,t-2}$. In the end, it has to invest on the new short and long assets, $I_{i,t}$ and $S_{i,t}$ as well. In addition, the bank gets bankrupted once $\pi_{i,t}$ becomes negative.

Repo market

The repo relation between the banks and investors is introduced in the following way: since one bank's return from investment, $R_i I_{i,t}$, is not verifiable for investors, i.e., the bank may claim to its investors that its return is not sufficient to repay them and therefore have to default, as a complement to the demand deposit contracts, the investors need to keep the bank's assets as collateral, and later the bank "repurchases" the collateral by repaying the promised return to the investors. Suppose that in each period t bank i's collateral for each unit of new deposit is $k_{i,t}$, then in period $t+1$ the bank repurchase the collateral only if the fundamental value of collateral exceeds the claim of the early investors, i.e., $R_i k_{i,t} \geq c_{1,t}$.

1.2.2 No-run equilibrium

As a reference case, now we characterize the equilibrium without bank runs, i.e., for each period t in the infinite time horizon the investors from the young generation make demand deposit contracts $(c_{1,t}, c_{2,t})$ with the banks and withdraw at the time they prefer.

The characteristics of such no-run equilibrium, as shown by the authors, are fairly intuitive. The banks are symmetric in their offers to the investors such that all the banks fix $c_{1,t}$ at the same level $\bar{c}$. They get fully leveraged to maximize their investment, or $I_i = \bar{I}_i$ for each period in equilibrium, and minimize their holdings of short assets, or $S_i = 0$ for each period in equilibrium. Each type of the investors gets repaid just in the period when they need liquidity (so that there is no bank run), and the late investors are just indifferent between waiting and withdrawing earlier. If the late investors of generation t mimic the early ones, they can withdraw at $t+1$, deposit again, and withdraw again at $t+2$. The expected return from doing so is $\bar{c}^2$. If the late investors' offer from the banks $c_{2,t}$ is lower than $\bar{c}^2$, they will have the incentive to take the contract for the early investors at t. Therefore, $c_{2,t}$ should be at least as high as $\bar{c}^2$ to induce the late investors to reveal their true type. However, if $c_{2,t}$ is higher than $\bar{c}^2$, the late investors will have the incentive to obtain short-term borrowing from the market with interest rate $\bar{c}$ and expand their deposit at t, getting a higher consumption $c_{2,t}$ at $t+2$. Therefore, in equilibrium the late investors' offer $c_{2,t}$ is exactly $\bar{c}^2$.

The dynamic feature of the model makes the equilibrium different from the one in the standard one-round Diamond–Dybvig game, because in the dynamic equilibrium the banks are able to repay the early investors in each period out of the return from the matured long assets. Therefore, after the banks have accumulated sufficient profit in the early periods, they do not need to invest on the short assets any more. With the non-run dynamic equilibrium as a reference, now we are able to show how robust the banking system with repo is if there is an unexpected liquidity shock.

1.2.3 Repo runs

Suppose that the system is already in its equilibrium, and the liquidity shock comes as a zero probability event. For a representative bank i, assume that at period $t+1$ there is a bank run such that the late investors of generation t demand repayment, together with the early ones. Assume that there is no market where the bank can sell its assets. At this moment, the bank's total liability to the investors is $[p\bar{c} + (1-p)\bar{c}^2]B_i$, and the bank also gets the return from the long assets that are invested two periods before, $(R_i - 1)\bar{I}_i$.

If $(R_i - 1)\bar{I}_i \geq [p\bar{c} + (1-p)\bar{c}^2]B_i$, the liquidity shock can be fully cushioned by the bank's profit and there is no need for the bank to restructure its balance sheet. If this is anticipated by the late investors, they will be indifferent between running and waiting.

If $(R_i-1)\bar{I}_i < [p\bar{c}+(1-p)\bar{c}^2]B_i$, the profit from the long assets will not be self-sufficient for the bank to escape from the liquidity shock unscathed. Especially, if the fundamental value of the long assets is below the bank's total liability, $R_i\bar{I}_i < [p\bar{c}+(1-p)\bar{c}^2]B_i$, the bank goes bankrupted. This is more likely to happen if the bank has too high exposure to the short-term debt, B_i, which is exactly the problem for many modern banks whose business heavily relies on short-term repos.

The intermediate case is when $(R_i-1)\bar{I}_i < [p\bar{c}+(1-p)\bar{c}^2]B_i$, but still $R_i\bar{I}_i > [p\bar{c}+(1-p)\bar{c}^2]B_i$, i.e., the bank is no longer self-sufficient but still solvent. In this case, the bank will have to downsize its investment and borrowing, and later converge to the steady state.

The interesting case happens when the bank is allowed to sell its assets to the market. Since besides the mature projects, the bank still holds some long assets that are invested on one period before. The bank is able to liquidate this part of assets and avoid bankruptcy even when $R_i\bar{I}_i < [p\bar{c}+(1-p)\bar{c}^2]B_i$. But because of inalienable human capital, the bank's projects only return γR_i if they are taken over by the investors, or $\hat{\gamma}R_i$ if by the other banks, with $0 < \gamma \leq \hat{\gamma} \leq 1$. This gives an upper bound of the asset price. To make it even worse, if the liquidity is an aggregate shock so that all the banks face the same liquidity shortage, the only buyer of the assets will be the investors who have a lower willingness to pay. In this situation, the assets can only be sold at a low, "fire sale" price so that the systemic bank failure is inevitable. We will explore this issue in Section 1.4.

1.3 The role of financial fragility

As one can easily see from the discussion in the previous sections, the fragility of banking emerges from the fragile debt contracts. The banks get trouble in liquidity once the creditors exit from the debt relationship. Although the financial intermediation is vulnerable to this unstable relationship, such fragile structure is a pivotal design in maintaining the credibility of banking. The fragility as a device aligning the incentives works through two mechanisms, a "passive" one and an "active" one.

Financial intermediation is subject to problems of asymmetric information, since the banks have superior information to the investors, leading to moral hazard in the banks' behavior and adverse selections. Because it is costly for the investors to acquire information by themselves, the debt contract offers a rather "passive" mechanism for the investors to guarantee their payoffs with least private information production, as argued by Dang *et al.* (2009). In other words, debt contract makes the value of debt least sensitive to public information, maximizing the ease of the banks' funding.

The fragile structure of banking also provides a device for the investors to actively defend their payoffs. Diamond and Rajan (2001) argue that the fragile banking based on the demand deposit contract is actually desirable for the banks as financial intermediaries between investors and entrepreneurs. In a stylized banking structure, as Figure 1.1 shows, financed by the investors' deposits the

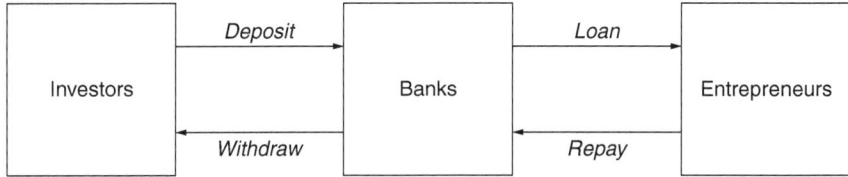

Figure 1.1 The stylized banking structure.

banks issue loans to the entrepreneurs running profitable projects, and the investors' return comes from the proceeds of the projects, collected by the banks.

However, one project can only achieve its highest return when it is run by the entrepreneur because she has the "inalienable human capital" (Hart and Moore, 1994). Therefore, the entrepreneur has a bargaining power over the profit of the project so that the lender can only collect a fraction of the project's return. The banks are justified as intermediaries simply because they have a better collection skill than the individual investors. The investors get better off from making the deposit contracts with the banks rather than lending directly to the entrepreneurs.

But in the absence of the demand deposit contract, there is a time consistency problem for such structure. No matter how much return the investors are promised when the contracts are signed, there is always an incentive *ex post* for a bank to renegotiate over the return after the projects' proceeds are collected for some rent; the investors therefore get worse off. On the other hand, this is not all good for the bank. Knowing that the bank can't commit to returning the collected proceeds on behalf of the others, the other investors won't take the bank's loans as collateral whenever the bank needs to raise more funds from the market. The bank loans thus remain illiquid.

The non-contingent demand deposit contract is a commitment device that prevents the banks from abusing the collection skill. Whenever a bank attempts to renegotiate and pocket any rent, its investors will run on the bank and force the bank to liquidate some or even all of the long assets. Such premature liquidation destroys the assets' value and makes the bank fail to capture any rent. Therefore, in equilibrium the bank will commit to using its collection skill on behalf of the investors. This is not all bad for the bank: knowing that the bank will take care of the investors' interest, the bank can expand its balance sheet by securitizing its loans, using the long assets as collateral, which increases the bank's profit from accessing more investment opportunities. This is a "win–win" solution: by tying its hands through the non-contingent demand deposit contract, the investors can get the promised return whenever they have a demand for liquidity, and the banks are able to access to fresh liquidity and explore more investment opportunities via securitizing the illiquid assets.

1.4 Fire sales, leverage, and unstable banking

The liquidity crunch in Diamond–Dybvig type bank runs comes out of the fact that the early liquidation of the long assets leads to a poor return, which substantially reduces the expected return of the late patient investors and forces them to run. The model itself doesn't explain why the assets have to be sold below their face value. Typically people attribute this to the "fire sale" phenomenon, as described in French *et al.* (2010):

> A bank that simply suffers large losses may be forced to reduce its risk by selling assets at distressed or fire-sale prices. If other banks must revalue their assets at these temporarily low market values, the first sale can set off a cascade of fire sales that inflicts losses on many institutions. Thus, whether through default or fire sales, one troubled bank can damage many others, reducing the financial system's capacity to bear risk and make loans.

Fire sale happens at the time when the financial institutions put a large volume of assets on sale that exceeds the financial system's capacity to absorb. However, the typical supply and demand relation in asset market is not sufficient to explain the plummeting price in the fire sale. The sharp decline of asset price is much due to the "limit of arbitrage," the term coined in Shleifer and Vishny (1997). When the financial institutions are all suffering from the market stress and have to liquidate their assets, they lack the capital for arbitrage – buying the assets at the low price. Therefore, the assets on sale can only be purchased with the investors whose willingness to pay is low. This depresses the asset price in the downturn.

Such "limit of arbitrage" makes the fire sale even more devastating in modern financial market, where the financial institutions actively disseminate the risks via securitization and rely on short-term repo market for funding. In the following, we show how repo market and asset price echo each other in a model based on Shleifer and Vishny (2010).

1.4.1 Model setup

Consider an economy that lives for three periods, $t = 1, 2, 3$. There are identical projects, each requiring one unit of investment, run by entrepreneurs. The projects can be initiated for either $t = 1$ or $t = 2$, and each of these projects returns $R > 1$ at $t = 3$.

Entrepreneurs get loans from the banks, and the banks raise funds via leveraging. Suppose each bank starts with equity E_0, and the equity level becomes E_t for period t. And the banks get a share γ, $\gamma \in [0, 1]$ out of the entrepreneurs' profit, $R - 1$.

For simplicity, assume that the entrepreneurs pay zero interest rate for their borrowing. After lending to the entrepreneurs, the banks securitize the loans and sell the securities in the market. To make it simple, there is no pooling or tranching in securitization, but one bank has to keep a share d, $d \in [0, 1]$ of the loans on its book. In this case, each security means one unit of loan which pays one unit at $t=3$. The price of the security in period t is denoted by P_t.

To focus on the interesting cases, assume $P_2<1\leq P_1$ and the banks have perfect information about P_2 at $t=1$, so that the banks are willing to securitize the loans at $t=1$ and keep the securities at $t=2$ (we will explain this later). To finance its activities, one bank can turn to repo market, raising L_t short-term debt using its entire security holding as collateral with a constant haircut h. Therefore, the maximum short-term borrowing one bank can initiate in period t is $L_t=(1-h)$ *collateral value.*

1.4.2 No repo equilibrium

As a reference case, suppose $h=1$ so that no repo lending is available. But the banks can still finance its loans to entrepreneurs via securitization. Since only a share d of the loans has to be financed directly out of a bank's own capital, at $t=1$ it is able to finance

$$N = \frac{E_0}{d}$$

projects and get a profit of

$$\gamma(R-1)\frac{E_0}{d}$$

from the loans.

When it comes to $t=2$, the bank will not engage in securitization since the security price is too low, $P_2<1$. But the bank may have the incentive to sell its assets to issue new loans. If the bank sells one security instead of getting one unit payoff at $t=3$, the opportunity cost is

$$\frac{1-P_2}{P_2},$$

and the profit from issuing a new loan is $\gamma(R-1)$. Assume from now on that the bank prefers to keep the security, i.e.,

$$\frac{1-P_2}{P_2} > \gamma(R-1). \tag{1.10}$$

In addition, the bank may have the incentive to keep some cash at $t=1$ to invest on the undervalued security at $t=2$. Suppose that the bank takes some cash C out of its endowment E_0 for this purpose, then the total profit is

$$\gamma(R-1)\frac{(E_0-C)}{d}+\frac{C}{P_2}(1-P_2).$$

Assume further that the bank has no incentive to keep cash at $t=1$, i.e., the profit when $C=0$ is strictly higher

$$\gamma(R-1)\frac{E_0}{d} > \gamma(R-1)\frac{(E_0-C)}{d} + \frac{C}{P_2}(1-P_2), \text{ or}$$

$$\frac{\gamma(R-1)}{d} > \frac{1-P_2}{P_2}. \tag{1.11}$$

If conditions (1.10) and (1.11) hold, banks will fully engage in securitization at $t=1$, and securitization improves social welfare: banks are able to finance more than if there is no securitization projects since

$$N = \frac{E_0}{d} > E_0,$$

and banks get higher profits with securitization,

$$\gamma(R-1)\frac{E_0}{d} > \gamma(R-1)E_0.$$

In the following, we concentrate on such full securitization case.

1.4.3 Equilibrium with repo

Now we extend the model to allow for leverage. Note that in each period t one bank posts all its assets, E_t+L_t, for raising the short-term debt L_t. This implies the haircut

$$h_t = \frac{E_t}{E_t+L_t}.$$

Suppose that $P_1=1$ and the bank maximizes its loan at $t=1$. The bank is able to finance the projects up to

$$N = \frac{E_0+L_1}{d}.$$

The haircut h_t must be maintained, and the maximum short-term borrowing the bank can make is

$$L_1 = (1-h_1) \cdot Nd, \tag{1.12}$$

using all the projects as collateral, the number of financed projects is therefore

$$N = \frac{E_0}{dh_1}.$$

Since $h_1 < 1$ one bank can further expand its balance sheet and finance more projects via leverage; and the lower h_1 is, the larger is the bank's initial balance sheet. Notice that the haircut

$$h_1 = \frac{E_1}{E_2 + L_1}$$

implies that

$$L_1 = (1 - h_1) \cdot \frac{E_1}{h_1}. \tag{1.13}$$

Comparing with (1.12) one can conclude that

$$Nd = \frac{E_1}{h_1}. \tag{1.14}$$

Now, when it comes to $t=2$ when price P_2 falls to a sufficiently low level so that the bank is not able to issue new loans, the bank has to liquidate some of its assets, denoted by S, to keep the haircut. By selling S assets at price P_2, the bank still holds $Nd-S$ assets, and $L_2 = L_1 - P_2 S$ liabilities to the investors. Computing from the balance sheet, the bank's equity is now

$$E_2 = (Nd - S)P_2 - (L_1 - P_2 S) = NdP_2 - L_1.$$

And the haircut is now

$$h_2 = \frac{E_2}{E_2 + L_2} = \frac{NdP_2 - L_1}{(Nd - S)P_2}. \tag{1.15}$$

Insert (1.13) and (1.14) into (1.15), S can be endogenized as

$$S = \frac{E_1}{h_1} \cdot \frac{h_2 P_2 + 1 - P_2 - h_1}{h_2 P_2} = Nd \frac{h_2 P_2 + 1 - P_2 - h_1}{h_2 P_2}. \tag{1.16}$$

In order to get the most important insight, first we assume that the haircut h is fixed for both $t=1$ and $t=2$, $h_1 = h_2 = h$. Equation (1.16) is therefore simplified as

$$S = \frac{E_1}{h} \left(\frac{1 - P_2}{P_2} \frac{1 - h}{h} \right) = Nd \left(\frac{1 - P_2}{P_2} \frac{1 - h}{h} \right). \tag{1.17}$$

Equation (1.17) has many implications. With a given h,

$$\frac{\partial S}{\partial P_2} < 0$$

means that the liquidation increases with a larger asset price shock. The bank even has to liquidate all its assets and exit the market, or $S=Nd$, when P_2 falls below $1-h$. In the following we focus on the partial liquidation case, i.e., $P_2>1-h$.

Differentiate (1.17) with respect to h, one can find that

$$\frac{\partial S}{\partial h} = -E_1 \frac{1-P_2}{P_2 h^2} - 2E_1 \left(\frac{1-P_2}{P_2} \frac{1-h}{h^3} \right) < 0.$$

When the haircut is smaller, or, when the bank gets more leveraged, the bank needs to liquidate more assets. Furthermore, one can find that

$$\frac{\partial^2 S}{\partial h^2} = 4E_1 \frac{1-P_2}{P_2 h^3} + 6E_1 \left(\frac{1-P_2}{P_2} \frac{1-h}{h^4} \right) > 0.$$

This implies that S is a strictly convex function of h with any given P_2, as Figure 1.2 shows. The bank needs to liquidate part of its asset holdings as long as $h<1$, and the lower h is, the more elastic S becomes. More leveraged financial institutions are forced to make more early liquidation, thus more vulnerable to economic downturns.

One can also find that

$$\frac{\partial^2 S}{\partial h \partial P_2} = E_1 \frac{1-P_2}{P_2^2 h^2} + E_1 \frac{1}{P_2 h^2} + 2E_1 \left(\frac{1-P_2}{P_2^2} \frac{1-h}{h^3} \right) = 2E_1 \frac{1-h}{P_2 h^3} > 0,$$

or, asset price and haircut are complementary to each other. The more the bank is initially leveraged, the more sensitive is S to the asset price shock. However, this fact does not fully reflect what happened in the financial crisis here because

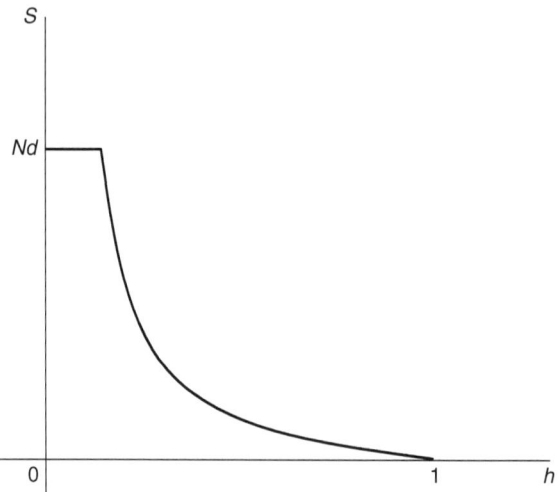

Figure 1.2 Haircut and liquidation.

the haircut h and asset price P_2 are both exogenously given and not correlated. However, if we allow h and P_2 to be endogenized from the model, they may reinforce each other, generating even higher asset price volatility. We will explore this later.

So far we assume that the haircut h remains the same for both periods. However, what has been often observed is that when the negative asset price shock on P_2 gets revealed, the value of the financial institutions' assets deteriorates so that they have to face a higher haircut. This will put a higher pressure on one bank's balance sheet and the bank has to "deleverage," leading to further liquidation. Given that all the banks are homogeneous in our model, the entire banking sector will run into a collective fire sale.

To see this, suppose that the haircut increases when P_2 gets revealed, i.e., $h_1 < h_2$. The quantity of liquidated assets S is given by equation (1.16). Again, in order to focus on the partial liquidation case we assume that $1 > P_2 > 1 - h_1$.

To see the impact of haircut on S, differentiate (1.16) with respect to h_1, one can find that

$$\frac{\partial S}{\partial h_1} = -E_1 \frac{(1-h_1) - P_2(1-h_2)}{h_1^2 h_2 P_2} - E_1 \frac{1}{h_1 h_2 P_2} < 0. \tag{1.18}$$

With low haircut at $t=1$ the bank becomes highly leveraged and has to liquidate more assets when time goes bad. To make it worse, haircut increases during the downturn, and banks have to put more assets on sale,

$$\frac{\partial S}{\partial h_2} = \frac{E_1}{h_1 h_2} \frac{P_2 - (1 - h_1)}{h_2 P_2} > 0. \tag{1.19}$$

The leverage's key contribution to financial instability through premature liquidation and fire sale is well unveiled by inequalities (1.18) and (1.19). Leverage allows the banks to expand their balance sheets for higher profit, and expansion is larger when the economy is booming and the haircut is low. However, high initial leverage also leads to more liquidation in the bad time, just as (1.18) shows. To make things worse, the leverage is often procyclical such that the banks have to face a higher haircut when the economy gets bust, and this leads to further inefficient liquidation of long assets, as (1.19) shows. The business cycle is much amplified by such leverage cycle.

1.4.4 Limits of arbitrage

So far we take P_2 as exogenously given. However, when the banks suffering from a negative asset price shock have to liquidate the long assets, such fire sale leads to further decline in asset price. To capture the feedback mechanism between fire sale and plummeting asset price, we need to endogenize P_2. To concentrate on the feedback mechanism, we assume that the haircut h remains constant, $h_1 = h_2 = h$.

The simplest approach to endogenizing P_2 is to introduce another group of long asset holders, the "noise traders" as Shleifer and Vishny (1997). The noise traders have deep pockets so that they are able to purchase all the assets in the market. The demand of the long assets from the noise traders follows a simple demand function which is the inverse of asset price and subject to the demand shock, σ,

$$D_n(P_2) = N\left(\frac{1-\sigma}{P_2}\right).$$

The demand of the long assets from the banks after the liquidation is

$$D_b(P_2) = Nd - S = Nd - Nd\left(\frac{1-P_2}{P_2}\frac{1-h}{h}\right).$$

The aggregate supply of the long assets is just the number of projects. Therefore, by market clearing condition,

$$D_n(P_2) + D_b(P_2) = N, \text{ or}$$

$$\frac{1-\sigma}{P_2} + d - d\left(\frac{1-P_2}{P_2}\frac{1-h}{h}\right) = 1.$$

The equilibrium asset price P_2 is thus characterized by

$$P_2 = \frac{h + hd - d - h\sigma}{h - d}$$

A regularity condition, $h > d > \sigma$ is needed to ensure $P_2 > 0$. P_2 falls in the presence of a demand shock from the noise traders,

$$\frac{\partial P_2}{\partial \sigma} = \frac{h}{d-h} < 0.$$

However, P_2 is more sensitive to σ when h is small since

$$\frac{\partial^2 P_2}{\partial \sigma \partial h} = \frac{d}{(d-h)^2} > 0.$$

Again, the higher the *ex ante* leverage is, the more *ex post* destabilizing effect there is in the economic downturn.

In summary, this compact model presents the key mechanism of financial instability arising from modern banking. Via "originate-to-distribute" model the banks expand the lending via securitizing the loans. Using the securities as collateral, the banks finance their investments through short-term repo market. The system exhibits a strong feature of procyclicality: the banks' balance sheets get further expanded when the time is good and haircut is low, but they suffer from a bigger blow when the time is bad. The companion procyclical leverage cycle aggravates the crisis: the rising haircut forces the banks to deleverage and make further liquidation. Furthermore, such liquidation implies that the banks are selling assets in a falling market, i.e., exactly at the time when the investors have plummeting willingness to pay. The limit of arbitrage finally turns the liquidation into a system wide fire sale, leading to a systemic melt down.

To concentrate on the key issues, we take it as an explicitly given that the haircut and asset price are negatively correlated. However, to understand the complete mechanism and its quantitative effect one needs to capture how such leverage cycle emerges; therefore, it is desirable to have a model where both haircut and asset price are endogenized from the model itself. In Section 5.2 we will come back to this issue and show how haircut and asset price reinforce each other in a different context.

1.5 The coordinative failure and the trigger of bank run

The existence of multiple equilibria in Diamond–Dybvig type bank run model much limits its application, since it is silent on the condition or the trigger of the bank runs. Therefore, one needs some equilibrium selection criteria that help reach clear-cut conclusions. One type of such criteria is based on the informational externalities, such as Chen (1999). There, similar as the banking framework in Diamond and Dybvig (1983), investors' time preferences get revealed in the intermediate date such that some of the investors prefer to withdraw early. Therefore banks have to finance the long-term and risky projects partially via short-term, demand deposit debts. Among both early and late investors, some of them are better informed about the quality of the projects.

The late investors' decision on running on the bank depends on their expected return, based on the information available about the quality of the banks' long assets. When in the intermediate period the information about the banks' fundamentals gets sequentially revealed, the better informed late investors will withdraw earlier than the uninformed ones if their private information about the banks is negative. However, the uninformed ones can infer the viabilities of their banks by observing the queues in front of the run banks: the private information generates an externality on the informed investors' behavior. If the banks' fundamentals are positively correlated, the failure of the other banks implies the prospects of the other banks are dull, too. Therefore, the observed bank failures may encourage the uninformed investors to run on their banks. If this happens, even the informed investors, whose private information about their banks' projects is positive, have to join the run. Reinforced by the "first come, first served" rule, the informational externality coordinates both the informed and uninformed investors, and the bank run equilibrium emerges.

Another type of equilibrium selection criteria is based on the investors' collective behavior coordinated by some imperfect information, such as the global game approach by Goldstein and Pauzner (2005). Different from the standard

Diamond–Dybvig model, assume that the probability of an investor being an early one, p, is a random variable drawn from some distribution function $F(p)$ with support $[0, 1]$. At the beginning of $t=1$, besides knowing her own type of time preference, each investor receives a private signal about the value of p – by the Law of Large Numbers, it is also the population of early investors. The signal of investor i, denoted by p_i, is her private information and cannot be observed by the others. The signal is noisy in the sense that $p_i = p + \varepsilon_i$ in which p is constant for all the investors while ε_i is i.i.d. and randomly drawn from a uniform distribution $[-\varepsilon, \varepsilon]$, $\varepsilon > 0$.

At $t=0$ the banks have to decide their demand deposit contract offer (c_1, c_2) and their holdings of liquid assets, α. The only information in this period about the liquidity demand in the next period is the expectation on p, $E[p]$. Here the liquidity preference shock is an aggregate shock in the sense that all the banks face the same percentage of early investors among their customers. As is shown later in Section 3.3, the banks' optimal strategy may be different from the first best solution. However, here we want to focus on explaining the mechanism leading to coordinative bank runs, therefore, we assume that the banks follow the first best allocation at $t=0$, as if the value of p is known as $E[p]$.

By getting the noisy signal of the liquidity shock, whether a late investor runs on a bank depends on two factors. The first one is what she can directly read from the signal. The higher p_i, the higher the true p is and thus the higher probability it is that the bank has to liquidate part of the long assets to meet the liquidity demand at $t=1$, and it becomes more likely that the remaining long asset cannot guarantee $c_2 > c_1$ which incentivize the late investors to run. The second one is what she can infer about the other investors' signals from her own signal. If p_i is high, it is likely that the other investors receive high signals and therefore are encouraged to run, too. By the "first come, first served" rule, the investor will certainly join the army of bank run if she believes the others will run as well. Here the noisy signal p_i also serves as a coordinative device for bank runs.

Such coordination mechanism provides an equilibrium selection criterion for the investors. When one's signal p_i exceeds some threshold, it becomes almost obvious that the true p should be high enough and the other investors mostly recognize this as well, the investors will coordinate to run. In contrast, when the signal p_i is not high and the bank is mostly likely to guarantee $c_2 > c_1$ even it liquidates some of the long assets to meet the early demand, the late consumers will choose to wait and the outcome is unambiguously the non-run equilibrium.

2 Financial network, interconnectedness, and contagion

Mellon pulled the whistle
Hoover rang the bell,
Wall Street gave the signal,
And the country went to hell
(Manchester, 1975)

The impressive feature in the financial crises is that the giant financial institutions jointly come to the brink of collapse. This is often claimed to be the eruption of the accumulated "systemic risk" in the financial system, the risk coming from each individual financial firm's activities but having the impact of destabilizing the entire system as a whole. In this and next chapters, we will discuss various sources of systemic risks.

Modern financial institutions are highly interconnected. As a division of labor, financial firms are getting more and more specialized their roles in financial intermediation, creating a sophisticated intermediation chain (to be discussed later in Chapter 4). The highly competitive financial firms may get involved in very similar investment portfolios or strategies, which increases the probability of joint failure. By heavily borrowing and lending to each other, the financial institutions are tightly interconnected via the web of claims. It has been for long time argued that the interconnection of financial institutions makes the financial risk widely disseminated among a large number of financial firms and thus increases the robustness of individual banks. However, the evolution of current crisis, especially the episode after the collapse of Lehman Brothers and the bailout of AIG, seems to suggest that we have paid too little attention to the other side of interconnection, the peril that financial interconnectedness raises systemic risk and amplifies the market turbulence.

Previous studies concentrate on the consequences of financial interconnectedness, especially the impact of interconnection in the crisis. The turbulence in the financial market can be propagated and amplified through the links between financial institutions via several channels. The most obvious channel is the "common assets" held by several institutions. When there is a loss on such assets, these holding institutions will be simultaneously hit.

Another more complicated channel is the price channel. The channel can work in several ways. One is directly through the asset prices: a bank in trouble may have to start liquidating its assets, causing the asset price to fall. Given that the banks' balance sheets are marked to market in real time, the fall in asset price will force the other banks to restructure their balance sheets as well. This is not necessarily an easy job and often brings more stress to the market. The other is indirectly through the cost of raising liquidity, which is to be discussed in Section 2.1. One bank in trouble may try to raise liquidity in the interbank market, this bids up the market rate for liquidity – to contain the rising demand for liquidity as well as to include the risk premium. However, the rising interest rate increases the other banks' funding cost as well, sending more banks on the verge to bankruptcy. The bank failure thus becomes contagious, when the banks get short-term funding from the interbank market.

The financial firms can also be connected by borrowing from and lending to each other. The borrowing and lending create a web of claims for the banks, as is modeled in Section 2.3. When part of the network is hit by the loss in the assets, these banks have to unwind their positions and impose a downward pressure on asset prices. With their balance sheets continuously marked to the market, the banks all over the network have to adjust their assets and liabilities, forcing the asset price to fall further. The local stress then spreads to the entire financial network through such Domino effect.

However, one should still keep it in mind that financial network also facilitates better risk sharing among the financial institutions; therefore, the more interesting question is the assessment on the benefit from better risk sharing and the cost from the devastating contagion – and the companion question is to what extent the interconnectedness is desirable. In Section 2.4, we will have a closer look at such benefit and cost for different network structure; and, surprisingly, such benefit and cost are not monotonic to the completeness of the financial network.

Most of previous studies focus on the contagion mechanism, or how the crisis evolves in a given structure of financial network with banks holding some certain investment portfolios. However, this strand of research says little about the true source of the systemic risk, i.e., the reason why the banks choose to be much interconnected in many ways even if they anticipate the devastating joint failure in the downturn. Therefore, the recent work starts explaining the incentive of the banks to get intertwined and become "too-interconnected-to-fail." The interconnectedness is thus an endogenous phenomenon rather than an exogenous setup.

One explanation is that the banks' investment strategy has some negative externality on the entire financial system – for example, one bank's fire sale in the crisis depresses the asset price in the market, bring more banks into trouble – and one bank's failure can spill over to the others. In Section 2.2, the banks can choose the degree of interconnection by choosing assets whose returns are correlated. Because of the negative externality, in equilibrium the banks neglect the cost from the recessionary spillover out of its failure in the crisis, leading to over-correlated investment portfolios and hence higher systemic risk.

2.1 The interest rate channel of contagion

This section is based on Diamond and Rajan (2005). In a partial equilibrium model, we show how the bank failure can spill over to the rest of the economy, through the cost of raising liquidity in the interbank market.

2.1.1 Model setup

Consider an economy that lives for three periods and four dates, $t=0, 1, 2$ with an intermediate date $t=0.5$. There are three groups of risk-neutral agents:

1　Investors, each of which is endowed with one unit of good at $t=0$. They have a short time preference, i.e., they only value the consumption at $t=1$ for their investments made at $t=0$. Investors only own an inferior storage technology so that they prefer to deposit their endowments in the banks as long as the expected return there exceeds 1.
2　Entrepreneurs, each of which has no endowment, but, instead, a production project (*ex ante* identical across the production sector) that needs one unit of fixed cost at $t=0$. The entrepreneurs are indifferent in the timing of consumption. There are more projects than the investors' endowments so that the entrepreneurs have to compete for funding.
3　A continuum of banks indexed by $i \in [0, 1]$, each of which has no endowment, but, instead, a special skill of collecting a share γ of the returns from the entrepreneurs' projects. This fact justifies the banks' role as intermediary, channeling the funds from the investors to the entrepreneurs while handing over the returns from the entrepreneurs to the investors.

There is an uncertainty concerning the timing of a project's return. After a project gets started at $t=0$, there is a probability p that it returns $R>1$ at $t=1$ – we call it an early project – and a probability $1-p$ that it is delayed and returns R at $t=2$ – we call it a late project. The value of p is public information once it gets revealed.

The banks, as lenders to the entrepreneurs, also have the authority to take over the projects and liquidate them before they mature. When a project, no matter early or late, is liquidated before $t=1$, it returns c. Early liquidation is costly so that

$$c < 1 < \gamma R < R.$$

The banks compete in the deposit market for the funds from the investors, by offering them the non-contingent demand deposit contracts. As argued in Section 1.3, such demand deposit contract, which is subject to the bank run and creates the fragility in the banking sector, is necessary to avoid the banks from abusing their intermediation expertise.

The timing of the model is sketched in Figure 2.1.

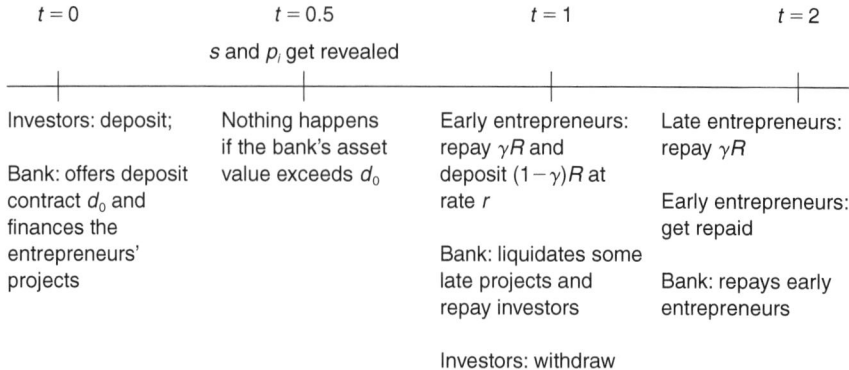

Figure 2.1 The timing of the model without bank run.

1   At $t=0$ the banks get deposits from the investors, using the demand deposit contracts promising a return d_0 at $t=1$ for each unit of deposit. Then the entrepreneurs get loans from the banks and start their projects.
2   At $t=0.5$ the probability of a project being an early one, p, gets revealed. The value p_i is heterogeneous for each bank i, which is randomly drawn from the same cumulative distribution function $F_s(p)$ in the state s. At $t=0$ the *ex ante* probability of getting into state s at $t=0.5$ is π_s. Without loss of generality, assume that p_i increases with the index i. Further, by the Law of Large Numbers, the probability p_i is also the share of early projects for bank i.

   Now the investors are able to compute the bank i's expected return from all the projects. If the return is below the face value of the deposit claims, the investors will run on the bank and the bank gets bankrupted, exits the market, as Figure 2.2 shows. Otherwise they wait and withdraw at $t=1$. Here any bank run caused plainly by panics is excluded.

   Notice that the banks have several resources of raising funds to repay the investors, including collecting the returns from the early projects, getting new deposits from the early entrepreneurs, and liquidating the long assets.

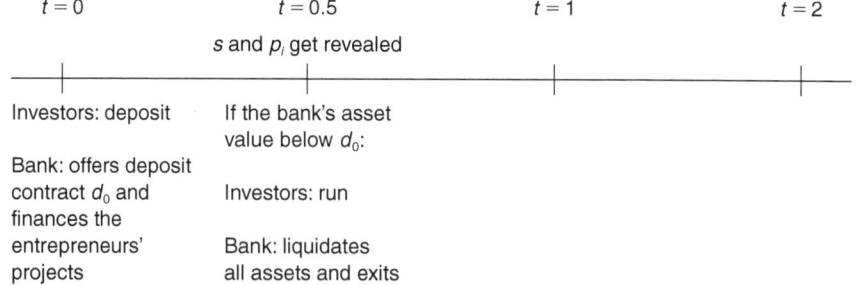

Figure 2.2 The timing of the model with bank run.

3   At $t=1$, if the bank survives, it collects the returns from the early projects and competes with the other surviving banks for the early entrepreneurs' funds; the deposit market is cleared by the equilibrium gross deposit rate r. Then the investors withdraw and consume.

4   At $t=2$, the surviving bank collects the returns from the late projects and repays deposits from the early entrepreneurs.

2.1.2 The market equilibrium

Since the banks engage in the perfect competition for the deposit at $t=0$, the representative bank i therefore simply aims to maximize the expected return from its depositors by liquidating a share μ_i of the late projects, i.e.,

$$\max\nolimits_{\mu_i} \ p_i \gamma R + \mu_i(1-p_i)c + (1-\mu_i)(1-p_i)\frac{\gamma R}{r},$$

$$s.t. p_i \gamma R + \mu_i(1-p_i)c + (1-\mu_i)(1-p_i)\frac{\gamma R}{r} \geq d_0.$$

In the object function, $p_i \gamma R$ is the return directly collected from the early projects, $\mu_i(1-p_i)c$ the return from liquidating the long assets, and

$$(1-\mu_i)(1-p_i)\frac{\gamma R}{r}$$

the present value of the late projects. The maximization problem only holds when the bank survives from runs, i.e., the bank is able to honor its liabilities to the depositors. If the bank experiences a run, the liquidated value of the bank's assets is constant at c and invariant to its strategy taken at $t=0$.

To solve the bank's problem, notice that the object function is linear in μ_i so that the optimal strategy on μ_i depends on the cost benefit comparison of asset liquidation. Therefore,

$$\mu_i = \begin{cases} 0 & if \quad 1 \leq r < \dfrac{\gamma R}{c}, \\ 1 & if \quad r > \dfrac{\gamma R}{c}, \\ \tilde{\mu} \in [0,1] & if \quad r = \dfrac{\gamma R}{c}. \end{cases}$$

The result here suggests that the bank's liquidation decision depends on the equilibrium deposit rate r, which reflects the bank's cost on raising funds in the intermediate period, and is hence a measure of market liquidity. On the other hand, r is endogenously determined by the liquidity supply and demand, therefore, it will be interesting to investigate how r is formed and see its feedback on the market outcome.

Although the failing banks are dissolved at $t=0.5$ while the surviving ones repay their investors at $t=1$, the consumers of the surviving banks just decide to wait at $t=0.5$ instead of run once they conclude that the banks will be solvent under the expected deposit rate r at $t=1$. Regarding the consumers' decision of running on a bank, it is easily seen that

1   The bank's present value at $t=1$,

$$p_i\gamma R + \mu_i(1-p_i)\left(c_1 + \frac{c_2}{r}\right) + (1-\mu_i)(1-p_i)\frac{\gamma R}{r},$$

is negatively correlated with p_i since

$$\gamma R \geq (1-\mu_i)\frac{\gamma R}{r} \text{ and } \gamma R \geq \mu_i\left(c_1 + \frac{c_2}{r}\right).$$

Therefore, if there are bank runs in the economy, the banks with the lowest p_i's, hence lowest i's, are the first ones who suffer from bank runs. In other words, the sequence of p_i gives the "pecking order" for bank runs.

2   Since the bank runs caused by panics are excluded by design, one bank is immune to bank runs if

$$p_i\gamma R + (1-p_i)\left(c_1 + \frac{c_2}{r}\right) \geq d_0.$$

That is, even if the bank has to liquidate all its long assets ($\mu_i=1$), the bank's present value at $t=1$ is still sufficient to repay the consumers. Therefore, if d_0 is not too high, the banks with the highest p_i's will stay solvent.

The intermediate interest rate r can be calculated by the aggregate demand and supply of liquidity at $t=0.5$ and $t=1$. From the demand side, the liquidity demand is d_0 for a surviving bank i and

$$c_1 + \frac{c_2}{r}$$

for a failing bank. From the supply side, the liquidity supply is

$$p_iR + \mu_i(1-p_i)\left(c_1 + \frac{c_2}{r}\right)$$

for a surviving bank i and c_1 for a failing bank. Depending on the demand and supply of liquidity, the market rate r can be characterized by one of the following three generic cases:

1   $r=1$ if there is excess liquidity supply at $t=1$, i.e., when

$$\int_0^{i^*(1)} c_1 dF(i) + \int_{i^*(1)}^1 p_i R dF(i) \geq \int_0^{i^*(1)} (c_1 + c_2) dF(i) + \int_{i^*(1)}^1 d_0 dF(i). \quad (2.1)$$

Let $i^*(1)$ be the "cut-off" value for case (1), which separates the failing banks from the solvent ones. Note that p_i increases with a bank's index i, therefore, the lower i is, the less liquid the bank's assets are and the more likely the bank suffers a run. The left hand side of the inequality is the aggregate liquidity supply in the market, including the liquidated value of the failed banks and the return from the early projects – note that in this case the solvent banks do not need to liquidate any assets when $r=1$, i.e., $\mu_i=0$, $\forall i \in (i^*(1), 1]$ as (2.1) argues; the right hand side is the aggregate liquidity demand, including the repayment to the consumers from both the failed and solvent banks, and the solvent banks that hold the residual of the failed ones.

2   $1 < r \leq \overline{R}$, when (2.1) fails to hold but

$$\int_0^{i^*(2)} c_1 dF(i) + \int_{i^*(2)}^1 p_i R dF(i) \geq \int_0^{i^*(2)} \left(c_1 + \frac{c_2}{\overline{R}} \right) dF(i) + \int_{i^*(2)}^1 d_0 dF(i), \quad (2.2)$$

and the interest rate r is determined by

$$\int_0^{i^*(2)} c_1 dF(i) + \int_{i^*(2)}^1 p_i R dF(i) = \int_0^{i^*(2)} \left(c_1 + \frac{c_2}{r} \right) dF(i) + \int_{i^*(2)}^1 d_0 dF(i). \quad (2.3)$$

Let $i^*(2)$ be the "cut-off" value for case (2), and (2.2) says that the solvent banks still do not need to liquidate any assets when $1 < r \leq \overline{R}$, i.e., $\mu_i=0$, $\forall i \in (i^*(2), 1]$, as long as the aggregate liquidity supply is still above the aggregate liquidity demand when r reaches the critical value, $r=\overline{R}$;

3   $r=\overline{R}$ otherwise, and r is determined by

$$\int_0^{i^*(3)} c_1 dF(i) + \int_{i^*(3)}^1 [p_i R + (1 - p_i)c_1] dF(i)$$
$$= \int_0^{i^*(3)} \left(c_1 + \frac{c_2}{r} \right) dF(i) + \int_{i^*(3)}^1 d_0 dF(i) \quad . \quad (2.4)$$

Let $i^*(3)$ be the "cut-off" value for case (3), and (2.4) says that even the solvent banks have to liquidate all the long assets given that $r > \overline{R}$, i.e., $\mu_i=1$, $\forall i \in (i^*(3), 1]$.

2.1.3 Contagion

The direct question from the result is by what factors the market equilibria are separated into these three cases. The most straight observation is that the cut-off value $i*$ in each case depends on the realized p_i at $t=0.5$, given that d_0 has been already contracted at $t=0$ and taken as given at $t=1$. Remember that p_i is randomly drawn from a state-dependent distribution $F_s(p)$, which varies each time when a specific state s is materialized, and each $F_s(p)$ corresponds to a different level of aggregate liquidity demand and supply. Regarding the three generic cases, this implies the following.

1 When an $F_s(p)$ is revealed with a very high average p_i across all the banks, denoted by $E_s(p_i)$, there will be more assets returning early, which leads to higher liquidity supply. In this case, only the banks in the tail, i.e., those with very low p_i, get bust from the bank run, and the abundant liquidity supply keeps the equilibrium interest rate at its lowest level, $r=1$.

2 When $E_s(p_i)$ is not very high for a revealed $F_s(p)$, there will be less long assets returning early. Then the surviving banks have to compete for the limited liquidity supply and the intermediate deposit rate, r, is bid up above one when $E_s(p_i)$ becomes low enough, but the surviving banks still don't have to liquidate their long positions as long as r is still below the threshold $\bar{R}$. However, a higher r means higher intermediate financing cost for all the banks, and those who could just be able to survive case (1) will be insolvent, implying a higher $i*$. It is easily seen by comparing the inequalities (2.1) and (2.2): when c_1+c_2 in the right hand side of (2.1) becomes

$$c_1 + \frac{c_2}{\bar{R}}$$

in (2.2),

$$c_1 + \frac{c_2}{\bar{R}} < c_1 + c_2 < 1 \le d_0$$

implies $i*(2)$ has to go up to depreciate the left hand side of (2.2), given $p_i R > 1 > c_1$, but this will further depress the value of critical level liquidity demand, i.e., the right hand side of (2.2), and so on. In equilibrium, $i*(2) > i*(1)$ and the bid-up interest rate drives more banks out of the market.

3 When $E_s(p_i)$ is very low for a revealed $F_s(p)$, there will be even less assets returning early. The intermediate deposit rate, r, is bid up to such a high level that the surviving banks even prefer liquidating their long assets to borrowing from the liquidity market. Since the early liquidation is very costly, making the banks with more illiquid assets more difficult to meet the demand deposit contract, more banks in the tail side will be insolvent. To see this, by comparing (2.2) and (2.4) notice

$$c_1 + \frac{c_2}{r} < c_1 + \frac{c_2}{\bar{R}}$$

in this case, $i^*(3)$ has to increase to reduce the liquidity supply, i.e., the left hand side of (2.4). However, since the surviving banks will have extra liquidity holdings coming from the early liquidation, i.e., $p_i R + (1-p_i) c_1 > p_i R$, $i^*(3)$ has to increase further to maintain the equality of (2.4), and this further depresses the right hand side of (2.4). In equilibrium, we must have $i^*(3) > i^*(2)$.

Therefore, the banks are interconnected through the liquidity market in the intermediate period, when the banks need raise liquidity to repay the consumers. The ease of raising funds is indicated by the market interest rate r, which is determined by the aggregate liquidity supply. Once the realized distribution of the early projects implies a shortage in the aggregate liquidity supply, the interest rate r will be bid higher, eroding the present value of the assets for all the banks and making more illiquid banks fail.

However, even for a given state of the world, s, the current model does not rule out multiple equilibria, i.e., with some exogenously given d_0 and a realized $F_s(p)$, the market outcome may fall in any of those three generic cases. To see this, remember that we do not explicitly model the feedback mechanism between the consumers' decision and the market rate r, i.e., the consumers' decision of running on a bank and the interest rate r are simultaneously formed. Although we exclude the bank runs coming from pure panics, one consumer's decision of running on a bank depends on her expectation of the other consumers' decisions, which pin down the aggregate liquidity demand – hence the market rate r because the supply side is more or less fixed by $F_s(p)$, and such expectation on r reinforces the consumer's belief on her bank's solvency. As long as we do not explicitly model the consumers' coordination mechanism, anything can happen. Regarding the three generic cases:

1   When consumers believe that only the consumers of most illiquid banks run, since there are still abundant liquidity supplied by the solvent banks, the interest rate will remain low at $r=1$. Therefore, the other consumers will choose to stay calm and wait till $t=1$.

2   When consumers believe that even the consumers of less illiquid banks run at $t=0.5$, implying the aggregate liquidity supply will be low at $t=1$ (because even the early projects of insolvent banks are liquidated at $t=0.5$) and r is bid up to exceed 1, making more banks difficult to raise liquidity. This invites more consumers to run. Now the aggregate the liquidity demand is characterized by the right hand side of (2.2),

$$c_1 + \frac{c_2}{r} < c_1 + c_2.$$

As argued before, this implies a higher cut-off value $i^*(2)$ – even some less illiquid banks become insolvent.

3   The worst case is that even the banks in seemingly good shape are believed to be insolvent, when their consumers are expected to run and the market rate r will be bid up so high that even the solvent banks have to completely liquidate the late projects – although the banks fulfilling

$$p_i \gamma R + (1 - p_i)\left(c_1 + \frac{c_2}{r} \right) \geq d_0$$

are immune to runs anyway.

Again, with given $F_s(p)$, the banks' solvency problems are interconnected via the liquidity market. Suppose, instead of having the consumers' decision of running on a bank and the equilibrium interest rate r simultaneously formed, we allow a short timeline for these two factors evolving together: when $F_s(p)$ gets revealed at $t=0.5$, the consumers of the least liquid banks start running. By observing how many banks become insolvent in this date, the other consumers can get their expectation on the aggregate liquidity demand and supply at $t=1$, hence r. When more banks become insolvent (this may be caused by some reasons which are not modeled here, for example, imperfect information about the banks' asset value, making the banks slightly above the cutoff line i^* vulnerable to runs), the expected r may exceed 1. This makes those previously slightly more liquid banks unable to observe their deposit contracts in the next period so that their consumers will join the army of run, which makes the expected r even higher. In the end, more banks fail, and the system is melted down by such contagion.

2.1.4 Discussion

In this simple model, we focus on the question how the failure of banking system evolves, interacting with the liquidity market interest rate as an indicator for both the degree of a bank's asset liquidity and the liquidity shortage in the aggregate level, as simplification, the liquidity shock and one bank's exposure to liquidity shock are taken as exogenously given. However, such partial equilibrium model doesn't explain why the bank failure happens in the first place, or it doesn't address the source of the failure and the need for policy intervention.

First, in the model, the demand deposit contract is featured by a given promise d_0 which is symmetric for all the banks. However, if *ex ante* a bank expects the bank failure in the future when it is unable to fulfill d_0, it should have the incentive to choose an optimal value of d_0 which maximizes its profit and minimizes the cost from the bank run. The regulation is only necessary when the market fails to insure the banks against the liquidity shocks. We will internalize the banks' decision on the deposit contract in Section 3.3.

Second, the banks in reality have many instruments to cushion against the shocks. One may hold a portfolio consisting of both liquid and illiquid assets to better accommodate the consumers' liquidity demand, as Section 8.2 argues, or hold equity as a capital buffer which can be used to cover the losses, as the prototype model, Diamond and Rajan (2005), does. In Section 8.2 we will explore the banks' optimal strategy on liquidity holding, and in Section 9.2 we extend the model with equity holding;

Finally, the banks in the current model are homogeneous *ex ante* but only exposed to heterogeneous, idiosyncratic risks *ex post*. However, if allowed the banks would have the incentive *ex ante* to diversify their investment to better hedge against the risks, i.e., the banks may have the opportunity to choose how much they are interconnected, or correlated in their asset returns, given some common factors such as interest rate in the market. The next section is dedicated to this purpose.

2.2 Strategic interconnectedness

As an analog to the "too-big-to-fail" phenomenon, the pioneer work of Acharya (2009) shows that the banks have the incentive to be "too-interconnected-to-fail." This section will explore the mechanism.

As Acharya (2009), in this economy, there are two groups of agents: investors and banks. The economy extends over three periods, $t=0, 1, 2$. It is assumed that the economy is divided into two regions, $i \in \{A, B\}$, and in region i there is

1   one bank, which is operated by some risk neutral bankers who own no wealth in the beginning of the world; and
2   a continuum of risk neutral investors with $d_{it}>0$ units of endowment for $t=0, 1$. The investors have no access to the investment technology, so they have to rely on the banks as intermediaries.

Both the bankers and investors are indifferent in the timing of consumption. Similar to the other standard banking models, the financial fragility comes from the fact that the banks offer the fixed deposit contract (see Section 1.1.3) for the investors and hence are subject to costly bank runs. Here the bank in each region is an abstraction of many perfectly competitive banks, therefore, the bank takes the market gross deposit rate $r_{dt}(t=0, 1)$ as exogenously given.

In periods $t=0$ and $t=1$ the banks can choose between investing on two types of assets:

1   Safe asset, which gives a gross return r_{St} at $t+1$ for one unit of investment made at t. The safe asset corresponds to some safe production technology, featured by the neoclassical production function $f(x)$, x being the aggregate investment on safe asset in the economy – which is of constant return to scale, strictly concave with $f'(x)>0$ and $f''(x)<0$. For regularity reason the Inada conditions are also assumed for $f(x)$: $\lim_{x \to 0} f(x)=+\infty$ and $\lim_{x \to +\infty} f(x)=0$. There is a perfectly competitive capital market so that the gross return of the safe asset is determined by the marginal return of the production technology, or $r_{St}=f'(x_t)$.

2   Risky asset, which gives a random gross return $R_{it} \in [0, \overline{R}]$ with probability density function $R_{it} \sim f_i(\cdot, \sigma)$ at $t+1$ for one unit of investment made at t by bank i. When investing on the risky asset, the bank can decide how much risk to take by choosing $\sigma_{it} \in [\underline{\sigma}, \overline{\sigma}]$. There is no interbank market, but the two banks' returns on their risky assets are correlated. The correlation ρ_t can take two values, $\rho_t \in \{\rho_H, \rho_L\}$, and $\rho_H > \rho_L$. There is a strictly convex cost in holding risky assets, $c(x)$, for x aggregate investment on risky assets in the economy. This assumption serves to limit the size of investments on the risky assets.

Since the banks are perfectly competitive in both regional level and economy level, the banks need to offer the deposit contracts that maximize the investors' expected returns. In order to increase the return from the investment, the banks must make strictly positive investments on the risky assets at $t=0$. But given that the demand deposit contract is not state contingent, when bank i's realized return at $t=1$, R_{i1}, is low the bank has to go bankrupt. Regarding the realized returns for both banks' risky assets at $t=1$, R_{11}, and R_{21}, there are three generic cases on both banks' viability.

Case 1: both R_{11} and R_{21} are high enough so that both banks are solvent.
Case 2: both R_{11} and R_{21} are low enough so that both banks are bankrupted.
Case 3: one bank's return is high but the other's is low. Then the solvent one can take over the insolvent one and serve at least part of its investors.

The third case is of special interest. Since there is a convex cost in holding risky assets, the solvent bank can only take over part of the investors from the insolvent bank, up to the point that the marginal profit of doing so is just offset by the marginal cost. Therefore, from $t=1$ to $t=2$ there is only one working bank in the economy serving for part of the investors. As a result, the aggregate investments on both safe and risky assets becomes lower, the riskless rate r_{S1} thus becomes higher because of diminishing marginal return in the production. Therefore, the solvent bank has to face a higher funding cost at $t=1$ and a poorer profit, with the other things equal. The bank failure hence generates a negative externality on the surviving bank. However, the downsize of the surviving bank's holding of risky assets also helps reduce the management cost, since the cost function $c(x)$ is strictly convex, hence improves the bank's profit. Therefore, the bank failure also imposes a positive externality on the surviving bank. The equilibrium of the model depends on these two diverting externalities.

   Note that at $t=1$ the banks' returns from the risky assets are correlated and the degree of correlation is chosen by the banks at $t=0$ as a strategic parameter. Therefore, when one bank's return is low and the correlation is high, it is very likely that the other's return is low as well. The negative externality means that one bank takes little account of its failure's impact on the other bank, and this leads to too high correlation in the banks' investment portfolios. The limited liability of the banks strengthens such incentive. Reversely, positive externality means that the banks tend to choose lower correlation.

The market equilibrium depends on which externality dominates. If the negative externality dominates, the banks will choose highly correlated investment portfolio at $t=0$ and maximize the probability of joint survival (Case 1) and joint failure (Case 2); if the positive externality dominates, the banks will choose less correlated investment portfolio at $t=0$ and maximize the probability of taking over the rivalry (Case 3).

In terms of the social welfare, the cost from the joint failure of the banks is too high. When there is a bank failure, it is *ex post* desirable to have a survival bank who is able to take over (part of) the investors and reduce the social cost. Therefore, the first best solution is the banks diversify their risks (in aggregate level. The incentive for the banks to diversify the components in their individual investment portfolios is examined in Wagner (2011)) and reduce the correlation of portfolios. However, in the presence of the negative externality, the banks' investments can be over-correlated, increasing the systemic risk of joint bank failure.

The externality of the bank failure is also the key mechanism of Wagner (2009), which considers a financial market with a continuum of banks rather than two banks, all offering fixed deposit contracts, their portfolios being invested in two types of assets. A bank suffers from bank run when it cannot meet the contract. Liquidation costs increase with the number of the bank runs. However, since each bank is atomistic in this economy, the marginal liquidation cost when one more bank fails is zero. Therefore, when deciding about its investment portfolio, each single bank never internalizes its impact on the social cost of bank runs, imposing a negative externality on the banking industry. As a result, the banks' equilibrium portfolios correlate in an inefficient way. Therefore, small banking failures may ripple to a large amount of banks with similar investment strategies. Hence banking regulation should take correlation of the banks' assets into account, encouraging heterogeneous investment.

The banks' decision on interconnectedness is modeled in Acharya and Yorulmazer (2008) as well, through a completely different channel. Here, incentives to correlate arise from informational spillovers. Starting from a two-bank economy, when the returns of bank's investments have a systemic factor, the failure of one bank conveys negative information about this factor which makes market participants skeptical about the health of the banking industry, inflating the borrowing cost of the surviving bank and increasing its probability to fail. Since such informational spillover is costly for banks, they herd *ex ante* (i.e., they choose perfectly correlated portfolio) to boost the likelihood of joint survival, given that bankers' limited liability mitigates concerns about their joint failure. Again, systemic risk arises out of endogenized excessive correlations.

2.3 Web of claims and the Domino effect

Financial network has a profound impact on financial stability. Besides investing on correlated assets, the financial institutions are networking through actively borrowing from and lending to each other, knitting a giant web of claims. Any shock to a part of the web may trigger all the banks in the network to unwind their positions, leading to a collective fire sale that destabilizes the entire financial system. In this section, we take a stylized banking network as in Shin (2008) to understand such Domino effect.

Consider an economy with a banking sector composed of n risk-neutral, leveraged banks, which finance their projects via raising debt and equity. There is also one non-leveraged sector (populated by households, pension funds, firms, etc.) in the economy that holds the equity and debts of the banks. Note that such non-leveraged sector is both the source of the banking network's funding (for example, households providing deposits for the banks) and the end customer getting the loans from the banks (for example, the households getting mortgage loans from the banks, and the firms borrowing from the banks), its total claims on the banks and by the banks net out. Without loss of generality, suppose that the non-leveraged sector holds a positive share of each bank's debt. The face value of the total debts issued by bank i is denoted by $\bar{x}_i$; among all the bank i's debts, the proportion held by bank j is denoted by π_{ij}. The book value of bank i's equity is denoted by $\bar{e}_i$, and $\bar{y}_i$ is the face value of bank i's loans. As Table 2.1 shows, the balance sheet implies that

$$\bar{y}_i + \sum_{j=1}^{n} \bar{x}_j \pi_{ji} = \bar{x}_i + \bar{e}_i .$$

There is an aggregate credit risk in the banking sector, such that at $t=1$ the total realized return from bank i's loans is $\tilde{y}_i = \gamma \bar{y}_i$, in which γ is randomly drawn from a distribution function with support $[0, 1]$.

Because of the credit risk, the bank may not be able to fully honor its debt, $\bar{x}_i$. Suppose that at $t=1$ the total realized repayment from bank i's debts is $\tilde{x}_i$. If $\tilde{x}_i < \bar{x}_i$, the bank has to default and the creditors share $\tilde{x}_i$ with equal seniority, for example, bank j gets $\tilde{x}_i \pi_{ij}$ from bank i. The realized value of bank i's assets is denoted by

$$\tilde{a}_i = \tilde{y}_i + \sum_{j=1}^{n} \tilde{x}_j \pi_{ji},$$

Table 2.1 The balance sheet of bank i

Assets	Liabilities
Loans $\bar{y}_i$	Equity $\bar{e}_i$
Bonds	Debt $\bar{x}_i$
$\sum_{j=1}^{n} \bar{x}_i \pi_{jt}$	

and this is the maximum value the bank i's creditors can claim, given that the bank's equity can be partially or even fully wiped out. Therefore, the total realized repayment from bank i's debts $\tilde{x}_i$ is

$$\tilde{x}_i = \min\{\tilde{a}_i, \bar{x}_i\}. \qquad (2.5)$$

Notice that $\tilde{a}_i$ depends on the realized repayment from all the banks' debts, denoted by a vector $x = (\tilde{x}_1, \ldots, \tilde{x}_n)$, (2.5) can be generalized as the realized repayments for the entire banking network, or a mapping $F(\cdot)$ that translates the realized value of all the banks' debts into the value that the banks realize from their debt holdings

$$x = F(x, \bar{x}) \qquad (2.6)$$

in which $\bar{x} = (\bar{x}_1, \ldots, \bar{x}_n)$ is the vector capturing the face value of all the banks' debts.

And the market value of equity is therefore

$$\tilde{e}_i = \tilde{y}_i + \sum_{j=1}^{n} \tilde{x}_j \pi_{ji} - \tilde{x}_i = \tilde{a}_i - \tilde{x}_i.$$

As is proved by Eisenberg and Noe (2001), which is based on Tarski's Fixed Point Theorem (see Topkis, 1998), there is a unique solution for x in (2.6). Therefore, one can find each bank's realized debt payment $\tilde{x}_1$ when the aggregate shock γ is realized.

The fixed point result also implies the algorithm of computing the equilibrium solution for $x = (\tilde{x}_1, \ldots, \tilde{x}_n)$. Starting from any arbitrary allocation for x, the mapping $F(\cdot)$ ensures the convergence to the fixed point. Suppose that we start from $x^0 = (0, \ldots, 0)$ such that the banks repay nothing on their debts. As long as $\gamma > 0$, any bank has a positive return from its loans, $\tilde{y}_i > 0$, implying a positive value for its debts, i.e., if we feed x^0 into the mapping $F(\cdot)$, the realized value should be positive at least for some banks,

$$x^1 = F(x^0, \bar{x}) \geq x^0.$$

We can continue feeding x^1 into the mapping $F(\cdot)$, and the outcome x^2 is off equilibrium if

$$x^2 = F(x^1, \bar{x}) \geq x^1.$$

The iteration is repeated until the t-th round, if

$$x^{t+1} = F(x^t, \bar{x}) \geq x^t.$$

The result x^t is the fixed point, or equilibrium solution for x.

Such banking network provides a powerful framework for analyzing the systemic impact of any financial stress, no matter whether it is local or global. It can also be used to test the robustness of an existing network, using any "worst possible scenario" as the input and see how much the likely damage is. It can be also shown that x is increasing with γ, i.e., a negative shock to the banks' returns ends up with a global decline in the value of the banks' debts, exhibiting the Domino effect. We will not go into further details, but rather see how such Domino effect propagates in a given network structure.

2.4 The network structure and financial stability

The network structure also matters for the resilience of the interconnected banks. In this section we will see how network structure affects systemic risk through a model taken from Allen and Gale (2000), which extends the banking structure of Diamond and Dybvig (1983) into a networked world.

2.4.1 Model setup

The agents, time preferences, and technology

In this economy, there are two groups of agents: investors and banks. The economy extends over three periods, $t=0, 1, 2$. It is assumed that:

1   The banking industry spreads over four *ex ante* identical regions, $i \in \{A, B, C, D\}$, each with one representative bank as regional financial intermediary.
2   In each region, there is a continuum of *ex ante* identical investors, each of which is endowed with one unit of consumption good at $t=0$. *Ex post*, the true preference of each investor gets revealed at $t=1$:

    a   with probability $p \in (0, 1)$ one investor is early investor so that she only values consumption at $t=1$, i.e., $U_e=u(c_1)$;
    b   with probability $1-p$ one investor is late investor so that she only values consumption at $t=2$, i.e., $U_l=u(c_2)$.

It is worth noting that in each region the banking industry is perfectly competitive in the deposit market. In the rest of this section, we focus on the pure strategy equilibrium so that it is reasonable to regard each of the regions, A, B, C, or D, as being represented by one bank. We call each representative bank A, B, C, or D for simplicity.

Similar as the settings in Diamond and Dybvig (1983), the banks offer demand deposit contracts. The difference here is that one bank can have both investors and the other banks as its customers, i.e., the banks can hold deposits of each other as interbank deposits. Assume that all the depositors are equal, so one bank has the same kind of claim as the investors' for its deposits in the other banks. More details about interbank deposits will be explained later.

The regions are heterogeneous in p, so the probability for an investor in region i being early investor is denoted by p_i. For each region there are two states with equal probability, i.e., $p_i \in \{p_H, p_L\}$ with $p_H > p_L$, and $Pr(p_i = p_H) = 0.5$. There are two states of the world $S_j = (p_A, p_B, p_C, p_D)$ with equal probability: either $S_1 = (p_H, p_L, p_H, p_L)$ or $S_2 = (p_L, p_H, p_L, p_H)$. One investor's preference is her private information; therefore, a late investor can imitate the early investor by withdrawing early and consuming late.

There are two linear technologies:

1 Storage technology. This technology is shared by both investors and banks, transferring one unit input at t into one unit output at $t+1$. The projects using such technology are *short assets*, or *liquid assets*.
2 Investment technology. This technology is only enjoyed by the banks, transferring one unit input at $t=0$ into $R>1$ units output at $t=2$. The projects using such technology are *long assets*, or *illiquid assets*. If the project is terminated at $t=1$ before it gets matured, it only gives a poor return $c \in (0, 1)$.

Timing

The timing of the model is summarized in Table 2.2, which is quite similar to Table 1.2 in the standard Diamond–Dybvig bank run model. One bank invests on both short and long assets at $t=0$. At $t=1$ the bank uses the proceeds from the short assets plus, if necessary, the liquidated value of some long assets, to repay the early investors. At $t=2$, the proceeds from all remaining long assets are paid to the late investors.

2.4.2 Equilibrium

The planner's problem

As a reference, the first best allocation is defined by the solution to the planner's problem. Suppose that the planner is able to identify the true type of the investors. Since the investors are *ex ante* identical, the planner's problem is to choose

Table 2.2 Timing of the model

$t=0$	$t=1$	$t=2$
Investors	$S_{i,j}$ gets revealed:	
Deposit	Early investors: withdraw c_1	
	Late investors: wait	Withdraw c_2
Bank *i*	Get returns from short assets	Get returns from the
Offer deposit contract	When necessary, liquidate interbank	remaining long assets
(c_1, c_2) along with α	deposits, then long assets	Repay late investors
Deposit in the other banks	Repay early investors	

a bank's investment portfolio $(\alpha, 1-\alpha)$ with α being the share invested in the liquid assets as well as the representative investor's consumption in period 1 and 2, denoted by (c_1, c_2), to maximize the investor's expected utility at $t=0$. Precisely, the planner's problem is choosing the optimal profile (α^*, c_1^*, c_2^*) to

$$\max_{\{\alpha, c_1, c_2\}} \bar{p}u(c_1)+(1-\bar{p})u(c_2), \tag{2.6}$$

$$s.t. \, \bar{p}c_1 = \alpha, \tag{2.7}$$

$$(1-\bar{p})c_2 = R(1-\alpha) \tag{2.8}$$

in which

$$\bar{p} = \frac{p_H + p_L}{2}$$

denotes the expected probability of a investor being an early one. The early investors are paid by the yields from the liquid assets, as budget constraint (2.7) says, and the late investors are paid by the yields from the illiquid assets, as (2.8) says. The optimal solution is featured by the first order condition, $u'(c_1)=Ru'(c_2)$, which implies that $c_1<c_2$ since $R>1$. Furthermore, $c_1<c_2$ means that a late investor doesn't have the incentive to mimic the early ones, therefore, the optimal allocation can be achieved even if the planner cannot observe the investor's true type. Since there is no aggregate uncertainty for the entire economy, at $t=1$ the planner just needs to reallocate the excess liquidity supply from regions with p_L to the regions with excess liquidity demand, i.e., where $p_i=p_H$.

The banking network and market equilibrium

Whether the first best allocation can be replicated by the market equilibrium crucially depends on the structure of the banking sector, i.e., how the banks are interconnected. In an interconnected banking network, the banks are able to exchange deposit before the liquidity shock is revealed at $t=1$ and insure against the uncertainty of the investors' time preferences. The first best allocation is never achieved by the regional banks isolated from the other regions. To see this, suppose that one bank in region i adopts (α^*, c_1^*, c_2^*), in which $\bar{p}c_1^*=\alpha^*$. However, when it turns out that $p_i=p_H$, the bank cannot meet the demands of early investors by only using the yields of the liquid assets since $p_H c_1^*>\alpha^*$; therefore, part of the illiquid assets have to be liquidated. As a result, the realized consumption for the late investors, c_2, must be smaller than c_2^*. To make it worse, if the liquidation return c is small enough such that $c_2<c_1^*$, the late investors will prefer to mimic the early ones and withdraw at $t=1$, leading to a bank run.

To see the impact of the structure of the banking sector on the market equilibrium, we start from the case of complete financial network. As Figure 2.3 shows, each region is connected with the other three, two being negatively correlated in

p and one positively correlated. The interbank deposit market allows the bank in region i to hold

$$d_i = \frac{p_H - \bar{p}}{2}$$

deposits in each of the other regions before $t=1$. It is assumed that the interbank deposit contract is the same as the deposit contract of the investors, i.e., the return of one unit of interbank deposit is c_1 (c_2) if it is withdrawn at $t=1$ ($t=2$).

To find the optimal strategic profile (α, c_1, c_2) of bank i, suppose that at $t=1$, p_i turns out to be p_H. The total deposit claims of the bank include the liquidity demand from the early investors and the other bank with p_H, and the total liquidity available includes its own investment on liquid assets plus the deposits in the other regions. The budget constraint of such bank is therefore

$$\left(p_H + \frac{p_H - \bar{p}}{2} \right) c_1 = \alpha + \frac{3(p_H - \bar{p})}{2} c_1, \tag{2.9}$$

and it's easily seen that (2.9) is equivalent to (2.7). Correspondingly, the bank from a region with low liquidity demand p_L has to meet the demand of both its early investors and the banks with p_H out of the yields of its liquid assets

$$\left[p_L + \frac{2(p_H - \bar{p})}{2} \right] c_1 = \alpha, \tag{2.10}$$

which is equivalent to (2.7), too.

At $t=2$, all the late investors and banks holding interbank deposits get repaid. The budget constraint of bank i is

$$\left[(1 - p_H) + \frac{2(p_H - \bar{p})}{2} \right] c_2 = R(1 - \alpha), \tag{2.11}$$

which is equivalent to (2.8), and the budget constraint of a bank with p_L is

$$\left[(1 - p_L) + \frac{p_H - \bar{p}}{2} \right] c_2 = R(1 - \alpha) + \frac{3(p_H - \bar{p})}{2} c_2, \tag{2.11}$$

which is equivalent to (2.8), too.

Since each bank maximizes the representative investor's expected utility, $\bar{p}$ $u(c_1)+(1-\bar{p})u(c_2)$, at $t=0$ – which is the same as (2.6) – and the budget constraints for the following periods are no different from (2.7) and (2.8), the market equilibrium outcome should be the same as the first best allocation defined by the planner's problem. Therefore, the first best allocation is achieved in the complete network where the banks can hedge against the liquidity shocks by holding deposits among each other.

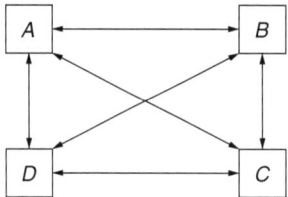

Figure 2.3 Complete financial network.

What happens if the network is incomplete and each bank has limited partici-pation in the interbank deposit market? One example is Figure 2.4, in which the banks are only able to hold deposits from its closest neighbors, e.g., *B* holds deposits from *A*, *C* holds deposits from *B*. Suppose the bank in region *i* holds $d_i = p_H - \bar{p}$ deposits in the connected region and p_H is revealed at $t=1$. The budget constraints for bank *i* and a bank with p_L are $p_H c_1 = \alpha + (p_H - \bar{p})c_1$ and $[p_L + (p_H - \bar{p})]c_1 = \alpha$ respectively, which are both equivalent to (2.7). Similarly, at $t=2$ the budget constraints for both types of banks are

$$[(1 - p_H) + (p_H - \bar{p})]c_2 = R(1 - \alpha) \tag{2.12}$$

and

$$(1 - p_L)c_2 = R(1 - \alpha) + (p_H - \bar{p})c_2 \tag{2.13}$$

and both are equivalent to (2.8). Therefore the market equilibrium outcome is again the same as the first best, as long as the entire economy stays connected despite the incompleteness of the network.

It can be further shown that the first best allocation can be achieved in a more incomplete financial network, such as Figure 2.5 shows. The economy is divided into two subsets, each containing two regions. Only banks in the same subset hold deposits from each other. When the bank in region *i* holds $d_i = p_H - \bar{p}$ depos-its in the connected region, it can be easily seen that the budget constraints are no different from (2.7) and (2.8).

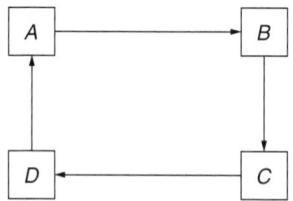

Figure 2.4 Incomplete financial network I.

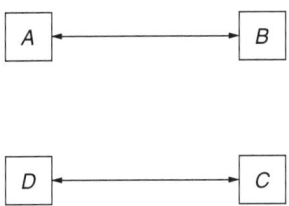

Figure 2.5 Incomplete financial network II.

2.4.3 Network and contagion

The analysis above shows that the banks achieve optimal risk sharing via inter-connection, as long as the liquidity shocks are idiosyncratic, i.e., for the inter-connected banks, the aggregate liquidity demand and supply remain the same under all states of the world. However, things may change when there is an aggregate liquidity shock. Take Figure 2.4 as an example: suppose that at $t=1$ the realized state of the world is $(p_H+\varepsilon, p_L, p_H, p_L)$, $0<\varepsilon<1-p_H$, instead of (p_H, p_L, p_H, p_L). Since this has not been expected at $t=0$, the strategic profile of each bank is still the first best one (α^*, c_1^*, c_2^*). However, bank A is now unable to meet the demand of its early investors even if it liquidates both its short assets and its deposits in bank B since $(p_H+\varepsilon)c_1^*>\alpha+(p_H-\bar{p})c_1^*$, therefore it needs to liquidate part of its long assets. But there is a limit for bank A to do so: since the return from early liquidation of the long assets, c, is very low, the expected return of bank A's late investors, $E[c_2]$, sharply declines. If the unexpected shock ε is so high that it makes $E[c_2]<c_1^*$, the late investors will have the incentive to mimic the early ones and run on the bank. This forces bank A to liquidate all its assets, including the deposit from bank D. Because of the costly bank run, all the investors of bank A and bank D receive very poor return at $t=1$. But bank D's late investors are partly paid out of the return from its interbank deposits at bank A, as the right hand side of (2.12) shows. When such return becomes low, the expected return of bank D's late investors declines, too. This may trigger a run on bank D – the contagion happens.

To formalize the idea, suppose that there exists another state of the world $\tilde{S}=(\bar{p}+\varepsilon, \bar{p}, \bar{p}, \bar{p})$, in addition to S_1 and S_2, with probability close to zero, i.e., bank A gets more early consumers than expected at $t=1$ while all the other banks' early consumer population remains the same as expected. Since the event $\tilde{S}$ rarely happens, the equilibrium allocation should be the same as before. Further, assume that the structure of banking network takes the form as Figure 2.4.

Since bank A now faces higher liquidity demand than expected in the inter-mediate period, it needs to raise funds from all the resources available, including

1   its own holding of liquid assets;
2   its deposits in the other banks;
3   its own holding of illiquid assets.

The decision on which asset should be liquidated first depends on the opportunity cost of early liquidation. Since liquid asset matures at $t=1$, its liquidation does not incur any opportunity cost. In contrast, withdrawing the deposit from the other banks in $t=1$ instead of $t=2$ implies a positive opportunity cost since bank A only gets c_1^* instead of c_2^*, $c_1^* < c_2^*$. Similarly, liquidating the long assets in $t=1$ means that bank A has to give up the high yield R to get the poor early return c. Since it is already known that

$$\frac{c_2^*}{c_1^*} > 1,$$

implying that bank A withdraws its interbank deposits only if all the liquid assets are exhausted, we can make sure that the bank won't liquidate its long assets before all its interbank deposits are withdrawn by further assuming

$$\frac{R}{c} > \frac{c_2^*}{c_1^*}.$$

In the presence of the liquidity shock, the survival of bank A at $t=1$ depends on whether its consumers run or not. Note that the bank run happens only if the late consumers' expected return falls below c_1^* so that they want to withdraw early. In the other words, when the bank run does happen, the bank has to liquidate all the assets and obtain (1) α from the liquid assets, (2) redeemed value from its $d_A = p_H - \bar{p}$ deposits in bank B, and (3) the liquidated value of its long assets, $c(1-\alpha)$ in order to meet (1) the claims from both its early and late consumers, 1, and (2) the $d_D = p_H - \bar{p}$ claim from bank D who made interbank deposit in bank A. The realized value for each unit of deposit claim is therefore

$$q_A = \frac{a + c(1-\alpha) + q_B d_A}{1 + d_D}. \tag{2.14}$$

The realized value, or "shadow value" of one unit deposit in bank i is denoted by q_i – obviously the value that bank A is able to redeem from its deposit in bank B is $q_B d_A$. Therefore, bank A suffers from a bank run only if $q_A < c_1^*$, i.e., q_i is the survival indicator for bank i at $t=1$.

Such shadow value q_i captures the feature that the banks are interconnected by the financial network. Note that the expression of q_A contains q_B, and q_B should be a function of q_C, and so on. Therefore, once there is a bank failure, its impact will soon ripple to the next bank through a falling shadow value of its interbank deposit. The liquidity crisis on an individual bank may become contagious and finally end up as a systemic event along the banking network.

However, as we argued in Section 2.4.2, by cross-holding deposits from each other, the network also provides a risk sharing mechanism which works as a buffer for each bank upon liquidity shocks. The bank failure becomes contagious only when the buffer fails. But even when the bank failure starts to spread, such buffer may prevent it from propagating further. To make it precise, we can characterize one bank's buffer in the following way. First, as a reference, consider one bank which is in autarky and not connected to the financial network follows the first best allocation (α^*, c_1^*, c_2^*). Given an arbitrary number $p \in [0, 1]$ as the realized share of early consumers, the bank is free from runs only if the late consumers get a return at least as high as c_1^*, i.e., the aggregate demand from the late consumers is at least $(1-p)c_1^*$. To meet the demand, the bank should keep at least

$$\frac{(1-p)c_1^*}{R}$$

long assets at $t = 1$, and can only liquidate at most

$$1 - \alpha^* - \frac{(1-p)c_1^*}{R}$$

in this period. The value from such early liquidation,

$$c\left[1 - \alpha^* - \frac{(1-p)c_1^*}{R}\right],$$

can be used to fill in the gap when the liquid asset holding, α^*, is not high enough to meet the demand of early consumers. This is exactly the buffer of the bank, denoted by $b(p)$,

$$b(p) = c\left[1 - \alpha^* - \frac{(1-p)c_1^*}{R}\right].$$

Regarding our model, when bank A gets a liquidity shock from a higher early demand, without joining the financial network, the bank's buffer is self-sufficient to avoid the bank run only if the buffer is high enough to cover the excess liquidity demand, i.e.,

$$\varepsilon c_1^* \leq b(\bar{p} + \varepsilon). \tag{2.15}$$

Now suppose that bank A is connected to the financial network as Figure 2.4 and inequality (2.5) holds. The liquidity shock makes little difference from the reference case of autarky. The other banks, together with bank A's late consumers, will suffer a loss from a lower c_2 than c_2^* but wait at $t = 1$ instead of run. However, if ε is so large that the condition (2.15) is violated, the bank will get bankrupted and all its depositors, including bank D, get a significantly low return $q_A < c_1^*$ so that the liquidity shock propagates to bank D through q_D. If the shock on bank D is smaller than its buffer, it can still survive and there is no further propagation of the bank failure. However, if D's buffer is not sufficient to contain the shock, bank D is going bust and the ripple goes on to bank C, or even further.

2.4.4 Discussion

Financial networks provide a risk sharing mechanism for its members. By holding deposits of each other, facing the idiosyncratic liquidity shock, one bank can easily raise funds from the other part of the network where cheaper liquidity supply is available, and the first best allocation can be achieved by the financial market with interbank deposit network. However, the network also increases the banks' exposure to each other, making the entire financial system vulnerable to contagions. One bank's failure may increase the other banks' exposure to risks, even lead to a systemic meltdown.

The role of network structure is rather subtle and ambiguous. As is shown in Section 2.4.2, the completeness of network doesn't seem to change the availability of efficient risk sharing, as long as there is no aggregate uncertainty. By connecting to the other banks, one bank gets insured from bank runs once the idiosyncratic liquidity shocks in the network cancel out altogether – no matter how these banks are connected.

Regarding financial contagion, given a failure from one bank, a more interconnected, or more complete financial network makes it seemingly easier for the failure to propagate. On the other hand, with a certain aggregate creditors' loss coming from the failed bank, a better interconnected network takes more connecting banks to buffer the loss, therefore, intuitively makes it more likely to absorb the loss and stop the propagation. However, such intuition may not be true. From Figure 2.5 to Figure 2.4, one bank's debt exposure to the rest of the network remains at $p_H - \bar{p}$, while from Figure 2.4 to Figure 2.3, the number increases to

$$\frac{3(p_H - \bar{p})}{2}$$

and makes the bank run more likely to happen in the first place when one bank is hit by a liquidity shock. Although more connecting banks provide a larger buffer in this case, it is ambiguous whether financial contagion is less likely or not. Therefore, the fragility of a banking network is not necessarily a monotone function of the network's completeness.

To focus on the network effect of the financial system, assumptions are made for simplification reasons. One of them is that the liquidity shock, the state $\tilde{S}$, happens with zero probability. This is a limiting case for a very small probability of $\tilde{S}$ so that the banks' optimal strategy should be the same as that in the first best solution. However, although in the state $\tilde{S}$ only bank A experiences the liquidity shock, the event leads to aggregate liquidity shortage because the shock is no longer to be offset by an opposite one in the aggregate level such as in the state S_1 or S_2. Therefore, if the probability for state $\tilde{S}$ is not small enough to be neglected, all the banks in the network will raise their investments on liquid assets at $t = 0$ to be better prepared for the bad event. To what extent the financial market is viable to solve the problem of aggregate liquidity shortage, and how the network structure affects such viability, remain as interesting questions for future research.

3 Endogenous exposure to systemic liquidity risks

In the previous chapters, the shocks to the banks are mostly exogenous, or unanticipated. In other words, the risks to the banks are not systemic since they are not internalized by the banks' investment decisions. Therefore, one may argue that in the general equilibrium framework where the banks take into account the risks in decision making, they will hold liquidity buffers to avoid the crunch.

The problem, however, is that due to limited liability some banks will be encouraged to free-ride on liquidity provision from the others. As a response, the banking competition will force the other banks to reduce their efforts for liquidity provision, too, generating the systemic risk. Chuck Prince, at that time chief executive of Citigroup, gave a perfect interpretation on such problem posed in fairly poetic terms on July 10, 2007 in an infamous interview with the *Financial Times*: "When the music stops, in terms of liquidity, things will be complicated. But as long as the music is playing, you've got to get up and dance. We're still dancing." And the key problem is best captured by the following remark about Citigroup in the *New York Times* report "Treasury Dept. Plan Would Give Fed Wide New Power" on March 29, 2008:

> Mr. Frank said he realized the need for tighter regulation of Wall Street firms after a meeting with Charles O. Prince III, then chairman of Citigroup. When Mr. Frank asked why Citigroup had kept billions of dollars in "structured investment vehicles" off the firm's balance sheet, he recalled, Mr. Prince responded that Citigroup, as a bank holding company, would have been at a disadvantage because investment firms can operate with higher debt and lower capital reserves.

Most existing literature on banking crises mainly focus on how banking crises evolve, rather than why the banking industry arrives at the brink of collapse. Therefore, liquidity shortage is usually introduced as an exogenous shock, instead of a strategic outcome. For example, Freixas, Parigi and Rochet (2000, 2004) model systemic liquidity risk out of coordinative failure from the interbank market, and a banking crisis may be triggered by an exogenous insolvency shock; therefore, closing insolvent banks helps cut off the contagion chain and save the system. Taking liquidity risk as (partially) exogenously given certainly works well for understanding the development of banking crisis, however, one has to be cautious when applying these models on banking regulation. As is stated in Acharya (2009), "Such partial equilibrium approach has a serious shortcoming from the standpoint of understanding sources of, and addressing, inefficient systemic risk." In other words, if we admit that it is equally important to establish proper regulatory rules *ex ante* as to bailout the failing banks *ex post*, it should be equally crucial to ask what causes the failure as to tell how severe the crisis can be, i.e., systemic liquidity risk should be an endogenous phenomenon.

This chapter bridges the gap and provides a theory explaining why the financial institutions systematically make underinvestment on liquid assets. The theory builds on the set up of Diamond and Rajan (2006) and extends it to capture the feedback from liquidity provision to risk taking incentives of financial intermediaries. As in Diamond and Rajan (2006), deposit contracts solve a hold up problem for impatient lenders investing in illiquid projects: these contracts give banks as financial intermediaries a credible commitment mechanism not to extract rents from their specific skills. But at the same time deposit contracts make non-strategic default very costly. Consequently, negative aggregate shocks may trigger bank runs with serious costs for the whole economy, thus destroying the commitment mechanism.

Here we extend the setup of Diamond and Rajan (2006) in several ways. In their model, the type of risky projects is exogenously given. Banks can either invest in risky, possibly illiquid projects or invest instead in a safe liquid asset with inferior return. In the equilibrium they characterize, banks invest all resources either in illiquid or liquid assets. In contrast, here we determine endogenously the aggregate level of illiquidity out of private investments. As in Diamond and Rajan (2006), illiquidity is captured by the notion that some fraction of projects turns out to be realized late. In contrast to their approach, however, we allow banks to choose the proportion of funds invested in less liquid projects continuously. These projects have a higher expected return, but at the same time also a higher probability of late realization. Because of that feature, some banks will have an incentive to free-ride on liquidity. Banks investing a larger share in illiquid projects with higher, yet delayed returns will always be more profitable as long as they stay solvent. Yet there is an economic role for liquidity to satisfy the need for early withdrawals by investors in our model. The problem is that the free-riding banks can always attract funds away from those prudent banks which had invested in more liquid, but less profitable assets (to use the poetic phrase by Mervyn King: "those financial institutions that sat out the dance").

In times of a liquidity crisis, the free-riding banks will run into trouble. They would have to leave the market, to make sure that in equilibrium the *ex ante* expected returns for depositors are the same for both free-riding and prudent banks. It is the banks' collective excess risk taking that leads to the aggregate liquidity shortage in the market. The systemic risk thus comes from the banks' endogenous investment decisions.

3.1 The maturity mismatch and liquidity

To capture the banks' endogenous exposure to the systemic liquidity risk in a tractable way, we first model the liquidity problem following Cao and Illing (2011).

The agents, time preferences, and technology

In this economy, there are three types of agents: investors, banks (run by bank managers), and entrepreneurs. All agents are risk neutral. The economy extends over three periods: $t=0$, 1, 2, and the details of timing will be explained later. We assume the following:

1 There is a continuum of investors, each initially (at $t=0$) endowed with one unit of resources. The resource can be either stored (with a gross return equal to one) or invested in the form of bank deposits.
2 There is a finite number N of active banks engaged in Bertrand competition, competing for investors' deposits. Using these deposits, the banks as financial intermediaries can fund projects of entrepreneurs.
3 There is a continuum of entrepreneurs. There are two types of them (denoted by i, $i=1$, 2), characterized by their project returns R_i.

    a Projects of type 1 (safe projects) are realized early at period $t=1$ with a safe return $R_1>1$.
    b Projects of type 2 (risky projects) give a higher return $R_2>R_1>1$. With probability p, these projects will also be realized at $t=1$, but they may be delayed (with probability $1-p$) until $t=2$. Therefore, in the aggregate, the share p of type 2 projects will be realized early. The aggregate share p, however, is not known at $t=0$. It will only be revealed between periods 0 and 1 at some intermediate period; call it $t=0.5$. In the following, we are interested in the case of aggregate shocks. We model them in the simplest way: the aggregate share of type 2 projects realized early, p, can take on just two values – either p_H or p_L with $p_H>p_L$. The "good" state with a high share of early type 2 projects p_H, i.e., the state with plenty of liquidity, will be realized with probability π. In the following, we assume that $1<p_sR_2<R_1$ ($s\in\{H, L\}$) to focus on the relevant case (to be explained later).

Investors are impatient: they want to consume early (at $t=1$). In contrast, both entrepreneurs and bank managers are indifferent between consuming early ($t=1$) or late ($t=2$). Focusing on the case of liquidity constraints being binding, we assume that resources of investors are scarce in the sense that there are more projects of each type available than the aggregate endowment of investors. Thus, in a first best market economy (in the absence of commitment problems, as explained in the next paragraph), total surplus would go to the investors. They would simply put all their funds in early projects and capture the full return.

We take this frictionless market outcome as our reference point and seek to minimize the distance in terms of the investors' welfare between this reference point and the equilibrium outcome under various policies. Hold-up problems prevent realization of the frictionless market outcome, creating a demand for liquidity. Since there is a market demand for liquidity only if investors' funds are the limiting factor, we choose the investors' payoff as the policy maker's objective and concentrate on deviations from this market outcome. With investors' payoff as the relevant criterion, we analyze those equilibria coming closest to implementing the frictionless market outcome.

Due to hold-up problems as modeled in Hart and Moore (1994), or Holmström and Tirole (1997), entrepreneurs can only commit to pay a fraction $\gamma < 1$ of their return with $\gamma R_i > 1$. Banks as financial intermediaries can pool investment; they have superior collection skills (a higher γ, which justifies their role as intermediaries). In the following, we also assume that $p_s \leq \gamma$ ($s \in \{H, L\}$) to concentrate on the relevant case that investors care about investment in liquid projects (see Section 3.3.1). Following Diamond and Rajan (2001), banks offer deposit contracts with a fixed payment d_0 payable at any time after $t = 0$ as a credible commitment device not to abuse their collection skills. The threat of a bank run disciplines bank managers to fully pay out all available resources pledged in the form of bank deposits. Deposit contracts, however, introduce a fragile structure into the economy: whenever investors have doubts about their bank's liquidity (the ability to pay investors the promised amount d_0 at $t = 1$), they run on the bank at the intermediate date, forcing the bank to liquidate all its projects (even those funding entrepreneurs with safe projects) at high costs: early liquidation of projects gives only the inferior return $c < 1$. In the following, we do not consider pure sunspot bank runs of the Diamond and Dybvig (1983) type. Instead, we concentrate on the runs happening if liquid funds are not sufficient to pay out investors.

Timing and events

At date $t = 0$, banks competing for funds offer deposit contracts with payment d_0 which maximize the expected return of investors. Banks compete by choosing the share α of deposits invested in type 1 projects, taking their competitors' choice as given. Investors have rational expectations about each bank's default probability; they are able to monitor all banks' investment. Remember that, at this stage, the share p of type 2 projects that will be realized early is not yet known.

At date $t = 0.5$, the value of p is revealed, as is the expected return of the banks at $t = 1$. A bank will experience a run if it cannot meet the investors' demand. If this happens, all the assets – even the safe projects – have to be liquidated. Those banks which do not suffer a run trade with early entrepreneurs in a perfectly competitive market for liquidity at $t = 1$, clearing at interest rate r. Note that because of the hold-up problem, entrepreneurs retain a rent – their share $(1 - \gamma)$ R_i. Since early entrepreneurs are indifferent between consuming at $t = 1$ or $t = 2$, they are willing to provide liquidity (using their rent to deposit at banks at $t=1$ at the market rate r). Banks use the liquidity provided to pay out investors. In this way, impatient investors can profit indirectly from the investment in high-yielding long-term projects. So banking allows the transformation between liquid claims and illiquid projects.

At date $t=2$, the banks collect the return from the late projects and pay back the early entrepreneurs at the predetermined interest rate r.

Note that the aggregate liquidity available at date $t=1$ depends on the total share of funds, α, invested in liquid type 1 projects at date $t=0$. As long as the banks are liquid, the payoff structure is described as in Figure 3.1. But if α is so low that the banks cannot honor deposits when p_L occurs, investors will run at $t=0.5$. The payoff in that case is captured in Figure 3.2.

The liquidity problem thus arises from the maturity mismatch. The banks would be better off if they can invest all the deposits on the illiquid assets; however, since the investors only value consumption one period after depositing, the banks need to raise liquidity in the intermediate date in order to meet the demand of the investors as well as to keep the long assets going.

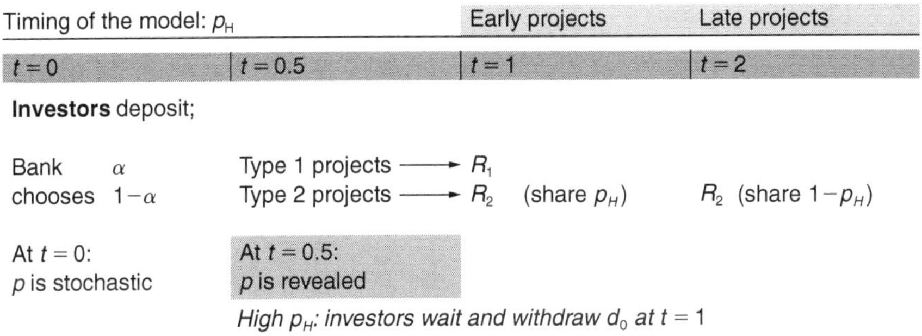

Timing of the model: p_H		Early projects	Late projects
$t=0$	$t=0.5$	$t=1$	$t=2$

Investors deposit;

Bank	α	Type 1 projects $\longrightarrow R_1$		
chooses	$1-\alpha$	Type 2 projects $\longrightarrow R_2$	(share p_H)	R_2 (share $1-p_H$)

At $t=0$:	At $t=0.5$:
p is stochastic	p is revealed

High p_H: investors wait and withdraw d_0 at $t=1$

Figure 3.1 Timing and payoff structure, when banks are liquid.

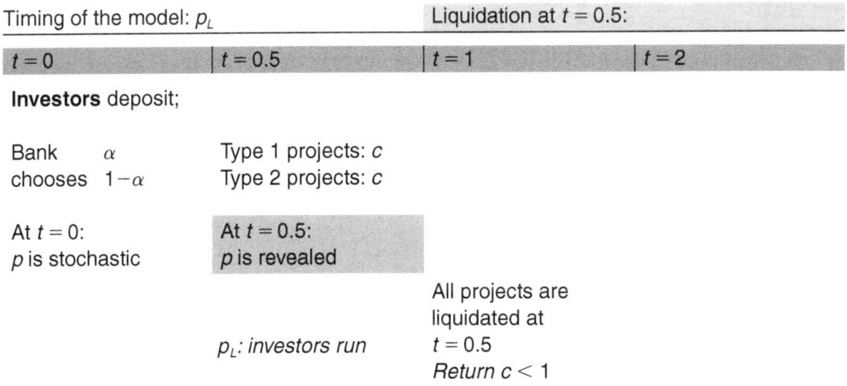

Timing of the model: p_L		Liquidation at $t=0.5$:
$t=0$	$t=0.5$	$t=1$	$t=2$

Investors deposit;

Bank	α	Type 1 projects: c
chooses	$1-\alpha$	Type 2 projects: c

At $t=0$:	At $t=0.5$:
p is stochastic	p is revealed

p_L: investors run | All projects are liquidated at $t=0.5$ Return $c<1$

Figure 3.2 Timing and payoff structure, when banks are illiquid.

3.2 The constrained efficiency

We first analyze the problem of a central planner maximizing the investors' payoff. This provides the reference point for the market equilibrium with banks as financial intermediaries characterized in the next section. Investors being impatient, the central planner would choose the share invested in illiquid projects so as to maximize the resources available to investors at period 1. Since $p_s R_2 < R_1$, in the absence of hold-up problems, the planner would invest only in liquid type 1 projects, this way maximizing resources available at period 1. But due to the hold-up problem caused by entrepreneurs, the central planner can implement only a constrained efficient solution. If the central planner had unlimited taxation authority, he or she could eliminate the hold-up problem completely by taxing the entrepreneurs' rent and redistributing the resources to the investors. Again, all resources would be invested only in liquid type 1 projects, and the entrepreneurs' rents would be transferred to the investors in period 1.

Obviously, allowing for non-distortionary taxation biases the comparison between market and planner's solution, giving the planner an unfair advantage. Effectively, redistribution via lump-sum taxation would make both hold-up and liquidity constraints non-binding, assuming the relevant issues away. To make the planner's constrained optimization problem interesting, we assume that non-distortionary taxation is not feasible in period 1. In order to impose sensible restrictions, we take private endowments as a binding constraint and assume that the entrepreneur has to receive an equivalent compensation when he or she is asked to give up resources in period 1. Being indifferent between consuming at $t=1$ and $t=2$, the entrepreneur needs to be compensated by an appropriate transfer in period 2. In order not to distort the comparison in favor of banks, we furthermore assume that the planner has the same collection skills (the same γ) as financial intermediaries.

Given these constraints, the constrained efficient solution is characterized in the following proposition.

Proposition 3.1 The optimal solution for the central planner's problem is as follows:

1   If there is no aggregate risk, i.e., when p_s is known at $t=0$, the planner invests the share

$$\alpha = \frac{\gamma - p_s}{\gamma - p_s + (1-\gamma)\dfrac{R_1}{R_2}} \quad (s \in \{H, L\})$$

in liquid projects and the investors' return is maximized at $\gamma E[R_s] = \gamma[\alpha_s R_1 + (1-\alpha_s)R_2]$.

2   In the presence of aggregate risk, the central planner implements the following state-contingent strategy, depending on the probability π for p_H being realized: the planner invests the share α_H in liquid projects as long as

$$\bar{\pi}_2' = \frac{\gamma E[R_L] - \kappa}{\gamma E[R_H] - \kappa} \leq \pi \leq 1$$

with $\kappa = \alpha_H R_1 + (1 - \alpha_H) p_L R_2$, and the share $\alpha_L > \alpha_H$ for $0 \leq \pi < \bar{\pi}_2'$.

Proof: see Appendix 3.4.1.

The first part of the proposition says that if p is known, the planner simply chooses α so as to maximize the investors' return. The second part says that if p is unknown, the planner faces a trade-off: the investors' return is maximized under p_H if the planner chooses α_H, but will be low if p_L is realized; the investors' return is maximized under p_L if the planner chooses α_L, but will be low if p_H is realized. So the optimal solution depends on the likelihood of p_H, that is, on π. When π is high enough, the planner will choose α_H; otherwise, he or she will pick α_L.

Obviously, hold-up and liquidity constraints are bound to have a distributional impact: if resources were taken away from investors in the initial period and redirected toward type 2 entrepreneurs, the commitment problem would no longer be relevant, nor would the need for liquidity provision. Even though such a reallocation would result in higher aggregate resources (all funds being invested in high-return projects), it would yield inferior payoff to investors. Since $p_s R_2 < R_1$, investing less than α_s in liquid projects reduces resources available in period 1 and so makes investors worse off.

In contrast to our modeling strategy, Holmström and Tirole (1998) assume that the lender of last resort has unlimited power to tax real resources and so is always able to redistribute resources *ex post*. This assumption, however, effectively makes liquidity constraints non-binding: the central planner can always redistribute resources *ex post* in such a way as to make them irrelevant. The planner could simply redirect resources to the constrained agents (and potentially compensate the unconstrained). Interestingly, in our model, giving the planner taxation power in period 2 cannot help to improve upon the investors' allocation: the investors being impatient, any redistribution from illiquid projects realized late at $t = 2$ is simply not feasible.

3.3 The market equilibrium and endogenous risk exposure

3.3.1 Market equilibrium without uncertainty

Let us now characterize the market equilibrium with banks as financial intermediaries. First, let us again start with the simplest case with no aggregate uncertainty; i.e., the share p of type 2 projects realized early is known at $t = 0$. The market equilibrium of the model is characterized by bank i's strategic profile (α_i, d_{0i}), $\forall i \in \{1, \ldots, N\}$ such that

1   Bank i's profit is maximized by

$$\alpha_i \arg\max_{\alpha_i \in [0,1]} \gamma \left\{ \alpha_i R_1 + (1-\alpha_i) \left[pR_2 + \frac{(1-p)R_2}{r} \right] \right\}. \tag{3.1}$$

Bank i chooses the share of liquid projects α_i so as to maximize expected discounted returns.

2   Bank i makes zero profit from offering deposit contract

$$d_{0i} = \max_{\alpha_i \in [0,1]} \gamma \left\{ \alpha_i R_1 + (1-\alpha_i) \left[pR_2 + \frac{(1-p)R_2}{r} \right] \right\}. \tag{3.2}$$

Investors deposit their funds at those banks offering the highest return. Thus, with Bertrand competition in the deposit market, the deposit rate d_{0i} offered to investors in equilibrium will be equal to expected returns, maximizing resources available at period 1.

3   The market interest rate is determined in the following way:

a   In equilibrium, all resources available at $t=1$ will be paid out to investors, so $d_{0i} = \alpha_i R_1 + (1-\alpha_i)pR_2$. Banks receive funds $\gamma[\alpha_i R_1 + (1-\alpha_i)pR_2]$ from those projects realized early. In addition, early entrepreneurs are willing to provide liquidity at $t=1$ (depositing their rent at the market rate $r \geq 1$) to solvent banks that are able to meet their liabilities to the investors, that is, to banks with

$$d_{0i} \leq \gamma \left\{ \alpha_i R_1 + (1-\alpha_i) \left[pR_2 + \frac{(1-p)R_2}{r} \right] \right\}.$$

So the liquidity supplied by early entrepreneurs is $(1-\gamma)[\alpha_i R_1 + (1-\alpha_i) pR_2]$ as long as bank i is expected to stay solvent – that is, as long as it is able to pay out early entrepreneurs at the market rate r at $t=2$ from its late project's return $\gamma(1-\alpha_i)(1-p)R_2$.

Furthermore, as the market clearing condition, aggregate liquidity supply and demand at $t=1$ have to be equal, given that banks stay solvent at the interest rate $r \geq 1$:

$$\sum_{i=1}^{N} r(1-\gamma)[\alpha_i R_1 + (1-\alpha_i)pR_2] = \sum_{i=1}^{N} r\gamma[(1-\alpha_i)(1-p)R_2.$$

b   Finally, when there is excess liquidity supply at $t=1$, i.e., when total intermediate output exceeds the payoff promised to the investors, $r=1$.

If there is no aggregate uncertainty, the market equilibrium with $r=1$ is equivalent to the solution of the social planner's problem: banks will invest such that – on aggregate – they are able to fulfill investors' claims in period 1, so there will be no run.

Proposition 3.2 If there is no aggregate uncertainty, the allocation in the market equilibrium with $r=1$ is identical to the solution of the social planner's problem, characterized by the following:

1 all banks set

$$\alpha = \frac{\gamma - p}{\gamma - p + (1-\gamma)\dfrac{R_1}{R_2}};$$

2 the market interest rate $r=1$.

Proof: see Appendix 3.4.2.

The proposition says that in the absence of aggregate uncertainty, the banks will choose α (the share invested in liquid projects) so as to maximize the depositors' return and to stay solvent at $t=1$, given that entrepreneurs are willing to provide liquidity at that time. This coincides with the solution of the social planner's problem. Since $R_1 > pR_2$ and $\gamma > p$, α will be strictly positive in equilibrium. For given p, there is a unique α maximizing resources available for investors at $t=1$. A bank investing less than this value of α would not be able to pay out the amounts promised to investors at $t=1$ and thus would experience a run at $t=0.5$. A bank investing more than α would be outbid by competitors offering a higher d_{0i}. Note that α is decreasing in p: the larger the share p of type 2 projects realized early, the less need for investment in liquid type 1 projects. For $p > \gamma$, liquid projects are dominated by the risky ones, so there would be no demand for liquid projects at $t=0$. Similarly, there would be no demand for liquid projects at $t=0$ either when $R_1 < pR_2$. Since liquidity is not an issue for these cases, they are ruled out by assumption.

One can go one step further and see that when there is uncertainty on p the market equilibrium with $r=1$ is also in line with the constraint efficient solution, as long as such uncertainty is idiosyncratic. That is, suppose that instead of assuming either p_H or p_L is realized for all the banks, the banks' liquidity risks are idiosyncratic in the sense that for one bank i, the probability p_i follows i.i.d. characterized by pdf $f(p_i)$ with a support $\Omega \in [0, \gamma]$. Then the market equilibrium is featured by:

1 all banks set

$$\alpha(E[p_i]) = \frac{\gamma - E[p_i]}{\gamma - E[p_i] + (1-\gamma)\dfrac{R_1}{R_2}};$$

2 the market interest rate $r=1$.

The result is pretty intuitive: as long as there are just idiosyncratic shocks, banks are always solvent via trade on the liquidity market.

3.3.2 Market equilibrium with aggregate uncertainty

It becomes tricky to find the market equilibrium when there is aggregate uncertainty. Let us briefly sketch the market equilibrium in the following proposition.

Proposition 3.3 When there is aggregate uncertainty:

1   there is a symmetric pure-strategy equilibrium such that all banks set $\alpha = \alpha_H$ for all $\bar{\pi}_2 < \pi \leq 1$, with

$$\bar{\pi}_2 = \frac{\gamma E[R_L] - c}{\gamma E[R_H] - c}$$

and $E[R_s] = \alpha_s R_1 + (1 - \alpha_s) R_2$, $(s \in \{H, L\})$;

2   there is a symmetric pure-strategy equilibrium such that all banks set $\alpha = \alpha_L$ for all $0 \leq \pi < \bar{\pi}_1$, with

$$\bar{\pi}_1 = \frac{\gamma E[R_L] - c}{\gamma R_2 - c};$$

3   there exists no symmetric pure-strategy equilibrium for all $\bar{\pi}_1 \leq \pi \leq \bar{\pi}_2$. However, there exists a unique equilibrium in mixed strategies such that

    a   at $t = 0$, with probability θ a bank chooses to be a free-riding bank that sets $\alpha_r^* = 0$ and with probability $1 - \theta$ a bank chooses to be a prudent bank that sets $0 < \alpha_s^* < \alpha_L$; and

    b   in the mixed-strategy equilibrium, investors are worse off than if all banks would coordinate on the prudent (non-equilibrium) strategy α_L.

Proof: see Appendix 3.4.3.

The intuition behind Proposition 3.3 is as follows: with uncertainty about p, a bank seems to have just two options available – it may either invest so much in safe type 1 projects (α_L) that it will be able to pay out the investors all the time (that is, even if the bad state occurs), or it may invest just enough, α_H, so as to pay out investors only in the good state and experience a run in the bad state. If π is very high (close to one), a bank should choose α_H – to reap the high yields in the good state, since the cost of the bank run in the bad state is rather low. Alternatively, if π is very low (close to zero), it always pays to be prepared for the worst case, so the bank should choose $\alpha_L > \alpha_H$ in safe projects. Since $\alpha_s (s \in \{H, L\})$ is the share invested in safe projects with return R_1, the total payoff by choosing α_s is $E[R_s] = \alpha_s R_1 + (1 - \alpha_s) R_2$, with $E[R_H] > E[R_L]$.

    With a high share α_L of safe projects, the banks will be able to pay out investors in all states. There will never be a bank run. So, independent of π, the expected payoff for investors is $\gamma E[R_L]$. In contrast, with strategy α_H there will be a bank run in the bad state, giving just the bankruptcy payoff c with probability $1 - \pi$. So the return to strategy α_H is $\pi\gamma E[R_H]+(1-\pi)c$, which is increasing in π. Investors get a higher payoff under α_H, if $\pi\gamma E[R_H]+(1-\pi)c>\gamma E[R_L]$, or

$$\pi > \bar{\pi}_2 = \frac{\gamma E[R_L]-c}{\gamma E[R_H]-c}.$$

For $\pi<\bar{\pi}_2$, the investors' payoff is higher with strategy α_L. But if all banks would choose strategy α_L, there will be excess liquidity at $t=1$ if the good state occurs (with a large share of type 2 projects realized early). A bank anticipating this event has a strong incentive to invest all funds in type 2 projects, reaping the benefit of excess liquidity in the good state. As long as the music is playing, such a deviating bank gets up and dances. In the good state, such a free-riding bank can credibly rely on entrepreneurs' excess liquidity at $t=1$, promising to pay back at $t=2$ out of highly profitable projects. After all, at that stage, this bank, free-riding on liquidity, can offer a capital cushion with expected returns well above what prudent banks are able to promise. Of course, if the bad state happens, there is no excess liquidity. Liquidity dries up. The free-riding banks would just bid up the interest rates, urgently trying to get funds. Rational investors, anticipating that these banks will not succeed, will have already triggered a bank run on these banks at $t=0.5$.

As long as the free-riding banks are not supported in the bad state, they are driven out of the market, providing just the return c. Nevertheless, these banks can offer the return $\pi\gamma R_2+(1-\pi)c$ as expected payoff for investors. Thus, a free-riding bank will be able to offer a higher expected return than a prudent bank, provided the probability π for the good state is not too low. The condition is

$$\pi > \bar{\pi}_1 = \frac{\gamma E[R_L]-c}{\gamma R_2 - c}.$$

Since $R_2>E[R_H]$, it pays to free-ride within the range $\bar{\pi}_1 \leq \pi \leq \bar{\pi}_2$.

Obviously, there cannot be an equilibrium in pure strategies within that range. As long as the music is playing, all banks would like to "get up and dance." But then, there would be no prudent bank left providing the liquidity needed to be able to free-ride. In the resulting mixed-strategy equilibrium, a proportion of banks behave prudently, investing some amount $\alpha_s^* < \alpha_L$ in liquid assets, whereas the rest free-ride on liquidity in the good state, choosing $\alpha=0$. Prudent banks reduce α in order to cut down the opportunity cost of investing in safe projects. Interest rates and α_s^* adjust so that investors are indifferent between the two types of banks. At $t=0$, both prudent and free-riding banks offer the same expected return to investors. The proportion of free-riding banks is determined by aggregate market clearing conditions in both states. Free-riding banks experience a run for sure in the bad state, but the high return in the good state R_2 compensates investors for that risk.

As shown in Proposition 3.3, free-riding drives down the return for investors. They are definitely worse off than they would be if all banks coordinated on the

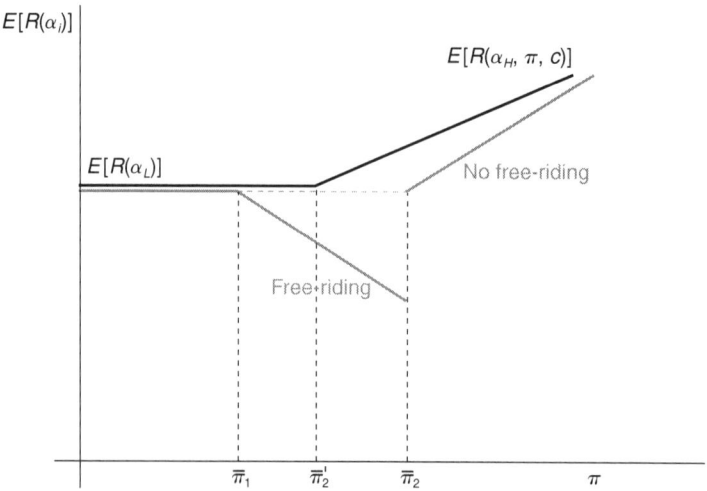

Figure 3.3 Investors' expected return under free-riding compared with the case of no free-riding and the central planner's solution.

prudent strategy α_L – similar to the inefficient mixed-strategy equilibrium in Allen and Gale (2004). The solid gray lines in Figure 3.3 illustrate the investors' expected return in the market equilibrium; as a result of free-riding behavior, the effective return on deposits for investors deteriorates in the range $\bar{\pi}_1 \leq \pi \leq \bar{\pi}_2$, compared with the outcome if all banks would coordinate (off equilibrium) on α_L as the dashed gray line shows.

Compared with the central planner's solution (the solid black line in Figure 3.3), the investor's payoff is lower in the market equilibrium with banks as financial intermediaries for two different reasons: first, free-riding banks reduce the investor's payoff in the mixed-strategy equilibrium in the intermediate case. Second, for high values of $\pi(\bar{\pi}_2 < \pi \leq 1)$, a representative bank, choosing α_H, accepts the risk of a bank run if the bad state occurs (with a low share p_L of illiquid projects realized early). If that state occurs, a bank run is triggered with inefficient liquidation, resulting in an inferior payoff $c < 1$.

Such inefficiencies of market equilibrium arising from a banking model with aggregate liquidity risks also emerge in other frameworks, such as Allen, Carletti, and Gale (2009). Their framework is based on the standard Diamond–Dybvig scenario (see Section 1.1) where the intermediate-date liquidity shock comes from the shock of investors' time preferences. They explicitly model the role of interbank market, and the impact of asset prices. The liquidity shock, the realized population of early investors for each bank contains two elements: one aggregate part that is symmetric across all the banks, plus an idiosyncratic part that is bank-specific. And similar as in Diamond and Dybvig (1983), funded by the demand deposits from the investors, the banks manage a portfolio consisting of both short and long assets. In the intermediate date when the liquidity shock gets revealed for all the banks, there is an interbank market where the banks can trade their holdings of long assets. If there is only idiosyncratic uncertainty, the interbank market facilitates the risk sharing among the banks, allowing the banks with high liquidity demand to sell their long assets to those with low liquidity demand. However, with the presence of the aggregate risk, there will be aggregate liquidity shortage or excess liquidity supply companioned by too low or too high price for long assets, which hinders the banks' capability of reallocating liquidity.

3.4 Appendix

3.4.1 Proof of Proposition 3.1

In the absence of aggregate risk, given p_s ($s \in \{H, L\}$), the social planner maximizes the investors' return by setting α_s such that

$$\alpha_s \ \arg\max_{\alpha_s \in [0,1]} \gamma \left\{ \alpha_i R_1 + (1-\alpha_s) \left[p_s R_2 + \frac{(1-p_s)R_2}{r_s} \right] \right\}, \text{ with } r_s \geq 1 \qquad (3.3)$$

Solve to get

$$\alpha_s = \frac{\gamma - p_s}{\gamma - p_s + (1-\gamma)\dfrac{R_1}{R_2}}, \ r_s = 1.$$

In the presence of aggregate risk, to find the social planner's optimal α which may depend on π, one just has to find the α that maximizes the investors' return for each $\pi \in [0, 1]$.

That the gross interest rate offered to the entrepreneurs at $t=1$ is no less than one implies that for any given α the investors' expected payoff is

$$E[R(\alpha)] = \pi \min\{\alpha R_1 + (1-\alpha)p_H R_2, \gamma[\alpha R_1 + (1-\alpha)R_2]\}$$
$$+(1-\pi)\min\{\alpha R_1 + (1-\alpha)p_L R_2, \gamma[\alpha R_1 + (1-\alpha)R_2]\}$$

which is linear in π. Then it is easy to depict $E[R(\alpha)]$ as a function of π, when $\alpha = \alpha_H$ or α_L, as Figure 3.4 shows. These two lines intersect at

$$\bar{\pi}_2' = \frac{\gamma E[R_L] - \kappa}{\gamma E[R_H] - \kappa}.$$

Note that $E[R(\alpha_H)] = \gamma E[R_H]$ when $\pi=1$, and $E[R(\alpha_H)] = \kappa$ when $\pi=0$.

For any $\alpha \in (\alpha_L, 1]$, $E[R(\alpha)] = \gamma[\alpha R_1 + (1-\alpha)R_2] < E[R(\alpha_L)]$ as the dotted gray lines in Figure 3.4.

For any $\alpha \in [0, \alpha_H)$, $E[R(\alpha)] = \pi[\alpha R_1 + (1-\alpha)p_H R_2] + (1-\pi)[\alpha R_1 + (1-\alpha)p_L R_2]$. Note that $E[R(\alpha)] < \kappa$ when $\pi=0$ and $E[R(\alpha)] < E[R(\alpha_H)]$ when $\pi=1$, as the dotted black lines in Figure 3.4.

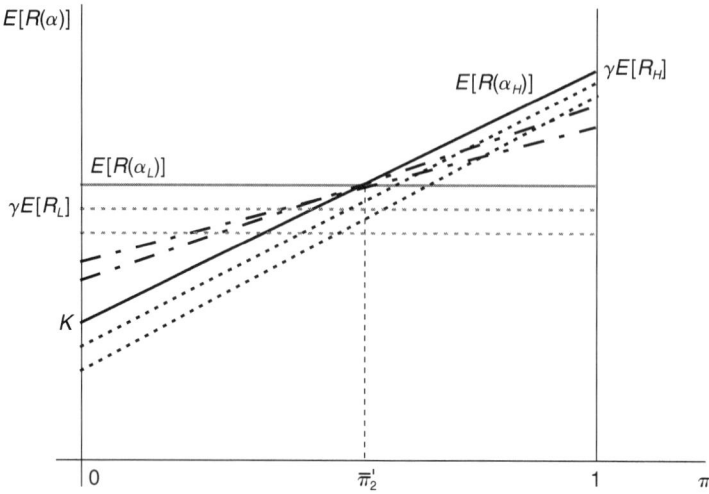

Figure 3.4 The investors' expected return for any $\pi \in [0, 1]$.

For any $\alpha \in (\alpha_H, \alpha_L)$, $E[R(\alpha)] = \pi\{\gamma[\alpha R_1 + (1-\alpha)R_2]\} + (1-\pi)[\alpha R_1 + (1-\alpha)p_L R_2]$. Denote $\alpha R_1 + (1-\alpha)R_2$ by $E[R_\alpha]$, and $\alpha R_1 + (1-\alpha)p_L R_2$ by κ'. Note that $E[R(\alpha)] = \kappa$ when $\pi = 0$ and $E[R(\alpha)] < E[R(\alpha_H)]$ when $\pi = 1$. The intersection between $E[R(\alpha)]$ and $E[R(\alpha_L)]$ is determined by

$$\bar{\pi}_2'' = \frac{\gamma E[R_L] - \kappa'}{\gamma E[R_\alpha] - \kappa'},$$

as the chain line in Figure 3.4.

To determine the value of $\bar{\pi}''_2$, note that $\bar{\pi}''_2 \gtrless \bar{\pi}_2$ only if

$$\frac{\gamma E[R_L] - \kappa'}{\gamma E[R_\alpha] - \kappa'} \gtrless \frac{\gamma E[R_L] - \kappa}{\gamma E[R_H] - \kappa}.$$

This is equivalent to

$$\gamma E[R_L](\gamma E[R_H] - \gamma E[R_\alpha]) + (\gamma E[R_\alpha] - \gamma E[R_L])\kappa + (\gamma E[R_L] - \gamma E[R_H])\kappa' \gtrless 0.$$

Using the fact that $\gamma E[R_s] = \alpha_s R_1 + (1 - \alpha_s)p_s R_2$ ($s \in \{H, L\}$), the left hand side of the inequality above can be written as

$$\gamma(R_1 - p_L R_2)\{E[R_H](\alpha_L - \alpha) - E[R_\alpha](\alpha_L - \alpha_H) + E[R_L](\alpha - \alpha_H)\}.$$

Further, note that $\alpha \in (\alpha_H, \alpha_L)$, therefore $\alpha = \omega\alpha_H + (1 - \omega)\alpha_L$ with $\omega \in (0, 1)$. Replace α by the linear combination of α_H and α_L, it is easily seen that

$$\gamma(R_1 - p_L R_2)\{E[R_H](\alpha_L - \alpha) - E[R_\alpha](\alpha_L - \alpha_H) + E[R_L](\alpha - \alpha_H)\} = 0,$$

which implies that $\pi'' = \pi_2$.

Combining all the cases, Figure 3.4 shows the investors' expected return for any $\alpha \in [0, 1]$. The social planner's optimal solution is given by the frontier of the investors' expected return, which is a state contingent strategy depending on the probability π. The investor invests the share α_H in liquid projects as long as $\pi_2' \le \pi \le 1$ and the share α_L as long as which $0 \le \pi < \pi_2'$.

3.4.2 Proof of Proposition 3.2

To show that the optimal allocation of the central planner's problem is supported by the market equilibrium, one has to show that (1) the allocation is feasible in the market economy, and (2) it is not profitable to unilaterally deviate from such allocation.

In the planner's economy, the central planner picks up the optimal α_s as equation (3.3) suggests, and transfers the maximized return to the investors. This coincides with equations (3.1) and (3.2), implying that claim (1) holds.

To show that claim (2) holds, suppose an arbitrary bank i deviates from such allocation by choosing $\alpha_i \ne \alpha_s$ for a given $s \in \{H, L\}$:

i   If $\alpha_i < \alpha_s$, by market clearing condition the liquidity market interest rate r' at $t = 1$ is now determined by

$$r'\{(1-\gamma)[\alpha_i R_1 + (1-\alpha_i)p_s R_2] + (N-1)(1-\gamma)[\alpha_s R_1 + (1-\alpha_s)p_s R_2]\}$$
$$= \gamma(1-\alpha_i)(1-p_s)R_2 + (N-1)\gamma(1-\alpha_s)(1-p_s)R_2.$$

Comparing with the condition in the central planner's problem in which $r = 1$, $r(1-\gamma)[\alpha_s R_1 + (1-\alpha_s)p_s R_2] = \gamma(1-\alpha_s)(1-p_s)R_2$, one can see that $r' > 1$. For the non-deviators, the depositors' return becomes

$$\gamma\left\{\alpha_s R_1 + (1-\alpha_s)\left[p_s R_2 + \frac{(1-p_s)R_2}{r'}\right]\right\} < d_0.$$

Knowing that the non-deviators will not be able to meet the contracted d_0 at $t = 1$, the depositors will only deposit at bank i at $t = 0$. If so, the deposit return that bank i can offer is at maximum $d_{0i} = \alpha_i R_1 + (1-\alpha_i)p_s R_2 < d_0$, implying that the deviator gets worse off.

ii   If $\alpha_i > \alpha_s$ the aggregate liquidity supply at $t = 1$ exceeds the the aggregate liquidity demand because

$$(1-\gamma)[\alpha_i R_1 + (1-\alpha_i)p_s R_2] + (N-1)(1-\gamma)[\alpha_s R_1 + (1-\alpha_s)p_s R_2]$$
$$> N(1-\gamma)[\alpha_s R_1 + (1-\alpha_s)p_s R_2] = N\gamma(1-\alpha_s)(1-p_s)R_2.$$

Therefore, the liquidity market interest rate remains at $r=1$ and the non-deviators are able to meet d_0. However, the deposit return that bank i can offer is $d_{0i} = \gamma[\alpha_i R_1 + (1-\alpha_i)R_2] < \gamma[\alpha_s R_1 + (1-\alpha_s)R_2] = d_0$, implying that the deviator will not get any deposit at $t=0$ and is hence worse off.

Therefore, the planner's optimal allocation is indeed supported by the market equilibrium.

3.4.3 Proof of Proposition 3.3

As is shown in Proposition 3.1 α_s maximizes the investors' expected return for a given p_s, $s \in \{H, L\}$. However, if the banks coordinate on α_H, they will experience bank runs and have to liquidate all the assets when $p_L < p_H$ gets revealed. In contrast, if the banks coordinate on α_L, they will survive on both states although the expected return is low when p_H gets revealed. It only pays off to coordinate on α_H instead of α_L if

$$\gamma E[R_H]\pi + (1-\pi)c > \gamma E[R_L], \text{ or } \pi > \bar{\pi}_2 = \frac{\gamma E[R_L] - c}{\gamma E[R_H] - c}.$$

There is a pure strategy equilibrium that all the banks coordinate on α_H for $\pi \in (\bar{\pi}_2, 1]$.

If the banks coordinate on α_L for $\pi \in [0, \bar{\pi}_2]$, when p_H gets revealed there will be excess liquidity supply and the market interest rate will be $r=1$ at $t=1$ since $\gamma E[R_L] = \alpha_L R_1 + (1-\alpha_L)p_L R_2 < \alpha_L R_1 + (1-\alpha_L)p_H R_2$. Knowing this, a deviating bank i may set a different α_i that maximizes its return

$$\gamma\left\{\alpha_i R_1 + (1-\alpha_i)\left[p_H R_2 + \frac{(1-p_H)R_2}{r}\right]\right\}$$

which is linear in α_i. It's easy to see that the optimal solution is $\alpha_i = 0$ and

$$\gamma\left\{\alpha_i R_1 + (1-\alpha_i)\left[p_H R_2 + \frac{(1-p_H)R_2}{r}\right]\right\} = \gamma R_2.$$

Obviously the deviating bank will experience bank run when p_L gets revealed, but it pays off to free-ride the cheap liquidity at p_H instead of coordinating with the other banks on α_L if

$$\gamma R_2 \pi + (1-\pi)c > \gamma E[R_L], \text{ or } \pi > \bar{\pi}_1 = \frac{\gamma E[R_L] - c}{\gamma R_2 - c}.$$

Therefore there is a pure strategy equilibrium that all the banks coordinate on α_L only of the profit from free-riding is too low, or, only if $\pi \in [0, \bar{\pi}_1)$. There is no pure strategy equilibrium for $\pi \in [\bar{\pi}_1, \bar{\pi}_2]$.

Now we characterize the market equilibrium for $\pi \in [\bar{\pi}_1, \bar{\pi}_2]$ by stepwise construction.

Step 1. The mixed strategy equilibrium can only have a two-point support $\{\alpha_r^*, \alpha_s^*\}$ such that one bank survives at both states by choosing α_s^* and survives at only one state by choosing α_r^*.

Suppose that α_1 and α_2 ($\alpha_1 \neq \alpha_2$) are two arbitrary elements in the support of the mixed strategies equilibrium, r_H and r_L are the corresponding equilibrium interest rates at p_H and p_L respectively. One bank shall be indifferent between choosing α_1 and α_2.

Suppose that one bank survives at both states by choosing either α_1 and α_2. So its expected return should be the same for both strategies,

$$\gamma \left\{ \alpha_1 R_1 + (1-\alpha_1) \left[p_H R_2 + \frac{(1-p_H)R_2}{r_H} \right] \right\} =$$

$$\gamma \left\{ \alpha_2 R_1 + (1-\alpha_2) \left[p_H R_2 + \frac{(1-p_H)R_2}{r_H} \right] \right\},$$

i.e., $\alpha_1 = \alpha_2$, a contradiction. Therefore there is at most one strategy by which one bank survives at both states.

Suppose that by choosing either α_1 and α_2 one bank survives at one state but suffers bank run in the other, so its expected return should be the same for both strategies:

$$\gamma \left\{ \alpha_1 R_1 + (1-\alpha_1) \left[p_H R_2 + \frac{(1-p_H)R_2}{r_H} \right] \right\} \pi + (1-\pi)c =$$

$$\gamma \left\{ \alpha_2 R_1 + (1-\alpha_2) \left[p_H R_2 + \frac{(1-p_H)R_2}{r_H} \right] \right\} \pi + (1-\pi)c,$$

i.e., $\alpha_1 = \alpha_2$, a contradiction.

Suppose that by choosing α_1 one bank survives at p_H and suffers bank run at p_L, and by choosing α_2 one bank survives at p_L and suffers bank run at p_H. This implies that

$$\gamma \left\{ \alpha_1 R_1 + (1-\alpha_1) \left[p_H R_2 + \frac{(1-p_H)R_2}{r_H} \right] \right\} >$$

$$\gamma \left\{ \alpha_1 R_1 + (1-\alpha_1) \left[p_L R_2 + \frac{(1-p_L)R_2}{r_L} \right] \right\},$$

i.e.,

$$p_H R_2 + \frac{(1-p_H)R_2}{r_H} > p_L R_2 + \frac{(1-p_L)R_2}{r_L},$$

as well as

$$\gamma\left\{\alpha_2 R_1 + (1-\alpha_2)\left[p_H R_2 + \frac{(1-p_H)R_2}{r_H}\right]\right\} <$$

$$\gamma\left\{\alpha_2 R_1 + (1-\alpha_2)\left[p_L R_2 + \frac{(1-p_L)R_2}{r_L}\right]\right\},$$

i.e.,

$$p_H R_2 + \frac{(1-p_H)R_2}{r_H} < p_L R_2 + \frac{(1-p_L)R_2}{r_L},$$

a contradiction.

Therefore there is at most one strategy by which one bank survives at one state and suffers from bank run at the other.

Therefore the equilibrium profile of mixed strategies is supported by $\{\alpha_r^*, \alpha_s^*\}$ such that one bank survives at both states by choosing α_s^* and survives at only one state by choosing α_r^*.

Step 2. In such equilibrium, interest rates at states p_H and p_L are $r_H > r_L > 1$.
By choosing α_s^* one bank should have equal return at both states, i.e.,

$$\gamma\left\{\alpha_s^* R_1 + (1-\alpha_s^*)\left[p_H R_2 + \frac{(1-p_H)R_2}{r_H}\right]\right\} >$$

$$\gamma\left\{\alpha_s^* R_1 + (1-\alpha_s^*)\left[p_L R_2 + \frac{(1-p_L)R_2}{r_L}\right]\right\}.$$

With some simple algebra this is equivalent to

$$\frac{1}{r_H} = \frac{1-p_L}{1-p_H}\frac{1}{r_L} - \frac{p_H - p_L}{1-p_H}.$$

Plot $\dfrac{1}{r_H}$ as a function of $\dfrac{1}{r_L}$, as Figure 3.5. The slope $\dfrac{1-p_L}{1-p_H} > 1$ and intercept $-\dfrac{p_H - p_L}{1-p_H} < 0$, and the line goes through (1, 1). But $r_H = r_L = 1$ cannot be equilibrium outcome here, because α_L is dominant strategy in this case and subject to deviation. So whenever $r_H > 1$ (suppose $\dfrac{1}{r_H} = A$ in the graph), there must be $r_H > r_L > 1$ (because $\dfrac{1}{r_H} < \dfrac{1}{r_L} = B < 1$).

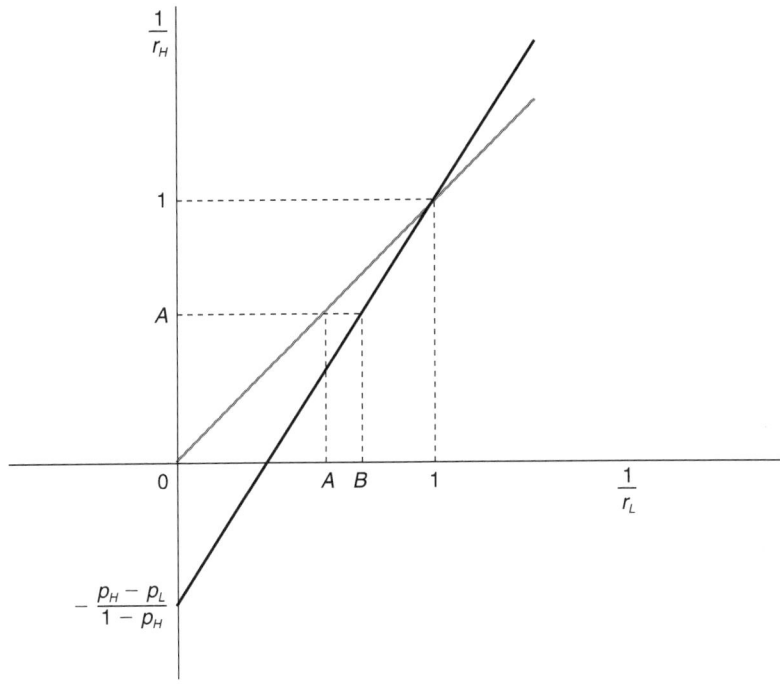

Figure 3.5 Market interest rate in the mixed strategy equilibrium.

Step 3. In such equilibrium, free-riding banks set $\alpha_r^* = 0$ and prudent banks $\alpha_s^* > 0$. Free-riding banks promise

$$d_0^r = \gamma \left[p_H R_2 + \frac{(1 - p_H) R_2}{r_H} \right]$$

and suffer from bank runs at p_L; prudent banks survive at both states by promising

$$d_0^s = \gamma \left\{ \alpha_s^* R_1 + (1 - \alpha_s^*) \left[p_s R_2 + \frac{(1 - p_s) R_2}{r_s} \right] \right\},$$

$s \in \{H, L\}$. Moreover, $d_0^r \pi + (1 - \pi) c = d_0^s$.

Since the free-riding banks' payoff is linear in α_r^*, it is optimal to set $\alpha_r^* = 0$. In equilibrium, the expected return from both types of banks must be equal, therefore, $d_0^r \pi + (1 - \pi) c = d_0^s$.

Step 4. In this step we show the existence of equilibrium solution for α_s^*. By expanding $d_0^r \pi + (1 - \pi) c = d_0^s$, one can get

$$\gamma\left[p_H R_2 + \frac{(1 - p_H)R_2}{r_H} \right]\pi + (1-\pi)c =$$

$$\gamma\left\{ \alpha_s^* R_1 + (1 - \alpha_s^*)\left[p_H R_2 + \frac{(1 - p_H)R_2}{r_H} \right]\right\}. \tag{3.4}$$

By expanding $d_0^s = d_0^s(p_H) = d_0^s(p_L)$, one can get

$$\gamma\left\{ \alpha_s^* R_1 + (1 - \alpha_s^*)\left[p_H R_2 + \frac{(1 - p_H)R_2}{r_H} \right]\right\} = \alpha_s^* R_1 + (1 - \alpha_s^*)p_L R_2. \tag{3.5}$$

Combining (3.4) and (3.5), we get a quadratic equation of α_s^*

$$(R_1 - p_L R_2)\alpha_s^{*2} - [\pi(\gamma R_1 - c) - (p_L R_2 - c) + \\ (1 - \pi)(R_1 - p_L R_2)]\alpha_s^* - (p_L R_2 - c)(1 - \pi) = 0. \tag{3.6}$$

Define left hand side of equation (3.6) as a function of α_s^*

$$f(\alpha_s^*) = \omega\alpha_s^{*2} + \phi\alpha_s^* + \varphi, \text{ with}$$

$$\begin{cases} \omega = R_1 - p_L R_2 > 0, \\ \phi = -[\pi(\gamma R_1 - c) - (p_L R_2 - c) + (1 - \pi)(R_1 - p_L R_2)], \\ \varphi = -(p_L R_2 - c)(1 - \pi) < 0. \end{cases}$$

Since $\phi^2 - 4\omega > 0$, the quadratic equation has two real roots, denoted by $\alpha_{s,2}^* < \alpha_{s,1}^*$. And by

$$\frac{\varphi}{\omega} < 0$$

and $f(0) = \varphi < 0$, we know $\alpha_{s,2}^* \alpha_{s,1}^* < 0$, i.e. $\alpha_{s,2}^* < 0 < \alpha_{s,1}^*$.
Moreover we find that

$$f(1) = \omega + \phi + \varphi = \pi(1 - \gamma)R_1 > 0,$$

which implies that $\alpha_{s,2}^* < 0 < \alpha_{s,1}^* < 1$. Further

$$f(1 - \pi) = -\pi(\gamma R_1 - c)(1 - \pi) < 0,$$

which implies that $\alpha_{s,2}^* < 0 < 1 - \pi < \alpha_{s,1}^* < 1$.
This implies that in current settings, there always exists a plausible solution $1 - \pi < \alpha_{s,1}^* < 1$, as Figure 3.6 shows.

Step 5. In this step, we characterize the market clearing condition.
The aggregate liquidity demand is equalized by the aggregate liquidity supply in both states. In the good state, with both types of banks surviving, denote the

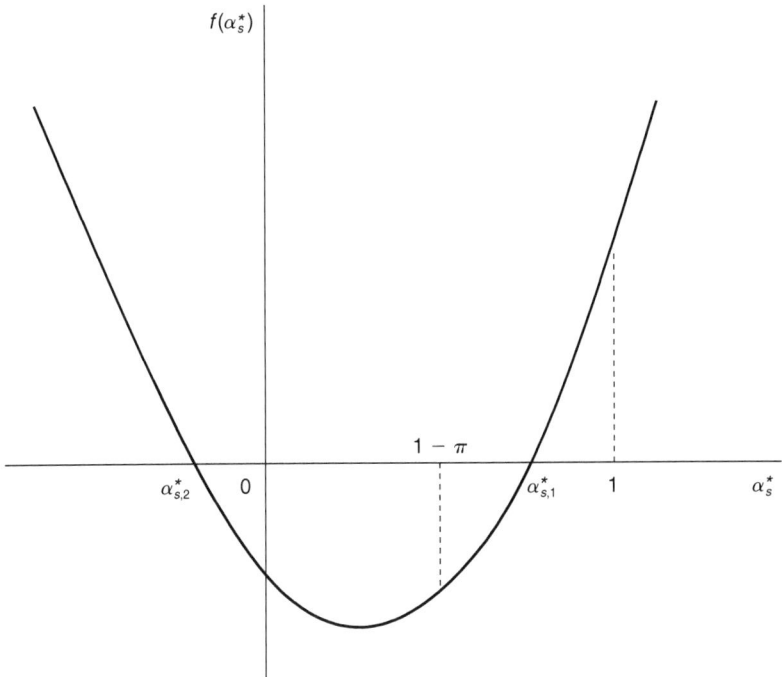

Figure 3.6 The solutions to α_s^*.

liquidity demand of a free-riding (prudent) bank by D_r (D_s) and the liquidity supply from the entrepreneurs of a free-riding (prudent) bank by S_r (S_s). Then

$$D_r = d_0^r - \gamma p_H R_2,$$

$$D_s = d_0^s - \gamma[\alpha_s^* R_1 + (1-\alpha_s^*)p_H R_2],$$

$$S_r = (1-\gamma)p_H R_2,$$

$$S_s = (1-\gamma)[\alpha_s^* R_1 + (1-\alpha_s^*)p_H R_2].$$

The market clearing condition at p_H is therefore $\theta D_r + (1-\theta)D_s = \theta S_r + (1-\theta)S_s$.

At p_H the free-riding banks get bankrupted. The aggregate liquidity supply from the surviving projects at $t=1$ meets the aggregate liquidity demand from the prudent banks by the market interest rate r_L

$$r_L(1-\gamma)[\alpha_s^* R_1 + (1-\alpha_s^*)p_L R_2] = \gamma(1-\alpha_s^*)(1-p_L)R_2.$$

4 Financial complexity and systemic risk

> How many other [financial] innovations can you tell me that have been as important to the individual as the automatic teller machine, which in fact is more of a mechanical than a financial one?
>
> (Paul Volcker)

The modern finance is a system of extremely high complexity, with structures and products that are hardly understandable by outsiders. The complexity of the financial system grows exponentially with financial innovation in the past decade, but what such complexity implies for financial stability is seldom discussed in the research (Brunnermeier and Oehmke (2009) is one of the few excellent reviews on this issue). During the current financial crisis, financial market is blamed to be over-complicated. In the financial turmoil, the panic grows mostly out of the suspicion that something indiscernible is rotten in the banks, and investors get tremendous loss from the financial products that are too complicated to understand.

The financial system gets more and more complicated in many ways. One prominent feature is that the intermediation structure becomes much more sophisticated than it used to be. An example by Shin (2010a) shows how the intermediation chain for mortgage evolves. Traditionally, as Figure 4.1 shows, the bank takes short-term deposits from the households and issues loans to long-term borrowers. The bank collects the mortgage repayments from the borrowers and then returns some of the proceeds to the depositors.

In contrast, the same thing is nowadays carried out through a very long intermediation chain (see Figure 4.2), involving many sophisticated financial products. First, the mortgages are pooled and financed by the mortgage-backed securities (MBS), and these securities are owned by the asset-backed securities (ABS) issuers and may be further tranched into new products such as collateralized debt

Figure 4.1 Short intermediation chain (source: Shin, 2010a, pp. 101).

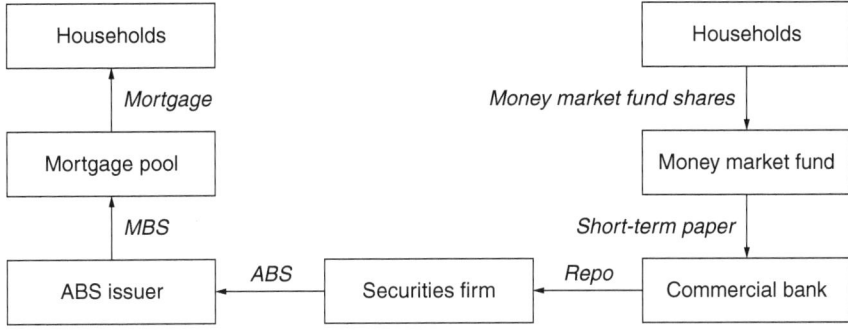

Figure 4.2 Long intermediation chain (source: Shin, 2010a, pp. 101).

obligations (CDO). The investment banks hold these CDO, but they get funding from the commercial banks in the repo market. The commercial banks raise funds by issuing short-term commercial paper. Money market funds buy such commercial paper, and the individual investors or the households hold the shares of the money market funds. This complicated procedure is not restricted to the mortgage business (whose failure is believed to be the trigger of the crisis), but also applies to many financial services such as credit cards and students' loans. The advantage, as people claim, is that the financial innovation such as CDO helps grease the wheels so that in the normal time the financial institutions can easily raise funds in a very liquid market. However, as is seen in the crisis, such complexity undermines the stability of the financial system and leaves all the financial institutions in the quagmire when time turns bad.

Financial complexity makes little trouble in the traditional theories of financial economics, where the economic agents are rational in the sense that they know all the details of the economy and they are able to make optimal decisions based on all the information they acquire. However, financial complexity makes much difference in a more realistic setup, where the agents are only boundedly rational. Rubinstein (1998) presents numerous occasions where bounded rationality needs to be considered, among which two are of special interest to our discussion. The first is that one can hardly get to know all the information in the financial system all the time; it is beyond anyone's capability. The second is that even there is no asymmetric information and the complete set of information is available – the development of information technology such as the Internet helps make information widely available – the quantity of information is likely to be too huge for anyone to process, due to the limited computation capacity. As a result, the market participants are only able and willing to possess a subset of information. In a complicated financial system, this implies that financial institutions along the long intermediation chain may gradually lose the tracking and control of some risks. The asset prices may fail to reflect the true risks, and the financial institutions may hold too thin buffer to weather the systemic events.

In Section 4.1, we will show how such "loss of information," or "loss of risk control," problem emerges from financial innovation. The example we take is securitization. The initial assets, for instance the mortgage loans, are first pooled and then sold as securities to the investors. Such asset-backed securities are often tranched into various degrees of subordination, each with different seniority and credit rating. It can be easily seen that the information and computation complexities grow exponentially in the securitization process and soon go beyond the capacity of any super computer. Finally the financial firms have to give up the complete tracking of risks and rely on the models where the risks are more or less exogenously assumed without having the sound foundation in and being clearly identified from economics.

The other question is why financial institutions are so keen on the complex structures and products. There still lacks a consistent theory for this question. Optimists argue that the complexity is the result of division of labor in a highly developed financial system, which facilitates to eliminate frictions and makes the market more liquid. But this argument is heavily questioned after the crisis got erupted. Pessimists argue that the complexity comes from the financial institutions' intention to abuse their market power, exploit the less informed investors, and get rid of financial regulation. In Section 4.2 we present a theory in which complexity can be indeed used as the financial institutions' strategy to generate price dispersion and capture the private rent.

Besides explaining why complexity increases in our financial system, an equally important question, especially for the regulator, is whether rising complexity raises systemic risk. Because of market participants' bounded rationality and the information loss, the financial institutions may lose track of some risks and the market price for assets may fail to reflect the true risks. This doesn't seem to be a problem as long as the banks are liquid; however, when the market is hit by the bad news, panic starts to arise from the investors' perception that some of the assets they hold may be "toxic." It is no longer clear whether a bank's trouble is only running short of liquidity or some of its assets are actually bad. The boundary between "illiquidity" and "insolvency" problems are much blurred. By extending the pure illiquidity model in Section 4.3, we will show how financial complexity induced illiquidity/insolvency uncertainty affects the banks' behavior, and how such uncertainty adds to systemic risk.

4.1 The computational complexity and loss of information

Along the intermediation chain, the computational complexity regarding estimating the value and risk of financial products grows exponentially, and can easily go beyond the capacity of any super computer. Then the financial institutions need to rely on approximation, simulation, and some less precise indicators about the quality of the assets. This is much like what is happening in engineering. For instance, when designing an aircraft, although theories of physics are sound enough to explain how each individual variable affects the aircraft's performance, to ease the computation engineers have to abstract from many minor factors and approximate their roles by semi-quantitative and semi-qualitative methods, which are often derived from experiments rather than theories. However, when the system becomes complicated, some minor factors that are *ex ante* neglected by assumption may *ex post* change the system in a disastrous way. The flap of a butterfly's wings in Brazil may set off a tornado in Texas.

It is widely believed that the growing intermediation chain in the past decade, particularly via heavy securitization, makes the complexity in financial market structure as well as products out of control, and financial institutions thus have to rely on either ad hoc assumptions or historical data which is not informative about the tail risks, sowing the seeds of the crisis. To what extent this is true is another question, which goes beyond the scope of this book. But in the following, we present the mechanism based on Gorton (2008) how securitization sharply increases the computational complexity, inducing the loss of information in asset pricing, hence the loss of tracking the risks.

4.1.1 Securitization and structural complexity

Figure 4.3 explains how securitization is worked out in a highly simplified chart. The stylized financial intermediary, call it the bank, issues loans to the borrowers. The loans are illiquid to the bank as long as they stay on the bank's balance sheet. In order to raise funds for the other investment opportunities, or to "liquidize" the illiquid assets, the bank has the incentive to remove the loans from the balance sheet. A special purpose vehicle (SPV) is thus established to buy the entire pool of illiquid assets and package them into securities. A characteristic feature in this process is tranching, that the asset pool is sliced into various

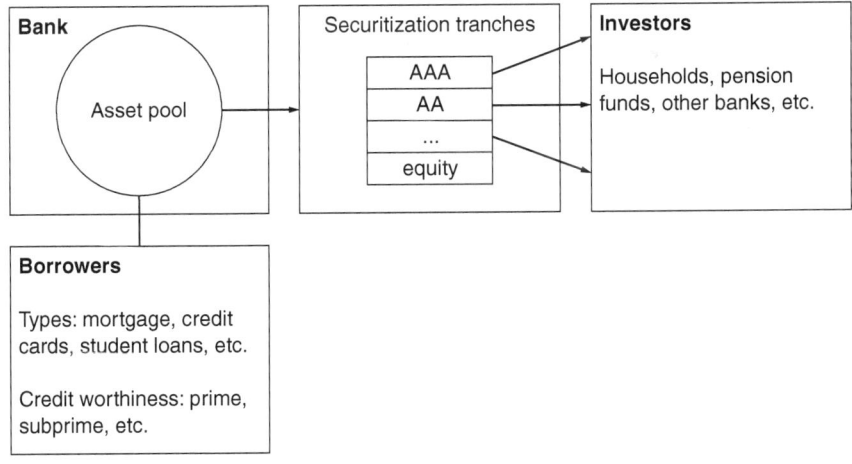

Figure 4.3 The securitization procedure: pooling and tranching.

Note
The credit ratings of tranches are listed in decreasing order, AAA being the highest, AA the next level ... and equity the lowest.

layers, or tranches. And each of the tranches is sold to investors with different appetite for risks.

The securitization process can go further. As Figure 4.4 shows, some of the securitization tranches may be purchased by CDO, and CDO may refine the securities and slice them again into CDO tranches, then sell them to finance the purchase.

In each stage of securitization, the tranches differ in their seniorities. A higher layer in the tranches enjoys higher seniority in the debt claim, and hence the priority in repayment. The most senior tranche gets paid out first, followed by the subordinated ones such as the mezzanine tranche, junior tranche, and equity tranche like a waterfall of cash. When it comes to a loss, the loss is first borne by the most junior tranche, and then the mezzanine tranche, and so on. Since the most senior tranche is supposed to bear the least risk, typically it gets the highest credit rating. The rating gets lower when moving down the tranches.

The most senior tranche with the highest credit rating is regarded as least risky, with default probability being next to none. In the orderly time before the crisis, it is generally seen as safe as the treasury bonds and widely accepted as

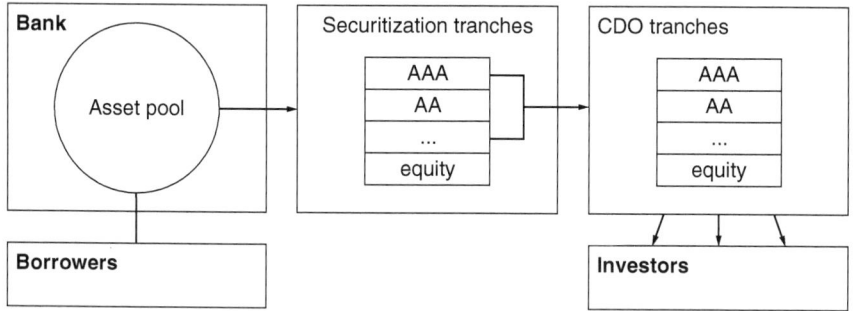

Figure 4.4 CDO and further securitization.

Note
The credit ratings of tranches are listed in decreasing order, AAA being the highest, AA the next level ... and equity the lowest.

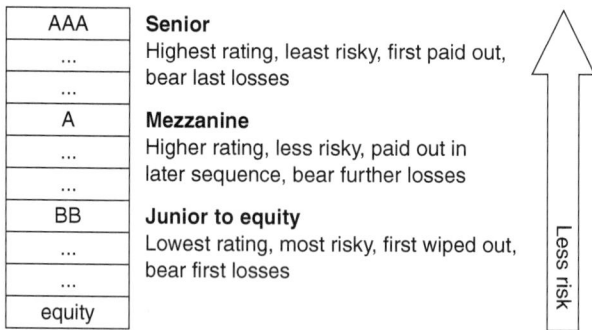

Figure 4.5 Seniorities of tranches.

eligible collateral in repo market. However, the financial institutions may find it more difficult to find buyers for the less senior tranches; the strategy to get rid of these tranches is to go on with the securitization procedure. These riskier tranches are repackaged, pooled, sometimes mixed up with fresh assets from elsewhere by the CDO operators, and sliced again into CDO tranches. The same procedure can go on to create a CDO of CDO, or CDO^2, then CDO^3, and so on.

4.1.2 Pricing and computational complexity

To see how the long securitization chain creates enormous computational complexity and induces the loss of information, let us consider the following simplified securitization procedure taken from Gorton (2008). Suppose that there are three financial instruments available in the stylized economy:

1 A single piece of (subprime) mortgage.
2 Mortgage-backed security (MBS) of this single mortgage. The MBS tranching is the simplest one: it only contains a junior tranche and a senior one.
3 A CDO with the simplest junior–senior tranches, which is based on purchasing the senior tranche of the MBS.

The economy lives for two dates, $t=0, 1$:

1 At $t=0$ the lender has to finance the mortgage which has a face value of W. The mortgage is financed by securitization, and the senior tranche of the MBS is purchased by the CDO. The details will be explained later.
2 At $t=1$ the mortgage needs to be refinanced – perhaps due to an unexpected increase in interest rate. If it doesn't get refinanced, it will default and the lender will be able to recover a value of R. In this case, the lender incurs a loss $L_M = W - R$. If it gets refinanced, the renewed mortgage has a new value of M. Obviously, the mortgage will not be refinanced if $M < R$.

During the securitization at $t=0$, the lender sells the mortgage to the security holders at its face value, W, and the aggregate return to the security holders at $t=1$ will be either W if the mortgage is refinanced or R if it defaults. The junior tranche in the securitization has a face value of N, and the senior tranche has a face value of $W-N$. This means that the first loss worth N will be shouldered by the junior tranche, and the senior tranche starts to incur the cost only if the loss exceeds N.

Thus, if the loss to the securities is below N, the senior tranche will stay intact; otherwise the senior tranche should take the remaining loss once the entire junior tranche is wiped out. Consequently, for the senior tranche, the loss at $t=1$ can be characterized by

$$L_S = \max[L_M - N, 0].$$

And the payoff to the senior tranche at $t=1$ is

$$V_S = \min\{\max[W - N, 0], W - N - L_S\}.$$

By regularity, N stands between 0 and W, $W-N$ is therefore greater than zero, so $\max[W-N, 0]=W-N$. Further, by definition $L_S \geq 0$, so $W-N-L_S \leq W-N$. Then $V_S = W-N-L_S = \min[W-N, W-L_S]$.

Also, note that the senior tranche of MBS, whose face value is $W-N$, is sold to a CDO, and the CDO is assumed to have two tranches, one junior and one senior, too. Suppose that the junior tranche in the CDO has a face value of N_C and the senior tranche has a face value of $W-N-N_C$. By the similar argument as before, the senior tranche stays intact if the loss to the CDO, or the senior tranche of MBS, is fully absorbed by the junior tranche of the CDO; otherwise the senior tranche has to take the remaining loss. Consequently, for the senior tranche of the CDO, the loss at $t=1$ can be characterized by

$$L_C = \max[L_S - N_C, 0],$$

and the payoff to the senior tranche at $t=1$ is

$$V_C = \min\{\max[W - N - N_C, 0], W - N - N_C - L_C\}.$$

Applying L_C in V_C yields

$$V_C = \min\left\{\begin{array}{l} \max[W - N - N_C, 0], \\ W - N - N_C - \max[L_S - N_C, 0] \end{array}\right\},$$

and further applying L_S yields

$$V_C = \min\left\{\begin{array}{l} \max[W - N - N_C, 0], \\ W - N - N_C - \max[\max(L_M - N, 0) - N_C, 0] \end{array}\right\}.$$

To get some idea about the value of V_C, note that $W-N-N_C \geq 0$ and $\max[\max(L_M-N, 0)-N_C, 0] \geq 0$, therefore, $\max[W-N-N_C, 0]=W-N-N_C$ and

$$W - N - N_C - \max[\max(L_M - N, 0) - N_C, 0] \leq W - N - N_C,$$

implying that

$$V_C = W - N - N_C - \max[\max(L_M - N, 0) - N_C, 0].$$

This Mickey Mouse example here is just used to present how securitization works, while the products in the market are far more complicated. Even though, the computation becomes fairly messy in the end. As to the securitization process in reality, there are many layers of tranches, and the tranches with lower seniorities may be repackaged and retrenched into CDO^2, CDO^3, and so on. Although in principle their values can be computed in the same way as in the simplified model above, the computational complexity grows exponentially with the securitization process. To make it worse, a financial institution on the intermediation chain may hold tens of thousands securities, and the underlying assets of these securities are changing in real time. As the computational complexity grows, at some point, the financial institutions have to give up the direct, quantitative analysis and turn to some qualitative reasoning to estimate the value and risk of the products. This makes the other market participants in the downstream of the intermediation chain hardly able to penetrate through the financial structure and products. Along the long intermediation chain, the originator of the securities will gradually lose track of the risks, and the buyers of the securities will be almost unable to perceive the location and size of the risks.

4.2 Complexity and market power

Over the last decade, financial innovation complicates the financial products and the market, leaving the market prices less informative about the assets' fundamental values. To understand the benefit and cost to social welfare, it is crucial to discover the reason why the financial institutions are so keen on making their products more complicated.

Theories in financial economics, much based on efficient market hypothesis and rational agent assumption, do not have much to say about this question. However, recent research from industrial organization may shed much light on this puzzle. Inspired by the sophisticated pricing schemes of Internet retailers, Ellison and Ellison (2009) argue that retailers can reduce the price sensitivity and capture some rent via obfuscation – practices that "frustrate investor search or make it less damaging to firms." Applying this idea, Carlin and Manso (2011) show that financial firms indeed have the incentive to increase wasteful obfuscation design, misguiding the investors who attempt to learn about the products.

The product complexity also relates to an old concept in industrial organization, the price dispersion, which may directly explain the reason why financial institutions actively engage in complex products. The idea is that complexity opens a second dimension of market competition, making it more difficult for the uninformed investors to discover the true cost of the products. Therefore, in the prevailing mixed strategy equilibrium, the financial firms can deviate from the competitive price by designing more sophisticated products, and the prices get dispersed with the degrees of complexity, generating higher profit from the uninformed investors who get disoriented and purchase those products. In the following, we present the mechanism how financial firms abuse their market power though creating product complexity via a model mainly based on Carlin (2009).

4.2.1 Model setup

The agents, time preferences, and technology

In this economy, there are N financial firms producing a homogeneous financial product. The product is universal in the sense that it can be used by the investors to buy consumption goods, or to be used as investment funds.

There is a continuum of risk neutral investors, who want to invest on a unit of financial product. The representative investor i's problem is to maximize her utility

$$U_i = v - P_i,$$

in which v is the fundamental value of the financial product and P_i is the price paid by investor i. The value v is public information among all the investors.

The investors are divided into two groups according to the information they obtain about the prices charged by the firms, denoted by $P_j, j \in \{1, \ldots, N\}$:

1   A fraction μ of the investors are financial experts, who are perfectly informed about the all the P_j in the market and only buy the financial product at the lowest price

$$\underline{P} = \min\{P_j\}_{j=1}^N.$$

The population of the financial experts, captured by μ, is endogenously determined by the overall "complexity" of the financial products, which we will explain later.

2   A fraction $1 - \mu$ of the investors are uninformed investors, who are completely uninformed about the P_j in the market and simply buy the financial product from a randomly chosen financial firm asking for a price P_j. Since all the firms have identical probability to be met by an informed investor, the expected price the representative informed investor pays is therefore

$$\bar{P} = \frac{1}{N} \sum_{j=1}^N P_j.$$

The uninformed investors are willing to buy the financial product only if $0 \leq P_j \leq v$.

Besides setting the price of financial product, a financial firm j can also choose the complexity of its product, denoted by $k_j \in [\underline{k}, \bar{k}]$. Assume that the firms can choose any k between $\underline{k}$ and $\bar{k}$ with zero cost, i.e., the cost for firm j on setting k_j is

$$C_j(k_j) = \begin{cases} 0, & \forall k_j \in [\underline{k}, \bar{k}] \\ +\infty, & otherwise. \end{cases}$$

The more the average complexity of financial products in the market is, the more difficult it becomes to get informed about all the P_j, i.e., the less investors are able to be financial experts. Therefore, the population of the financial experts, μ, shrinks if the financial firms successfully coordinate to increase the financial complexity. Precisely, given $k_j \in [\underline{k}, \bar{k}]$, $\forall j \in \{1, \ldots, N\}$, μ is a function of overall financial complexity

$$\mu : [\underline{k}, \bar{k}]^N \to (0,1),$$

with

$$\frac{\partial \mu}{\partial k_j} < 0,$$

$\forall j$, while zero complementarity between the financial firms,

$$\frac{\partial^2 \mu}{\partial k_m \partial k_n} = 0,$$

$\forall m, n \in \{1, \ldots, N\}$, and $m \neq n$.

The investors and financial firms are engaging in a two-period game. In the first period, $t=0$, each financial firm simultaneously chooses the complexity of its product, k_j, and posts the price P_j of the product. Then, in the second period, $t=1$, the investors purchase the products from the firms with the posted prices.

4.2.2 *The market equilibrium and price dispersion*

The market equilibrium is solved by backward induction. Starting from $t=1$, given the strategic profile of the financial firms, (P_j, k_j), $\forall j \in \{1, \ldots, N\}$, chosen at $t=0$, and without loss of generality the prices are ranked in the following order, $P_1 \leq P_2 \leq \ldots \leq P_N$, the firm(s) with lowest price(s) will serve all the financial experts plus part of the uninformed investors, and the other firms will only serve the rest of the uninformed investors. Suppose that M firms choose the lowest price P_1, i.e., $P_1 = \ldots = P_M$ and they share the demand of the financial experts. Then the strategic profile for each of these firms, (P_1, k^*_1), $\forall l \in \{1, \ldots, M\}$, is the equilibrium outcome only if it maximizes the expected profit when the firms set their strategies at $t=0$

$$(P_1, k^*_l) = \arg\max\nolimits_{(P_1, k_l)} \Pi_1(P_1, k_l),$$

in which

$$\Pi_1(P_1, k_l) = P_1\left(\frac{\mu}{M} + \frac{1-\mu}{N}\right).$$

And for the firms with higher prices, the strategic profile for each of these firms, (P_h^*, k_h^*), $\forall h \in \{M+1, \ldots, N\}$, is the equilibrium outcome only if it is profit maximizing at $t=0$ as well

$$(P_h^*, k_h^*) = \arg\max_{(P_h, k_h)} \Pi_h(P_h, k_h),$$

in which

$$\Pi_h(P_h, k_h) = P_h \left(\frac{1-\mu}{N} \right).$$

The existence of equilibrium is proved by Carlin (2009), which applies the Dasgupta–Maskin Existence Theorem (see Dasgupta and Maskin, 1986). Here we will not present the details of proof, but rather concentrate on the characteristics of the equilibrium.

First, it is not difficult to find out that there doesn't exist any equilibrium in which all the firms are symmetric in P. To see this, assume that all the firms choose the same price level P^*, although they may differ from each other in k. We distinguish several cases:

1   If P^* is equal to the marginal cost, i.e., $P^*=0$, so that all the firms earn zero profit, one firm j will profit from setting $P_j>0$ because it makes strictly positive profit from serving

$$\frac{1}{N}$$

of the uninformed investors, although it loses all the financial experts.

2   If P^* is strictly positive, i.e., $0<P^* \leq v$, all the firms share both financial experts and uninformed customers and each one earns a profit

$$\frac{p^*}{N}.$$

a   If there is at least one firm z who sets $k_z > \underline{k}$, one firm j will profit from setting $P_j = P^* - \varepsilon$, in which ε is arbitrarily small, and $k_j = \underline{k}$. By undercutting its competitors, it gets all the financial experts while still maintaining

$$\frac{1}{N}$$

of the uninformed investors; by setting $k_j = \underline{k}$ it lowers the average financial complexity and increases the population of the experts, further increasing its profit.

b   Even if all the firms choose $\underline{k}$, the deviator can secure the increase in profit by simply undercutting its competitors.

Therefore, there must be price dispersion in equilibrium, i.e., it is a mixed strategy equilibrium in which the equilibrium price P_j^*, $\forall j \in \{1,\ldots, N\}$, is randomly drawn from a cumulative distribution function $F^*(P)$.

Further, it can be seen that there is no mass point P^m on $F^*(P)$, because one deviator can profit from assigning a bit higher probability on the price level $P^m - \varepsilon$ and a bit lower probability on P^m.

Second, one can also see that the firms get dispersed in product complexity as well. Since the conditional probability of being the one offering the lowest price is high when a low price is drawn from $F^*(P)$, it will be better for the firm to set the lowest possible k, i.e., $\underline{k}$, to maximize the population of the financial experts, hence its expected profit. Similarly, it will be better for the firm to set the highest possible k, i.e., $\overline{k}$, to maximize the population of the uninformed investors. Therefore, the equilibrium is characterized by a mixed strategy equilibrium in which a representative financial firm j chooses a strategic profile $(P_j^*, k_j^* (P_j^*))$ in which P_j^* is randomly drawn from a cumulative distribution function $F^*(P)$ and the complementary complexity of the financial product is set to be

$$k_j^*(P_j^*) = \begin{cases} \underline{k} & for \quad P_j^* < \hat{P}, \\ \overline{k} & for \quad P_j^* > \hat{P}, \\ k \in [\underline{k}, \overline{k}] & for \quad P_j^* = \hat{P}, \end{cases}$$

and $\hat{P}$ is the cutoff value.

To get some knowledge about the cutoff value, $\hat{P}$, suppose that in a materialized equilibrium outcome firm j makes a random draw for price P_j and sets a corresponding complexity $k_j(P_j)$. The firm can certainly sell its product to

$$\frac{1}{N}$$

of the uninformed investors and get a profit

$$P_j \frac{1-\mu}{N},$$

but whether it is able to attract the financial experts depends on whether P_j is the lowest price among all the financial firms, i.e., $P_j = P_1$ in our notation. The probability that P_j is the lowest price is equal to the probability that each of the other firms' prices is higher than P_j, i.e., $Prob(P_n > P_j, \forall n \in \{1,\ldots, N\}, n \neq j) = \Pi_{n \neq j} Prob (P_n > P_j) = [1 - F(P_j)]^{N-1}$.

Therefore, the expected profit of firm j is

$$\Pi_j(P_j, k_j) = P_j \left\{ [1 - F(P_j)]^{N-1} E[\mu \mid P_j = P_1] + \frac{1-\mu}{N} \right\}.$$

Note that firm j only gets the financial experts when its price is the lowest, therefore, the corresponding population of the experts is the conditional expectation on μ.

Taking derivative of $\Pi_j(P_j, k_j)$ with respect to k_j, one can get

$$\frac{\partial \Pi_j}{\partial k_j} = P_j \left\{ [1 - F(P_j)]^{N-1} \frac{\partial E[\mu \mid P_j = P_1]}{\partial k_j} - \frac{1}{N} \frac{\partial \mu}{\partial k_j} \right\}.$$

By assumption,

$$\frac{\partial^2 \mu}{\partial k_j \partial k_n} = 0, \ \forall n \in \{1, \ldots, N\},$$

and $n \neq j$, i.e., the choice of the other firms on k doesn't change the firm j's marginal contribution on μ; therefore,

$$\frac{\partial E[\mu \mid P_j = P_1]}{\partial k_j} = \frac{\partial \mu}{\partial k_j}.$$

Then,

$$\frac{\partial \Pi_j}{\partial k_j} = P_j \frac{\partial \mu}{\partial k_j} \left\{ [1 - F(P_j)]^{N-1} - \frac{1}{N} \right\}.$$

When $P_j < \hat{P}$, from the *ex post* point of view the firm can always make higher profit by increasing the population of the financial experts, i.e., to reduce its complexity k_j, therefore

$$\frac{\partial \Pi_j}{\partial k_j} < 0, \ \forall P_j < \hat{P}.$$

Since it is already known that

$$\frac{\partial \mu}{\partial k_j} < 0,$$

it must be that

$$[1 - F(P_j)]^{N-1} - \frac{1}{N} > 0.$$

This fact will be reversed when $P_j > \hat{P}$, which implies that

$$[1 - F(P_j)]^{N-1} - \frac{1}{N} = 0$$

when $P_j = \hat{P}$, hence

$$\hat{P} = F^{-1}\left(1 - \left[\frac{1}{N}\right]^{\frac{1}{N-1}}\right).$$

4.2.3 Market power from product complexity

One can learn two lessons from the model. First, in the mixed strategy equilibrium, the firms set prices higher than zero, the marginal cost. Although one firm can undercut the rivalries and attract all the financial experts, there is a reversed incentive by the other firms to raise their prices, hence the profit, because they are guaranteed to get part of the uninformed investors anyway; second, the price dispersion along with a substantial average financial complexity is not solved by raising the competition in the banking sector. To see this, notice that $\hat{P}$ is declining with N, or

$$\frac{\partial \hat{P}}{\partial N} < 0,$$

i.e., more firms will set a higher product complexity $\bar{k}$ as a result, therefore, the overall complexity in the market increases. This is because increasing competition erodes the firms' profit by reducing the share of uninformed investors for everyone, therefore, the firms will coordinate to complicate their products and enlarge the population of the uninformed, since each firm's decision on k changes μ in the margin,

$$\frac{\partial \mu}{\partial k_j} < 0, \forall j.$$

The result is much in line with the models of search, which have been much explored in the theories of industrial organizations, for example, d'Aspremont (1979), Varian (1980), Stahl (1989), among many others. It has been shown that with the presence of search cost, a firm may gain local monopoly around its neighborhood and increase its profit from setting a price higher than the marginal cost. In Carlin (2009) the firms compete in two dimensions, financial complexity and price, and the two dimensions interact with each other: one firm may either undercut its competitors to win all the financial experts – in this case a lower level of average complexity is desired to make a larger expert group, or raise its price to maximize the profit from the uninformed investors – in this case a higher level of average complexity is desired to make a larger group of the uninformed. As a result, the equilibrium is featured by the firms dispersed in the prices and heterogeneous in their product complexity.

On the other hand, it is obvious that the product complexity here implies a pure dead weight loss in social welfare. It distorts the market competition and leaves the investors worse off, not to mention that such wasteful complexity may disguise the risks (although not explicitly modeled here) and increase the systemic risk (we will see this in the next section). But this does not necessarily mean that the regulator shall completely deter any complexity in the market and make all the products plain and standardized. There is still a long way to go to fully understand the social benefit and cost of financial complexity.

4.3 Financial complexity and illiquidity/insolvency uncertainty

In the banking literature, illiquidity and insolvency problems have been intensively studied for decades. Illiquidity means that one financial institution is not able to meet its short-term liability via monetizing the future gains from its long-term projects – in other words, there's a mismatch between the time when the long-term projects return and the time when its liability is due, i.e., it is "cash flow trapped" but "balance sheet solvent." In contrast, insolvency of a financial institution generally means that liabilities exceed assets in its balance sheet, i.e., it is not able to meet due liabilities even by perfectly monetizing the future gains from its long-term projects. Existing banking models usually focus on either problem. If a financial firm's ailment is diagnosed to be one of them, the solution is (at least intuitively) clear. For example, illiquid banks may be bailed out by central bank's liquidity injection (against their illiquid assets "good" collateral, suggested by the Bagehot principle), and insolvent banks have to be closed down in order to avoid contagion (see Freixas *et al.*, 2004).

However, as is observed in the current crisis, one prominent feature about this crisis is the ambiguity in the financial institutions' health, especially the daunting question whether the problem for the large banks is illiquidity or insolvency. Financial innovation in the past two decades doesn't only help improve market efficiency, but also creates high complexity (hence, asymmetric information) which blurs the boundary between illiquidity and insolvency. The over complicated financial products, as Gorton (2009) states, finally "could not be penetrated by most investors or counterparties in the financial system to determine the location and size of the risks." For example, subprime mortgages, a financial innovation from which the current crisis broke out, were designed to finance riskier long-term borrowers via short-term funding. So when the trend of continuing US house price appreciation started to stagger and giant investment banks ran into trouble, the trouble seemed to be a mere illiquidity problem – as long as house prices were to increase in the future, the long-term yields of subprime mortgage-related assets would be juicy, too. However, since the location and size of the risks in these complicated financial products could not be fully perceived even by the designer banks themselves, there was a probability that these financial institutions were actually insolvent. In this vague scenario banks could hardly get sufficient liquidity from market and the crisis erupted.

We explore such scenario in a model based on Cao (2010). In this model, banks are intermediaries financing entrepreneurs' short-term (safe) and long-term (risky) projects via short-term deposit contracts, as in Diamond and Rajan (2006). Illiquidity is modeled as Section 3.1: some fraction of risky projects turns out to be realized late. The aggregate exposure to the risks is endogenous; it depends on the incentives of financial intermediaries to invest in risky, illiquid projects. This endogeneity captures the feedback from liquidity provision to risk taking incentives of financial intermediaries.

Unlike in the models with pure illiquidity or insolvency problems, in the intermediate period the market participants only observe the aggregate amount of early returns from the risky projects. However, they don't know whether these risky assets are just illiquid (i.e., the majority of high yield risky projects will return late), or whether the banks are insolvent (i.e., a substantial amount of the risky projects will fail in the next period). The introduction of such ambiguity has both significant impacts on equilibrium outcomes.

The market equilibria of the model include two types of pure strategy equilibria – the banks coordinate to be risky when the sun always shines and be prudent when it always rains – and a mixed strategy equilibrium for an intermediate probability of having good luck. However, the gap between the expected return from the risky projects in the good state and that in the bad state gets larger with the uncertainty on the true problem – asset price is more inflated in the good state, while it is more depressed in the bad state. The bigger gap makes the interval for mixed strategy equilibrium wider in current setting, making free-riding more attractive (more excessive liquidity supply when time is good).

The mostly closely related work is probably the model considered in Bolton, Santos, and Scheinkman (2009, henceforth, BSS). The feature that the market participants can hardly distinguish between illiquidity and insolvency is captured in their model, while they mainly focus on the supply side of liquidity, i.e., liquidity from financial institutions' own cash reserve (inside liquidity) or from the proceeds from asset sales to the other investors with longer time preference (outside liquidity), and the timing perspective of liquidity trading. I take BSS's view that (outside) liquidity shortage arises from the banks' coordinative failure, but the timing of liquidity trading is not going to be my focus. Rather, I provide a different explanation of systemic liquidity risk, i.e., liquidity under-provision may come from the banks' incentive of free-riding on each other's liquidity supply, which is not covered in BSS (in which they restrict attentions to pure strategy equilibria); and clear-cut results from a more compact and flexible model lead to clear-cut policy implications (we will see this later in Section 8.3).

4.3.1 Model setup

In the economy, there is a continuum of entrepreneurs of two types, denoted by type i, $i = 1, 2$. Each type of entrepreneur is characterized by the return R_i of their projects:

1   type 1 projects (safe projects) are realized early at period $t = 1$ with a certain return $R_1 > 1$;

2 type 2 projects (risky projects) give a higher return $R_2 > R_1 > 1$. These projects may be realized at $t=1$, but they may also be delayed until $t=2$ or fail with zero return.

The exact payoff structure of type 2 projects is shown in Figure 4.6.

1 With probability p the project returns in $t=1$. For those projects with early returns

    a   with probability η the project is successful, returning R_2;
    b   with probability $1-\eta$ the project fails, returning zero.

2 With probability $1-p$ the project is delayed. For those projects with late returns

    a   with probability η the project is successful, returning R_2;
    b   with probability $1-\eta$ the project fails, returning zero.

The values of p and η, however are not known at $t=0$. They will be only revealed between periods 0 and 1 at some intermediate period, call it $t=0.5$. In the following, we are interested in the case of aggregate illiquidity/insolvency shocks. We model them in the simplest way. Assume that p can take three values, $p_L < \bar{p} < p_H$, and η can take three values as well, $\eta_L < \bar{\eta} < \eta_H$. To concentrate on the cases where there is a demand for liquidity, we assume that $\eta R_2 > R_1$ such that the expected return of risky asset is higher than that for safe asset, but

Timing of the model:

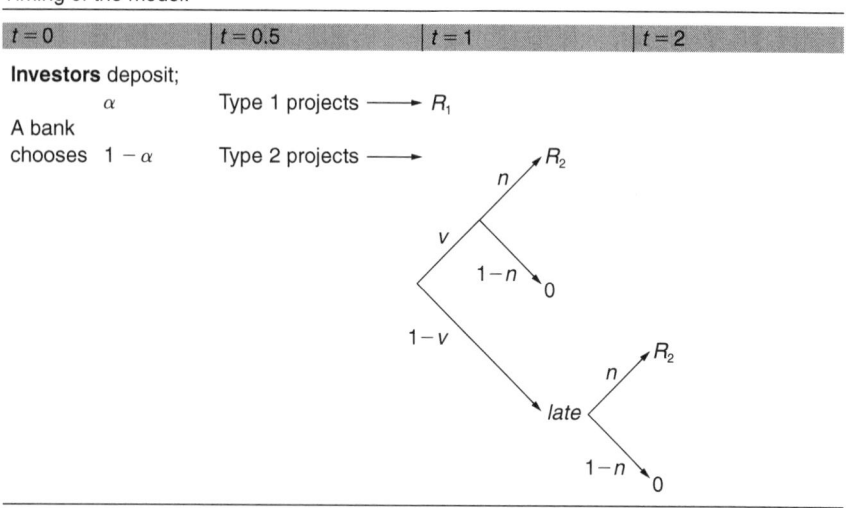

At $t = 0$:   At $t = 0.5$:

p,η *are stochastic* $p \cdot \eta$ *revealed*

Figure 4.6 The timing of the model and illiquidity/insolvency uncertainty.

$p\eta R_2 < R_1$ such that the early return of risky asset is lower than the return for safe asset.

At $t=0.5$, $(p \cdot \eta)$, or the early return from the risky projects, becomes public information. It can take two values, $(p \cdot \eta)_H$ and $(p \cdot \eta)_L$, but no player knows the exact values of p and η. Further, assume that there can be only one shock at $t=1$, i.e., it may be either p or η that takes its "extreme" value, but not both. Assume that $(p \cdot \eta)_L = \bar{p}\eta_L = \bar{\eta}p_L < \bar{p}\eta_H = \bar{\eta}p_H = (p \cdot \eta)_H$, and $(p \cdot \eta)_H$ occurs with probability π. Therefore,

1   if one observes $(p \cdot \eta)_H$, it may come from either p_H (with probability σ) or η_H (with probability $1 - \sigma$);
2   if one observes $(p \cdot \eta)_L$, it may comes from either p_L (with probability σ) or η_L (with probability $1 - \sigma$).

Such $p - \eta$ setting captures both of the concerns in banking industry. The value p defines how likely the cash flow is materialized earlier, i.e., the liquidity of the risky projects, and η defines the quality of the projects – or, how likely the banks stay solvent.

Investors are impatient so that they want to consume early (at $t=1$). In contrast, both entrepreneurs and bank managers are indifferent between consuming early ($t=1$) or late ($t=2$). This again creates the liquidity problem. At $t=0.5$, when $(p \cdot \eta)$ gets revealed, the investors can infer whether they are fully repaid at $t=1$. If the answer is negative, they run on the bank and all the bank's assets have to be liquidated at the poor return $c < 1$.

4.3.2 The planner's problem and the first best solution

If all the agents are patient, it is *ex ante* optimal to allocate all the resources to the high yield risky projects so that the expected aggregate return is maximized. However, because the investors are impatient and there is no way to reshuffle the output between periods, the central planner should take the investors' expected return as the welfare criteria.

Proposition 4.1 The optimal solution for the central planner's problem is:

1   In the absence of aggregate risk, the planner invests the share

$$\alpha = \frac{\gamma - p}{\gamma - p + (1-\gamma)\dfrac{R_1}{\eta R_2}} = \frac{1}{1 + (1-\gamma)\dfrac{R_1}{\eta R_2 (\gamma - p)}}$$

in liquid projects and the investors' return is maximized at $\gamma E[R] = \gamma[\alpha R_1 + (1-\alpha)\eta R_2]$.

2   In the presence of aggregate risk, the central planner implements the following state contingent strategy, depending on the probability π for $(p \cdot \eta)_H$
being realized: the planner invests the share

$$\alpha_H = \frac{1}{1 + (1-\gamma) \dfrac{R_1}{\gamma E\left[R_2 \mid (p \cdot \eta)_H\right] - (p \cdot \eta)_H R_2}},$$

in which $E[R_2|(p \cdot \eta)_s] = (p \cdot \eta)_s R_2 + [(1-\bar{p})\bar{\eta} + (1-\bar{p}-\sigma)(\eta_s - \bar{\eta})]R_2$, $(s \in \{H, L\})$
in liquid projects as long as

$$\pi \geq \pi_2' = \frac{\gamma E[R_L] - \kappa}{\gamma E[R_H] - \kappa + \gamma E[R_L] - \gamma E[R_{L|H}]},$$

in which $\gamma E[R_s] = \gamma\{\alpha_s R_1 + (1-\alpha_s)E[R_2|(p \cdot \eta)_s]\}$, $(s \in \{H, L\}$, $\kappa = \alpha_H R_1 +$
$(1-\alpha_H)(p \cdot \eta)_L R_2$, $\gamma E[R_{L|H}] = \gamma\{\alpha_L R_1 + (1-\alpha_L)E[R_2|(p \cdot \eta)_H]\}$, and the share

$$\alpha_L = \frac{1}{1 + (1-\gamma) \dfrac{R_1}{\gamma E\left[R_2 \mid (p \cdot \eta)_L\right] - (p \cdot \eta)_L R_2}},$$

otherwise, that is, for $0 \leq \pi < \pi_2'$.

Proof: see Appendix.

When there is no aggregate risk, i.e., $p \cdot \eta$ is deterministic, the central planner
implements the α that maximizes the investors' return. It can be seen that

$$\frac{\partial \alpha}{\partial \eta} > 0,$$

i.e., when insolvency risk is less severe, illiquidity problem dominates so that
more funds should be invested on the safe assets. Moreover,

$$\frac{\partial \alpha}{\partial p} < 0$$

implies that more funds should be invested on the safe assets when the long-term
projects get more illiquid. In the presence of aggregate risk, the central planner
faces the tradeoff between reaping the high return from the risky projects in the
good state (which corresponds to the lower α_H) and securing the return from the
safe projects in the bad state (which corresponds to the higher α_L). The solution
is hence a contingent plan which depends on the probability π.

4.3.3 The market equilibrium and systemic risk

In this section, we will characterize the market equilibrium with banks as financial intermediaries. For the simplest case, if there is no aggregate uncertainty and $p \cdot \eta$ is deterministic, the market equilibrium of the model is characterized by the bank i's strategic profile (α_i, d_{0i}), $\forall i \in \{1, ..., N\}$ such that

1 bank i's profit is maximized by

$$\alpha_s \arg \max_{\alpha_i \in [0,1]} \gamma \left\{ \alpha_i R_1 + (1 - \alpha_i) \left[p\eta R_2 + \frac{(1-p)\eta R_2}{r} \right] \right\}; \qquad (4.1)$$

2 bank i makes zero profit from offering deposit contract

$$d_{0i} = \max_{\alpha_i \in [0,1]} \gamma \left\{ \alpha_i R_1 + (1 - \alpha_i) \left[p\eta R_2 + \frac{(1-p)\eta R_2}{r} \right] \right\}; \qquad (4.2)$$

3 it is not profitable to deviate from (α_i, d_{0i}) unilaterally;
4 the market interest rate is determined in a way such that

   a when the aggregate liquidity supply at $t=1$ is equalized by the aggregate demand, $r \geq 1$;
   b when there is excess liquidity supply at $t=1$, $r=1$.

If there is no aggregate uncertainty the market equilibrium is in line with the solution of the social planner's problem which is constrained-efficient: banks will invest such that – on aggregate – they are able to fulfill investors' claims in period 1, so there will be no run.

Now if there is aggregate uncertainty, when $(p \cdot \eta)_s$, $(s \in \{H, L\})$ is revealed in $t=0.5$, the expected return of the risky projects at $t=2$ is given by

$$R_2^s = [(1 - \bar{p})\bar{\eta} + (1 - \bar{p} - \sigma)(\eta_s - \bar{\eta})]R_2,$$

and the aggregate expected return from the risky projects is

$$E[R_2 \mid (p \cdot \eta)_s] = (p \cdot \eta)_s R_2 + [(1 - \bar{p})\bar{\eta} + (1 - \bar{p} - \sigma)(\eta_s - \bar{\eta})]R_2 = \\ [\bar{\eta}\sigma + (1 - \sigma)\eta_s]R_2. \qquad (4.3)$$

It can be seen that $E[R_2|(p \cdot \eta)_H] > E[R_2|(p \cdot \eta)_L]$, since $\eta_H > \eta_L$.

If there's only illiquidity risk as in Section 3.1, the expected return from the risky projects is just R_2 (the only thing that matters is the timing of cash flow). Now with coexistence of insolvency risk, such return is determined by the probability and scale of insolvency, as (4.3) suggests: in good time, the confidence in the risky assets (more likely to have good quality) raises the expected return (hence asset price at $t=1$), and vice versa.

The market equilibrium is then characterized in the following proposition:

Proposition 4.2 The market equilibrium depends on the value of π, such that,

1   There is a symmetric pure-strategy equilibrium such that all banks set $\alpha = \alpha_H$ as long as $\bar{\pi}_2 < \pi \leq 1$, with

$$\bar{\pi}_2 = \frac{\gamma E[R_L] - c}{\gamma E[R_H] - c}.$$

In addition

   a   at $t=0$ the banks offer the investors a deposit contract with $d_0 = \gamma E[R_H]$;
   b   the banks survive at $(p \cdot \eta)_H$, but experience a run at $(p \cdot \eta)_L$;
   c   the investors' expected return is $E[R(\alpha_H, c)] = \pi d_0 + (1 - \pi)c$.

2   There is a symmetric pure-strategy equilibrium such that all banks set $\alpha = \alpha_L$ as long as $0 \leq \pi \leq \bar{\pi}_1$, with

$$\bar{\pi}_1 = \frac{\gamma E[R_L] - c}{\gamma E[R_2 \mid (p \cdot \eta)_H] - c}.$$

In addition

   a   at $t=0$ the banks offer the investors a deposit contract with $d_0 = \gamma E[R_L]$;
   b   the banks survive at both $(p \cdot \eta)_H$ and $(p \cdot \eta)_L$;
   c   the investors' expected return is $E[R(\alpha_L)] = d_0$.

3   There exists no symmetric pure-strategy equilibrium for all $\bar{\pi}_1 \leq \pi \leq \bar{\pi}_2$. However, there exists a unique equilibrium in mixed strategies such that

   a   with probability θ one bank chooses to be a free-rider – setting $\alpha_r^* = 0$, offering high return for investors at $(p \cdot \eta)_H$ and experiencing bank run at $(p \cdot \eta)_L$; and with probability $1 - \theta$ the bank chooses to be prudent – setting $\alpha_s^* > 0$ and surviving both $(p \cdot \eta)_H$ and $(p \cdot \eta)_L$;
   b   at $t=0$ a free-riding bank offers a deposit contract with higher return

$$d_r^0 = \gamma \left[(p \cdot \eta)_H R_2 + \frac{R_2^H}{r_H} \right],$$

but the bank suffers bank run when $(p \cdot \eta)_L$ is observed; a prudent bank offers a deposit contract with lower return

$$d_s^0 = \gamma \left[\alpha_s^* R_1 + (1 - \alpha_s^*)(p \cdot \eta)_H R_2 + \frac{(1 - \alpha_s^*) R_2^H}{r_H} \right],$$

but the bank survives in both states;

c   the expected returns for both types are equal, and the probability θ is
     determined by market clearing condition, which equates liquidity
     supply and demand in both states.

Proposition 4.2 says that when π is low the banks coordinate on the higher α_L to
always get prepared for the bad state, while when π is high the banks coordinate
on the lower α_H to benefit from the high return in the good state since the risk of
experiencing a bank run is rather low. But what makes the model more interesting is the equilibrium for an intermediate value of π. In this case choosing α_H is
not optimal since the cost of bank run is still high. But if all the banks choose α_L,
there will be excess liquidity at $t=1$ when the good state occurs. A bank anticipating this event has a strong incentive to free-ride, investing all the funds in the
risky projects to benefit from the excess liquidity in the good state. Those
prudent banks which still invest on the safe projects have to set a lower $\alpha_s^* < \alpha_L$
to cut down the opportunity cost of holding liquid assets. In the end, there will
be a mixed strategy equilibrium.

   Moreover, when a state of the world is realized, there is an uncertainty about
the true type of the risk. The potential illiquidity and insolvency risks will have
contradicting impacts on the prudent banks' decision of α_s^*. Suppose $(p \cdot \eta)_H$ is
revealed at $t=0.5$:

1   It may imply a lower insolvency risk (higher η) at $t=2$, therefore the value
     of risky assets at $t=1$ gets higher so that the banks are able to get more
     liquidity from the entrepreneurs (hence, offer higher d_s^0 for the investors at
     $t=0$). Such "income effect" encourages prudent banks to set a higher α_s^*.
2   It may imply less delay (higher p) for the risky projects, making it easier to
     fulfill d_s^0. Such "substitution effect" discourages prudent banks to set higher
     α_s^*.

The exact value α_s^* in equilibrium then depends on the cost of the banks' liquidity financing at $t=1$, i.e., the interest rate r_H. Since r_H is bid up by the free-riders,
it reflects the incentive for free-riding, which hinges on the probability of being
in a good state, π.

1   When π is just a bit higher than $\bar{\pi}_1$, the profitability of free-riding in the
     good state is not much higher than being prudent. Therefore, there won't be
     many free-riders and r_H won't be that high. In this case "substitution effect"
     dominates and prudent banks will choose to set a higher α_s^*.
2   When π is much higher than $\bar{\pi}_1$, the profitability of free-riding is much
     higher. Therefore, there will be many free-riders and r_H will be high. In
     this case "income effect" dominates and prudent banks will choose to set a
     lower α_s^*.

The investors' expected return in equilibrium as a function of π is summarized
in Figure 4.7.

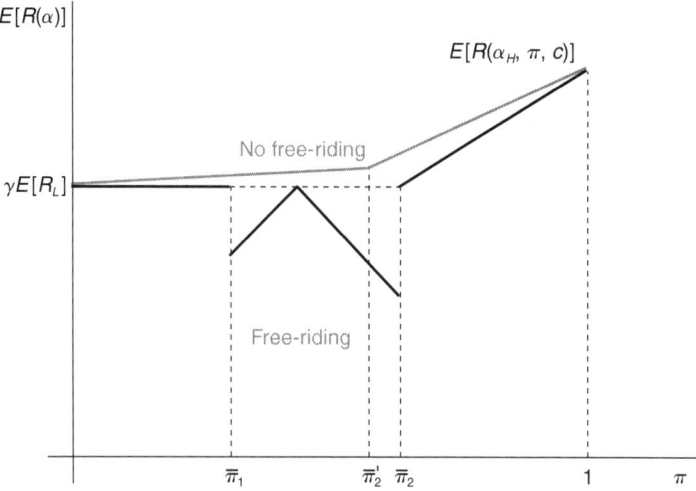

Figure 4.7 The inefficient market equilibrium.

Comparing with the solution of the central planner's problem, when the liquidity and insolvency problem coexist, the inefficiencies arise from (1) the inferior mixed strategy equilibrium, and (2) the costly bank runs when π is high. Banking regulation is therefore needed to restore the efficiency.

4.4 Appendix

4.4.1 Proof of Proposition 4.1

In the absence of aggregate risk, given $p \cdot \eta$, the social planner maximizes the investors' return by setting α such that

$$\alpha = \arg\max_{\alpha \in [0,1]} \gamma \left\{ \alpha R_1 + (1-\alpha) \left[p\eta R_2 + \frac{(1-p)\eta R_2}{r} \right] \right\},$$

and the interest rate r is determined by

$$r(1-\gamma)[\alpha R_1 + (1-\alpha)p\eta R_2] = \gamma(1-\alpha)(1-p)\eta R_2, \text{ with } r \geq 1.$$

Solve to get

$$\alpha = \frac{\gamma - p}{\gamma - p + (1-\gamma)\dfrac{R_1}{\eta R_2}} = \frac{1}{1 + (1-\gamma)\dfrac{R_1}{\eta R_2(\gamma - p)}}, \text{ with } r = 1$$

In the presence of aggregate risk, the social planner's optimal α may depend on π. First, solve for the α that maximizes the investors' return for each possible $\pi \in [0, 1]$. The gross interest rate offered to the entrepreneurs at $t=1$ is no less than one, this implies that for any given α the investors' expected payoff is

$$E[R(\alpha)] = \pi \min\{\alpha R_1 + (1-\alpha)(p \cdot \eta)_H R_2, \gamma(\alpha R_1 + (1-\alpha)E[R_2 \mid (p \cdot \eta)_H])\} + (1-\pi)\min\{\alpha R_1 + (1-\alpha)(p \cdot \eta)_L R_2, \gamma(\alpha R_1 + (1-\alpha)E[R_2 \mid (p \cdot \eta)_L])\},$$

which is a linear function of π.

Denote α_H as the value of α such that

$$\alpha R_1 + (1-\alpha)(p \cdot \eta)_H R_2 = \gamma(\alpha R_1 + (1-\alpha)E[R_2 \mid (p \cdot \eta)_H]), \text{ or}$$

$$\alpha_H = \frac{1}{1 + (1-\gamma)\dfrac{R_1}{\gamma E[R_2 \mid (p \cdot \eta)_H] - (p \cdot \eta)_H R_2}}.$$

Denote α_L as the value of α such that

$$\alpha R_1 + (1-\alpha)(p \cdot \eta)_L R_2 = \gamma(\alpha R_1 + (1-\alpha)E[R_2 \mid (p \cdot \eta)_L]), \text{ or}$$

$$\alpha_L = \frac{1}{1 + (1-\gamma)\dfrac{R_1}{\gamma E[R_2 \mid (p \cdot \eta)_L] - (p \cdot \eta)_L R_2}}.$$

Depict $E[R(\alpha_H)] = \pi\gamma E[R_H] + (1-\pi)\kappa$ (the solid black line) and $E[R(\alpha_L)] = \pi\gamma E[R_{L|H}] + (1-\pi)\gamma E[R_L]$ (the solid gray line) in Figure 4.8. The intersection is denoted as

$$\bar{\pi}_2' = \frac{\gamma E[R_L] - \kappa}{\gamma E[R_H] - \kappa + \gamma E[R_L] - \gamma E[R_{L|H}]}.$$

For any $\alpha \in (\alpha_L, 1]$, $E[R(\alpha)]$ is always below $E[R(\alpha_L)]$ (the dotted gray line in Figure 4.8 is an example) since

$$E[R(\alpha)] = \pi\gamma(\alpha R_1 + (1-\alpha)E[R_2 \mid (p \cdot \eta)_H]) + (1-\pi)\gamma(\alpha R_1 + (1-\alpha)E[R_2 \mid (p \cdot \eta)_L]) < \pi\gamma E[R_{L|H}] + (1-\pi)\gamma E[R_L] = E[R(\alpha_L)].$$

For any $\alpha \in [0, \alpha_H)$,

$$E[R(\alpha)] = \pi[\alpha R_1 + (1-\alpha)(p \cdot \eta)_H R_2] + (1-\pi)[\alpha R_1 + (1-\alpha)(p \cdot \eta)_L R_2].$$

$E[R(\alpha)]$ is always below $E[R(\alpha_H)]$ since both ends of $E[R(\alpha)]$ are lower (the dotted black line in Figure 4.8 is an example): $E[R(\alpha)] < \kappa$ when $\pi=0$ and $E[R(\alpha)] < \gamma E[R_H]$ when $\pi=1$.

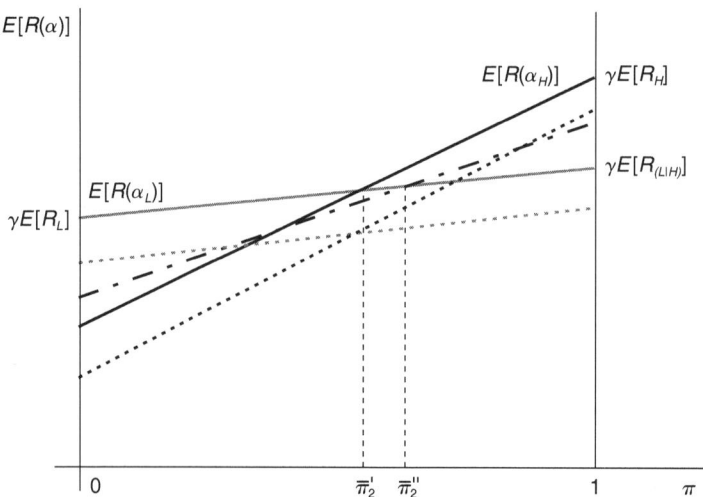

Figure 4.8 The constrained efficiency.

For any $\alpha \in [\alpha_H, \alpha_L]$,

$$E[R(\alpha)] = \pi\gamma(\alpha R_1 + (1-\alpha)E[R_2 \mid (p \cdot \eta)_H]) + (1-\pi)[\alpha R_1 + (1-\alpha)(p \cdot \eta)_L R_2] \quad .$$

Depict $E[R(\alpha)]$ as the chain line in Figure 4.8. Denote $E[R_\alpha] = \alpha R_1 + (1-\alpha) E[R_2 \mid (p \cdot \eta)_H]$ and $\kappa' = \alpha R_1 + (1-\alpha)(p \cdot \eta)_L R_2$. Note that $\kappa < E[R_\alpha] < \gamma E[R_L]$ when $\pi = 0$ and $\gamma E[R_{L|H}] < E[R_\alpha] < \gamma E[R_H]$ when $\pi = 1$. Denote the intersection of $E[R(\alpha)]$ and $E[R(\alpha_L)]$ as

$$\pi_2'' = \frac{\gamma E[R_L] - \kappa}{\gamma E[R_\alpha] - \kappa' + \gamma E[R_L] - \gamma E[R_{L|H}]}.$$

$\pi_2'' \gtrless \pi_2'$ only if

$$\frac{\gamma E[R_L] - \kappa}{\gamma E[R_\alpha] - \kappa' + \gamma E[R_L] - \gamma E[R_{L|H}]} \lessgtr \frac{\gamma E[R_L] - \kappa}{\gamma E[R_H] - \kappa + \gamma E[R_L] - \gamma E[R_{L|H}]}, \text{ or}$$

$$\gamma E[R_L](\gamma E[R_H] - \gamma E[R_\alpha]) + (\gamma E[R_\alpha] - \gamma E[R_L])\kappa + (\gamma E[R_L] - \gamma E[R_H])\kappa' + (\gamma E[R_L] - \gamma E[R_{L|H}])(\kappa - \kappa') \gtrless 0.$$

Further, note that

$$\gamma E[R_L](\gamma E[R_H] - \gamma E[R_\alpha]) + (\gamma E[R_\alpha] - \gamma E[R_L])\kappa + (\gamma E[R_L] - \gamma E[R_H])\kappa' = 0 \text{ and}$$

$$(\gamma E[R_L] - \gamma E_{[L|H]})(\kappa - \kappa') > 0,$$

implying that $\bar{\pi}_2'' > \bar{\pi}_2'$, or $E[R(\alpha)]$ is always below the upper frontier formed by $E[R(\alpha_L)]$ and $E[R(\alpha_H)]$. Therefore the social planner's optimal solution is given by the frontier of the investors' expected return, which is a state contingent strategy depending on the probability π. The planner invests the share α_H in liquid projects as long as $\pi \in [\bar{\pi}_2', 1]$, and the share α_H in liquid projects as long as $\pi \in [0, \bar{\pi}_2')$.

5 Leverage and leverage cycle

The role of leverage that played in aggravating the credit crunch in the current crisis has been gaining much attention in research. A financial institution's leverage is defined as the size of its total assets to equity (or, net worth, the term often used later in this book). The leverage of the financial market exhibits strong pro-cyclicality: it rises sharply in the boom, but falls heavily in the bust. As Adrian and Shin (2010) pointed out, this reflects the financial firms' *active* management on their balance sheets – otherwise, if one firm's balance sheet doesn't respond to the business cycle, the firm's leverage ratio should be counter-cyclical: falling in the boom since its net worth increases, and vice versa. Therefore, the leverage ratio is a crucial indicator of the firm's investment and risk management, as well as a key to understanding the financial institutions' risk taking incentive, helping the regulators see through the murky veil of their daily activities.

The leverage ratio captures the feedback mechanism between the banks' balance sheets and the fluctuations of asset prices, as argued by Adrian and Shin (2011). As the asset prices rise, since one bank's balance sheet is marked to market in real time, the bank's net worth increases immediately. This improves the bank's borrowing condition, and the bank has a strong incentive to expand its balance sheet, searching for yield. This further increases the market demand for assets and raises asset prices even further. On the contrary, as the asset prices go down, the bank's net worth drops immediately. This makes the bank's borrowing condition binding, and the bank is forced to "deleverage" by selling its assets, which further depresses the asset prices. Given that the bank has been already leveraged up in the good time, such deleverage across the entire financial sector often turns an initial market stress into a full-scale crunch.

Of course, the rigid mark-to-market accounting principle is the key catalyst for such mechanism to work. The contribution of mark-to-market principle to financial instability has been intensively studied and well understood by large existing literature, for example, Allen and Carletti (2008a, b), so we will not spend much space on it in this chapter. Rather, we will focus on several other questions: (1) how does leverage cycle emerge along with the asset price cycle? We want to explain the incentive that the financial institutions actively manage their balance sheets and the mechanism how such practice affects financial stability and contributes to systemic risks. (2) How does leverage cycle amplify the boom and bust of financial market? This question is the mirror of the first one. We want to see how the leverage cycle feeds back to asset prices, which yields higher market volatilities. Only if the incentive that makes market participants engage in inefficient leverage ratios is better understood, can the regulators fix the market imperfections; and only if the impact of leverage cycle on market outcome is clearly estimated, can the authority raise better crisis policies.

Section 5.1 shows how leverage cycle arises as a natural consequence of the financial institutions' operational exercises. The risk management is a continuous response of the banks to the changing market conditions, and it is based on the real time assessment about its expected loss from an imaginary but sufficiently bad situation in a certain time horizon. Such assessment defines the minimum buffer one bank needs to hold to weather the potential market shocks, in practice is often measured by Value-at-Risk (*VaR*). The banks have to actively manage their balance sheets in order to meet *VaR* requirements all the time. It is this active management that generates the strong procyclical leverage cycle.

Suppose that the fundamental value of assets improves, raising the asset price. The banks' net worth therefore gets higher, which relaxes the *VaR* constraints. This gives the banks an opportunity to "leverage up," expanding their balance sheets by raising more (short-term) debts to finance more lucrative investment projects. With a higher demand for assets, the asset price flies even higher. In contrast, when the banks' net worth shrinks in the downturn and makes the *VaR* constraints binding, the banks have to restructure their balance sheets. Often they are forced to sell their assets instead of raising new capital because of the typical "debt overhang" problem, explained by Myers (1977), that the issuance the new equity will be barred by the existing shareholders since the new equity dilutes the value of their share holdings. But such asset fire sale imposes further downward pressure on asset price, dragging the initial deleveraging into a vicious cycle.

In Section 5.2, we go one step further by lifting up the exogenous *VaR* constraints and model leverage as an endogenous market outcome in a general equilibrium framework. The trick of endogenizing leverage into a general equilibrium model is to introduce some heterogeneity in the agents' belief in the long asset's expected return. Those optimistic agents are willing to invest on the long, but risky assets, and buy the assets at a higher price; they become natural borrower. Those pessimistic agents are not willing to invest on the risky assets, but they are willing to lend to the borrowers for better return; they become natural lender. The leverage ratio in the economy is thus endogenized as the ratio of the aggregate assets to the borrowers' net worth, with asset price endogenously determined as well.

The business cycle and leverage cycle reinforce each other through general equilibrium effect. In the boom, more agents are optimistic enough to become borrowers, and their demand for risky assets raises asset price and leverage simultaneously. In the bust, the most optimistic agents become bankrupted and have to liquidate their assets. Only less optimistic agents continue to be borrowers and the aggregate demand for risky assets diminishes. Furthermore, the assets on the sale can only be purchased by the less optimistic agents, whose willingness to pay is lower. This makes the asset price drop even further. The downward spiral in the deleveraging is thus a feedback between asset price and leverage, reinforced by the "limit of arbitrage" type fire sale.

5.1 Leverage cycle and risk management

In this section, we show how leverage cycle emerges as a result of mark-to-market principle and the financial institutions' active adjustment on their balance sheets, using the model based on Shin (2010a, 2010b).

The risk management practice in the financial institutions is widely based on the *VaR*. The *VaR* of a portfolio defines the worst loss over a certain time horizon such that with a pre-specified probability the realized loss is larger. Quantitatively, the *VaR* of a portfolio at confidence level α means that the event that the realized loss L exceeds *VaR* happens at a probability no higher than $1-\alpha$, i.e., $Prob(L>VaR) \leq 1-\alpha$, or equivalently $Prob(L<VaR) \geq \alpha$.

For example, the *VaR* of a portfolio over one month at confidence level 99 percent means that the probability of having a loss larger than *VaR* does not exceed 1 percent, or with 99 percent probability the realized loss is below *VaR* within the next month. Since *VaR* gives a clear assessment on a financial firm's potential loss during a certain period and a reference about the buffer the firm needs to hold to avoid bankruptcy, it is widely adopted as a key indicator in risk management. The theory and application of *VaR* are available in almost all risk management textbooks, see Pearson (2002), Jorion (2007), Saita (2007), etc.

5.1.1 Market equilibrium and asset price

The financial firms' active management of their balance sheets using *VaR* brings extra volatility to asset prices and amplifies the market turbulence in the crises. The mechanism can be seen from the following model based on Shin (2010a, 2010b). Consider an economy that extends to two periods, $t=0$, 1. There are two kinds of assets in the economy:

1   The risky asset. It is traded in the initial period, $t=0$, at the price level P, and the investors get the return from the asset at $t=1$. The stochastic return from one unit of risky asset holding, R, follows a uniform distribution with the support $[\bar{R}-z, \bar{R}+z]$, with $z>0$. The expected value of R, $E[R]$ is $\bar{R}$, and the variance of R,

$$\mathrm{var}[R] = \frac{z^2}{3}.$$

2   The riskless asset, which pays zero interest rate for the investors.

There are also two groups of agents, or investors, with a continuum for each group, in the economy:

1   the risk-neutral leveraged investors, such as banks, who manage their port-
    folio using *VaR*;
2   the risk-averse non-leveraged investors, such as pension funds, who don't
    actively adjust their balance sheets. To capture the risk aversion, assume
    that the non-leveraged investors have mean-variance preference with utility
    function of consumption *c* being

$$U = E[c] - \frac{1}{2\tau} \text{var}[c],$$

in which τ indicates the degree of investors' tolerance on risks: the higher τ
is, *ceteris paribus*, the more the investors are tolerant on taking risks.

At $t=0$, a representative investor finances q units of risky asset, with the worth Pq,
via issuing equity e and debt $Pq-e$. Its balance sheet is summarized as Table 5.1.
    The expected return is therefore

$$c = Rq - (Pq - e).$$

If the investor is a non-leveraged one, her investment decision at $t=0$ is defined
by maximizing her expected utility

$$\max_q U = E[Rq - (Pq - e)] - \frac{1}{2\tau} \text{var}[Rq - (Pq - e)]$$

$$= \bar{R}q - (Pq - e) - \frac{1}{2\tau} \frac{z^2}{3} q^2.$$

The first order condition

$$\frac{\partial U}{\partial q} = 0$$

gives the unleveraged investor's optimal level of holding risky assets, $q_P(P)$

$$q_P(P) = \begin{cases} \frac{3\tau}{z^2}(\bar{R} - P), & \bar{R} > P, \\ 0, & \textit{otherwise.} \end{cases}$$

Table 5.1 The investor's balance sheet at $t=0$

Assets	Liabilities
P_q	Equity e Debt $P_q - e$

If the investor is a leveraged one, her investment decision at $t=0$ is defined by maximizing her expected return, given the *VaR* constraint

$$\max_q E[Rq - (Pq - e)] = (\bar{R} - P)q - e,$$

$$s.t. \, e \geq VaR.$$

Since the expected return is linear in q and e, the leveraged investor will maximize q and minimize e as long as $\bar{R} > P$, i.e., the *VaR* constraint becomes binding.

The *VaR* requirement is designed in a way that the investor should be able to stay solvent even in the worst state, i.e., be able to repay the debtors even the payoff from the risky asset is the lowest, $\bar{R} > z$. This implies $(\bar{R} - z)q \geq Pq - e$. When the *VaR* constraint is binding, $e = (P - \bar{R} + z)q$. Rewrite it as

$$q_A(P) = \frac{e}{P - \bar{R} + z} \tag{5.1}$$

for the demand of risky assets from the leveraged investor. The balance sheet is now featured by Table 5.2.

To concentrate on the key mechanism, assume that in the short run the aggregate supply of risky assets is fixed at S, or, equivalently, the asset price adjustment is much faster than quantity. Therefore, we have $q_A + q_P = S$. Depict $q_A(P)$ and $q_P(P)$ in the same space, as Figure 5.1 shows, the equilibrium asset price P and the demand from both types of investors are determined simultaneously.

5.1.2 VaR, asset price, and the leverage cycle

The impact of economic fundamentals on asset price is visualized in Figure 5.2. Suppose that the fundamentals of the risky assets improves and the expected return rises from $\bar{R}$ to $\bar{R}'$, both demand curves are shifted upwards, leading to a higher price level. This fits perfectly the observed fact that the asset price increases in the economic boom.

Although the equilibrium price P is simultaneously determined once the shock to the fundamental value of the risky assets gets realized, we may break the entire process in several steps to see how the impact of $\bar{R}$ evolves through the balance sheet channel:

Table 5.2 The balance sheet at $t=1$

Assets	Liabilities
P_q	Equity e Debt $(\bar{R} - z)q$

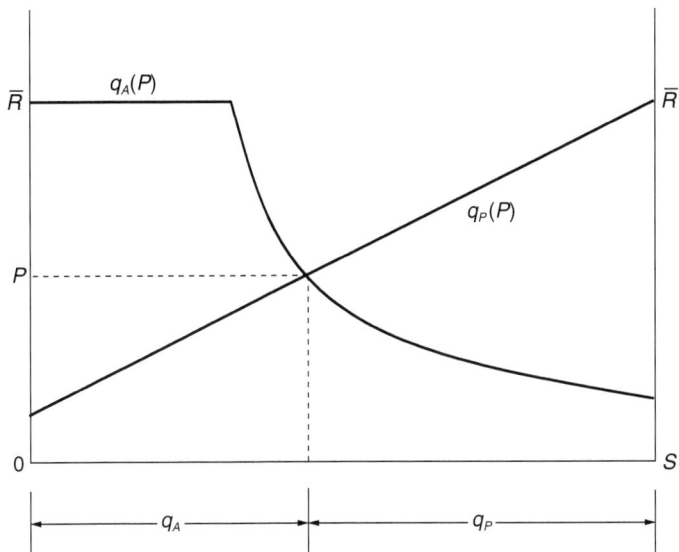

Figure 5.1 The equilibrium asset price.

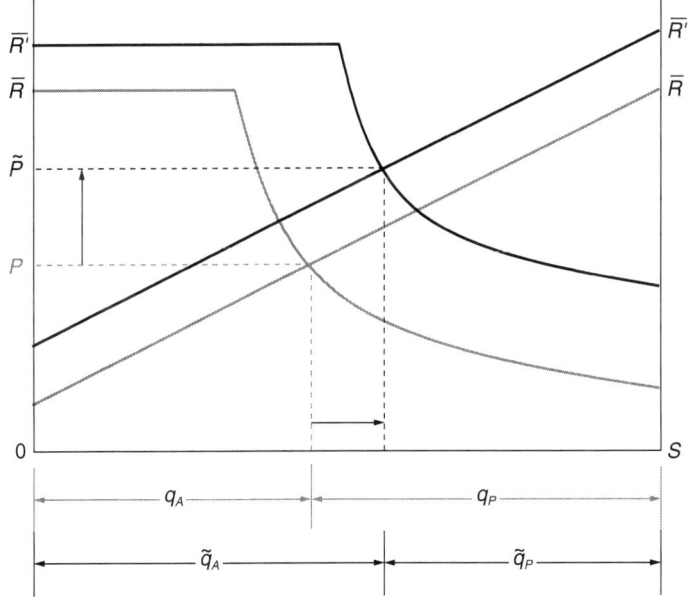

Figure 5.2 Asset price dynamic.

1 The rising $\bar{R}$ increases the unleveraged investors' demand of the risky assets, which is characterized by

$$q_P = \frac{3\tau}{z^2}(\bar{R} - P).$$

With all other things equal, an upward shifted $q_P(P)$ line has a positive impact on the price level P.

2 With a higher price level, call it $\tilde{P}$, the value of the leverage investors' risky assets, $\tilde{P}q_A$, increases. From its balance sheet, Table 5.2, this implies a higher level of equity

$$\tilde{e} = \tilde{P}q_A - (\bar{R} - z)q_A,\tag{5.2}$$

given its starting debt level $(\bar{R} - z)q_A$.

3 With a higher equity level, the investors' *VaR* constraint becomes relaxed since $\tilde{e} > e = VaR$. This allows the investor to expand her balance sheet, take in more borrowing and purchase more risky assets to $\tilde{q}_A > q_A$ in order to catch up with an improved fundamental value $\bar{R}'$. The expanded balance sheet is then featured by

$$\tilde{e} = \tilde{P}\tilde{q}_A - (\bar{R}' - z)\tilde{q}_A.\tag{5.3}$$

Comparing equation (5.2) with (5.3), we can express the new demand level of risky assets from the leveraged investors, using the old demand level

$$\tilde{q}_A = \frac{\tilde{p} + z - \bar{R}}{\tilde{p} + z - \bar{R}'} q_A = \left(1 + \frac{\bar{R}' - \bar{R}}{\tilde{p} + z - \bar{R}'}\right) q_A.\tag{5.4}$$

4 Under the new circumstance, the demand level of risky assets from the non-leveraged investors is

$$\tilde{q}_P = \frac{3\tau}{z^2}(\bar{R}' - \tilde{P}) = S - \tilde{q}_A.\tag{5.5}$$

Both equations (5.4) and (5.5) determine the equilibrium demand for both types of investors,

$$\tilde{q}_A = \left[1 + \frac{\bar{R}' - \bar{R}}{z + (\tilde{q}_A - S)\dfrac{z^2}{3\tau}}\right] q_A.\tag{5.6}$$

Denote the right hand side of (5.6) by $f(\tilde{q}_A)$. Note that its denominator part,

$$z + (\tilde{q}_A - S)\frac{z^2}{3\tau},$$

comes from $\tilde{P}+z-\overline{R'}$ of (5.1) which is positive. Therefore $f(\tilde{q}_A)$ is a downward sloping curve of $\tilde{q}_A$ and the solution to (5.6) is the intersection between $f(\tilde{q}_A)$ and $\tilde{q}_A$, as Figure 5.3 shows.

As in the figure, with a higher $\overline{R'}$ the $f(\tilde{q}_A)$ curve is shifted upwards, leading to a higher demand $\tilde{q}_A$ for risky assets. As a mirror case, $\tilde{q}_A$ falls when $\overline{R'}-\overline{R}<0$.

Furthermore, note from (5.6) that $\tilde{q}_A$ becomes more sensitive to the fundamental shock $\overline{R'}-\overline{R}$ when z is smaller, or *VaR* is smaller since the assets are less risky. In this case, the banks get more leveraged, and the asset price becomes more volatile. This generates higher flying asset price in the boom phase, while more devastating collapse when the economy comes to the downturn.

5.2 The general equilibrium effect and the leverage cycle

The leverage cycle even arises without the explicit *VaR* constraint, as Geanakoplos (2010) demonstrates. This is due to the fact that the borrowers and lenders can choose to enter and exit market when their expected returns on assets vary. The aggregate demand for and supply of credit nail down the equilibrium asset price, and the leverage cycle is thus endogenized through the general equilibrium effect.

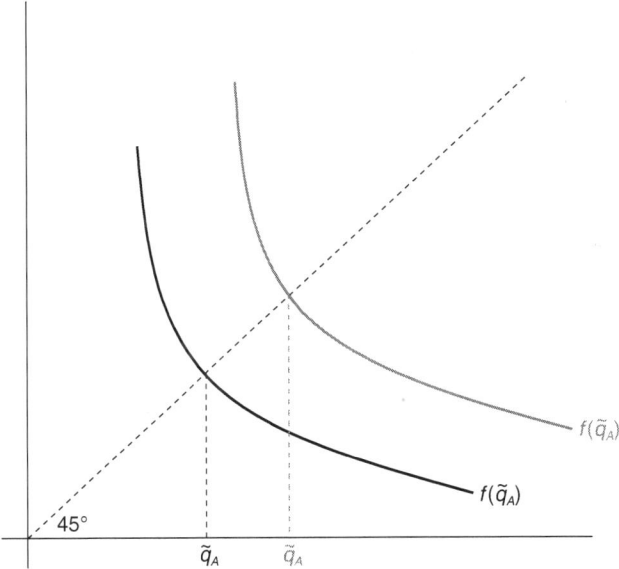

Figure 5.3 Equilibrium demand for risky assets.

5.2.1 Model setup

The agents, time preferences, and technology

As Geanakoplos (2003, 2010a, 2010b), consider an economy that extends to two periods, $t=0$, 1. The only commodity in the economy is a consumption good C, which can be consumed at any time, stored, or used for investment. There are two states of the world, $S \in \{U, D\}$, as in Figure 5.4, namely "up" or "down," for $t=1$. The only asset in this economy is a risky asset Y, at $t=1$ each unit of Y returns $R_U(R_D)$ units of consumption good in the state $U(D)$. As a regularity condition, it is assumed that $R_U \geq 1 > R_D > 0$.

There is a continuum of investors, each of which is endowed with one unit of the asset Y and one unit of consumption good C at $t=0$. The investors are indifferent in the timing of consumption. The investors are heterogeneous in their belief at $t=0$ of the probability π that the economy goes up at $t=1$. For simplicity, suppose π is uniformly distributed and $\pi_i = i$ for a investor indexed by $i \in [0, 1]$. The more the index gets close to 1 (0), the more optimistic (pessimistic) the investor becomes.

Assume that the short selling is not allowed in this economy. When the price of the asset Y is P at $t=0$, the investor i is (weakly) willing to buy the asset as long as she believes that P is (weakly) below the asset's expected value, i.e., $iR_U + (1-i)R_D \geq P$, otherwise she wants to sell the asset. Therefore the more optimistic investors tend to buy the assets and hence are natural buyers of the risky assets, and the more pessimistic ones tend to be natural sellers. Here we have the first novelty of this model: the types of investors are endogenized by their subjective expectation on the risky asset's return.

5.2.2 Market equilibrium without borrowing

To get some flavor about the market equilibrium, we start from the reference case in which no borrowing is allowed, i.e., the buyers can only buy with their own endowments. For a representative investor i, let c^i_0 denote her consumption at $t=0$, and c^i_U (c^i_D) denote her consumption at $t=1$ if the state of the world is $U(D)$. Then at $t=0$ her subjective expected utility is

$$u^i = c^i_0 + ic^i_U + (1-i)c^i_D. \tag{5.7}$$

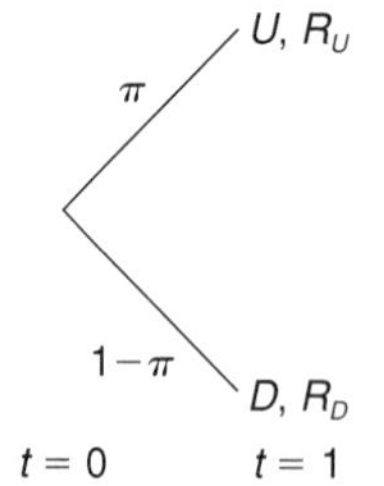

Figure 5.4 The payoff of the risky assets.

Besides consuming c_0^i at $t=0$, the investor can also invest w_0^i as storage which can be consumed at $t=1$. Let y_0^i denote the investor's holding of risky assets for $t=1$. Given some risky assets are traded between the two types of the investors at price P, the investor's budget constraint at $t=0$ is therefore

$$c_0^i + w_0^i + P(y_0^i - 1) = 1. \tag{5.8}$$

With the payoff structure of the risky assets, the expected consumption at $t=1$ for each state is

$$c_U^i = w_0^i + R_U y_0^i, \tag{5.9}$$

$$c_D^i = w_0^i + R_D y_0^i. \tag{5.10}$$

The market clearing conditions must hold:

1   the aggregate $t=0$ consumption and storage is equal to the aggregate endowment of consumption good,

$$\int_0^1 (c_0^i + w_0^i) di = 1; \tag{5.11}$$

2   the aggregate $t=0$ holdings of risky assets is equal to the aggregate endowment of risky assets,

$$\int_0^1 y_0^i di = 1; \tag{5.12}$$

3   the expected aggregate $t=1$ consumption in each state is equal to the expected return from all the risky assets plus the aggregate storage made at $t=0$,

$$\int_0^1 c_U^i di = R_U + \int_0^1 w_0^i di, \tag{5.13}$$

$$\int_0^1 c_D^i di = R_D + \int_0^1 w_0^i di. \tag{5.14}$$

The investor's problem is to choose the optimal $(c_0^i, w_0^i, y_0^i, c_U^i, c_D^i)$ to maximize the object function (5.7) with the budget constraints (5.8)–(5.10) and market clearing conditions (5.11)–(5.14).

Remember that the equilibrium price P divides the investors into two groups: with the boundary i^*, buyers are those with indices $i \in (i^*, 1]$, and seller are those with $i \in [0, i^*)$. Therefore, the equilibrium price P can be solved from the boundary buyer who is indifferent between buying and selling:

$$i^* R_U + (1-i^*) R_D = P. \tag{5.15}$$

Further, note that without borrowing the buyers, whose measure is $1-i^*$, spend all their endowment of consumption good, to purchase the endowment of risky assets from the sellers, whose measure is i^*. The equilibrium price of the risky asset is therefore denoted by the ratio between the total expenditure and the purchased quantity, i.e.,

$$P = \frac{1-i^*}{i^*}. \tag{5.16}$$

The equilibrium price and the boundary buyer are jointly determined by (5.15) and (5.16), as Figure 5.5 shows.

5.2.3 Market equilibrium with borrowing

In our reference case, the buyers' demand of risky assets is limited by their endowments of consumption goods, given that borrowing is not allowed.

What will happen if borrowing is allowed in this economy? Obviously the buyers tend to become borrowers to purchase more risky assets – so long as their subjective expected return is higher than the asset price, and the sellers tend to become lenders so long as the market interest rate is weakly higher than one. The extreme case is the buyer $i=1$: since her subjective expected return is $R_U > P$, she is willing to borrow infinite amount with interest rate R_U. However, the lenders, those $0 \le i < i^*$, won't offer the lending because they believe that the probability of the state D at $t=1$ is strictly positive in which the borrower will have to default. Therefore, in order to avoid default, the lenders must require collateral from the borrowers as a commitment device.

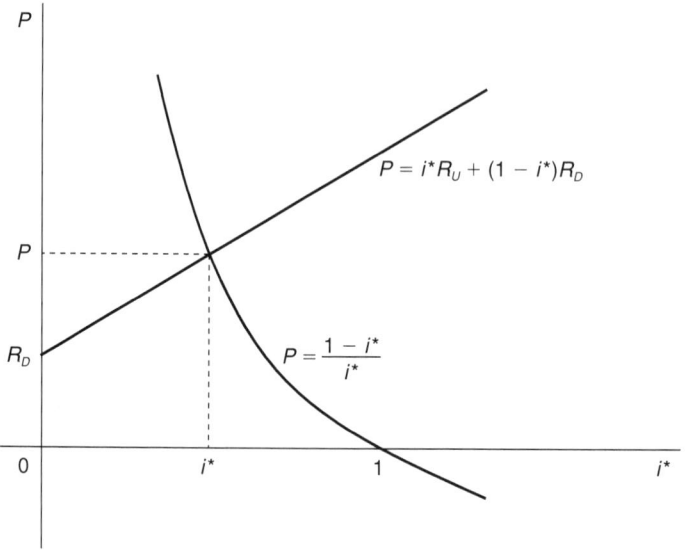

Figure 5.5 The equilibrium price and the boundary buyer.

Assume now that buyers can borrow from the sellers at $t=0$ and the loan contract between the borrowers and lenders is featured by

1   the contract is non-contingent, i.e., the lenders get the same return in the both states, U and D;
2   in order to guarantee the safe return in both states, the lenders take the borrowers' risky assets as collateral.

To find the market equilibrium, suppose that borrower i borrows

$$\frac{\varphi_0^i}{1+r}$$

at $t=0$ with interest rate r and promises to repay φ_0 at $t=1$. The collateral requirement guarantees that the collateral value is sufficient to repay the loan even when the borrower has to default in the D state, i.e.,

$$R_D y_0^i \geq \varphi_0^i. \tag{5.17}$$

This gives the limit of the buyer's borrowing capacity. Now the buyer's budget constraint at $t=0$ becomes

$$c_0^i + w_0^i + P(y_0^i - 1) = 1 + \frac{\varphi_0^i}{1+r}. \tag{5.18}$$

The expected consumption at $t=1$ for each state is now

$$c_U^i = w_0^i + R_U y_0^i - \varphi_0^i, \tag{5.19}$$

$$c_D^i = w_0^i + R_D y_0^i - \varphi_0^i. \tag{5.20}$$

The market clearing conditions must hold:

1   for the aggregate $t=0$ consumption and storage,

$$\int_0^1 (c_0^i + w_0^i)\,di = 1; \tag{5.21}$$

2   for the aggregate $t=0$ holdings of risky assets,

$$\int_0^1 y_0^i\,di = 1; \tag{5.22}$$

3   for the expected aggregate $t=1$ consumption in each state,

$$\int_0^1 c_U^i\,di = R_U + \int_0^1 w_0^i\,di, \tag{5.23}$$

$$\int_0^1 c_D^i di = R_D + \int_0^1 w_0^i di; \tag{5.24}$$

4   for any investor i, she is a borrower if $\varphi_0^i > 0$ and lender if $\varphi_0^i < 0$. The lending and borrowing cancel out in aggregate, which makes

$$\int_0^1 \varphi_0^i di = 0. \tag{5.25}$$

Now the investor's problem is to choose the optimal $(c_0^i, w_0^i, \varphi_0^i, y_0^i, c_U^i, c_D^i)$ to maximize the object function (5.7) with the borrowing constraint (5.17), budget constraints (5.18)–(5.20) and market clearing conditions (5.21)–(5.25).

Similar to the reference case, the market equilibrium price P can be solved by the boundary buyer i^* with

$$i^* R_U + (1 - i^*) R_D = P. \tag{5.26}$$

In equilibrium, the buyers will hold the risky asset of the entire economy, which means a collateral value R_D. This allows all the buyers to borrow up to

$$\frac{R_D}{1+r}$$

in total from the sellers to finance their purchase of risky asset, i^*, besides their endowment of consumption good, $1 - i^*$. Suppose that R_D is so low that the total collateral value of the economy is below the lenders' aggregate endowment of consumption good, $R_D \leq i^*$. The competition among the lenders will drive the equilibrium interest rate r down to zero. The equilibrium price of the risky asset is therefore

$$P = \frac{1 - i^* + R_D}{i^*}. \tag{5.27}$$

The equilibrium price and the boundary buyer are jointly determined by (5.26) and (5.27), as Figure 5.6 shows.

Comparing with the reference market equilibrium without borrowing, which is depicted in gray as Figure 5.6 shows, the access to tapping the credit from the lenders enables the borrowers to increase their expenditure on risky assets and this shifts the asset price to a higher level, given the aggregate supply of risky assets is inelastic. Facing a higher asset price, only those investors who are more optimistic are still willing to purchase, and this crowds out those who are less optimistic and raises the bar for one investor becoming a natural buyer.

One may doubt that such market equilibrium comes from the fact that the loan contract is assumed to be non-contingent, i.e., the lenders must get the same return in both states, so that one buyer's borrowing is upper bounded by $R_D y_0^i$ and the aggregate borrowing is limited to R_D. The optimistic investors would

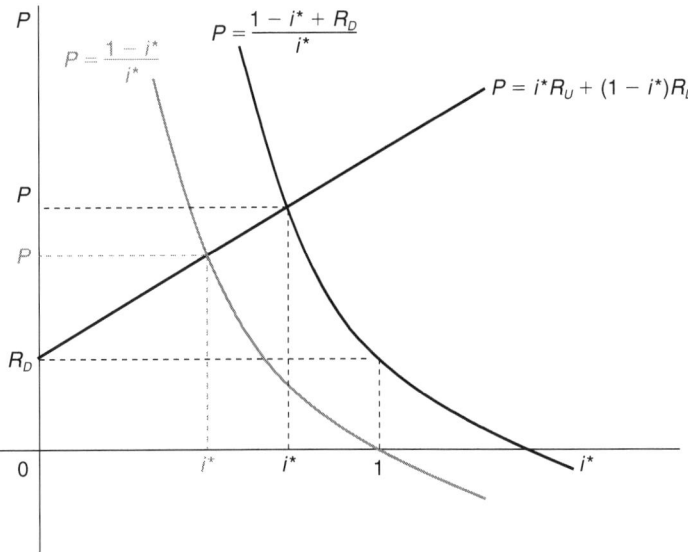

Figure 5.6 The impact of borrowing.

seemingly be able to borrow more if we lift the non-contingency restriction on the loan contract. For example, the most optimistic investor $i=1$ may promise $\tilde{R}y_0^1$, $R_D<\tilde{R}<R_U$, as $t=1$ return, to attract more loans from the lenders. However, this will not happen because of the heterogeneous beliefs of the investors. A natural seller, or a lender, believes that the collateral is worth $\tilde{R}y_0^1$ only with a low probability $i<i^*$, and with a fairly high probability $1-i$ it is worth just $R_Dy_0^1$. Therefore, if the lender agrees to borrow, she must take into account that with probability $1-i$ her loan is not fully pledgeable. Therefore, she has to ask for a higher interest rate to insure against the high probability of default. However, the borrower $i=1$ believes that she will come up with state U with certainty so that she always has to pay the high interest rate to the lender. This is obviously dominated by just promising $R_Dy_0^1$ and paying zero interest rate.

Note that in the market equilibrium with borrowing, the total value of risky assets is P, which is financed by the borrowers' endowment and the debt R_D raised from the lenders. The leverage ratio of the economy is therefore

$$L = \frac{P}{P-R_D}. \tag{5.28}$$

Now we have the second novelty of this model: in the market equilibrium, not only the asset price, but also the leverage of the economy is endogenized.

Using the simplest framework constructed by (5.26), (5.27), and (5.28), we are able to analyze the impact of economic fundamentals on the equilibrium leverage. For example, suppose that the investors become more optimistic such that at $t=0$ investor i believes that the economy goes down at $t=1$ with a lower probability $\pi=(1-i)^2<1-i$, and the chance that the economy goes up gets higher since $1-\pi=1-(1-i)^2>i$. As a result, the boundary investor becomes the one with $[1-(1-i^*)^2]R_U+(1-i^*)^2 R_D=P$. Given that the borrowing constraint

$$P = \frac{1-i^*+R_D}{i^*}$$

remains the same as before, it is easily seen that the equilibrium price P goes up and the boundary i^* goes down. Intuitively, when the investors get more optimistic, those who were previously marginally below the boundary i^* now realize the expected payoff gets higher so that they will switch to be buyers. This increases the total expenditure on risky assets and imposes a positive pressure on asset price through (5.27). But when asset price gets higher, it makes the risky asset less appealing for the marginal buyers which prevents more sellers from joining the buyers. The equilibrium P and i^* thus reflect the balance between these two diverting effects.

Instead of a shock on π, now suppose the expected return of the risky asset in the upside, R_U, gets improved. As Figure 5.7 shows, this means a higher slope for $P=i^*R_U+(1-i^*)R_D$, leading unambiguously to a higher asset price P and lower equilibrium boundary i^*. That is, a higher R_U means a higher fundamental value of risky assets, implying a higher asset price. On the other hand, with

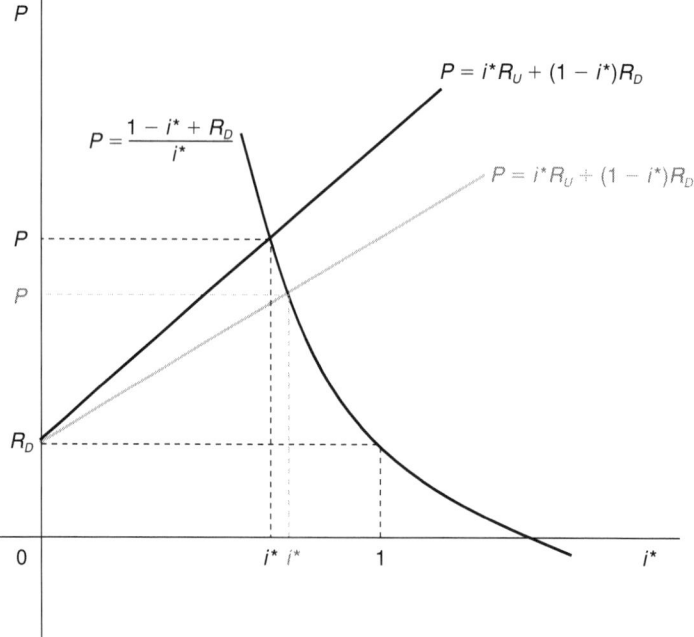

Figure 5.7 The impact of improving fundamentals I.

higher R_U even previously less optimistic investors will find it worthwhile to hold risky assets since the expected return gets higher. Therefore, some of the natural sellers will be converted to buyers. The leverage

$$L = \frac{P}{P - R_D}$$

becomes lower because of the higher asset price. The equilibrium price would have been higher, should there be no shift in boundary i^*. In other words, the impact of higher R_U on asset price has been dampened by the fall in leverage.

Now suppose the expected return of the risky asset in the downside, R_D, gets improved. This means that both

$$P = \frac{1 - i^* + R_D}{i^*}$$

and $P = i^* R_U + (1 - i^*) R_D$ are shifted upwards in Figure 5.8, and $P = i^* R_U + (1 - i^*)$ R_D gets flatter, implying a higher asset price P. To see impact on the equilibrium boundary i^*, combine (5.26) and (5.27) to get the implicit function $i^*(R_D)$

$$\frac{1 - i^* + R_D}{i^*} = i^* R_U + (1 - i^*) R_D.$$

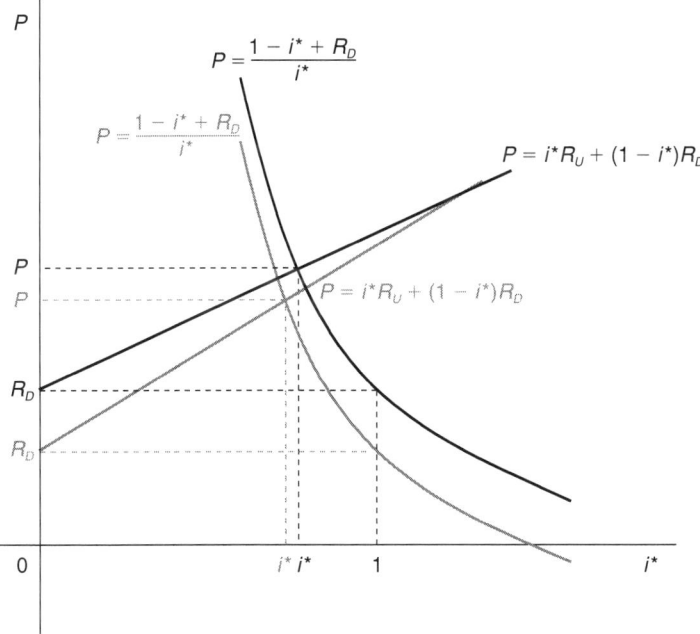

Figure 5.8 The impact of improving fundamentals II.

Differentiating with respect to R_D yields

$$\frac{\partial i^*}{\partial R_D} = \frac{1 - i^* + i^{*2}}{1 + R_D + 2i^*(R_U - R_D)} > 0. \tag{5.28}$$

This means the equilibrium boundary i^* gets higher, too.

Here the rising boundary i^* comes as a result of the general equilibrium effect, which amplifies the impact of R_D through the feedback mechanism between the asset price and the leveraged investors' balance sheet. The improvement of the expected return on the downside relaxes the buyers' borrowing constraint through the improved collateral value, and this is immediately translated to a higher asset price through the multiplier:

$$P = \frac{1 - i^* + R_D}{i^*}$$

implies that the shock to R_D is amplified by

$$\frac{1}{i^*} > 1.$$

However, the sharp rise in asset price also makes the buyers' feasibility constraint, $iR_U + (1-i)R_D \geq P$, less likely to hold. In the end, the marginal buyers who were previously just above the boundary i^*, are now crowded out, and only the more optimistic investors will stay as buyers. But when i^* rises, the total endowment of consumption good from the buyers falls, which brakes the rising trend in asset price through

$$P = \frac{1 - i^* + R_D}{i^*}$$

as a feedback. Finally, equation (5.28) suggests that in equilibrium the amplification effect outweighs the dampening effect.

5.2.4 The business cycle and the leverage cycle

As the simplest general equilibrium model shows, by comparative analysis one can see the impact of fundamental value on asset prices through the lenders' balance sheet. One interesting extension to this baseline model is to explain the leverage cycle through investors' expectation on the fundamental value, i.e., the building up of leverage after good news or the asset price crash caused by excessive deleveraging after the bad news.

To capture such leverage cycle, the model needs at least three periods. Keeping the settings almost the same as in the baseline model, there is one additional intermediate date, $t=0.5$, in which investors can observe a signal regarding the risky asset's payoff in the future. For investor i with subjective probability $\pi(1-\pi)$ the signal is $U(D)$. At $t=1$ the investors observe another signal, which is independent on, but of the same distribution of, the previous one, as Figure 5.9 shows. The $t=1$ payoff of the risky asset is R_D only if both signals are D. Again, suppose π is uniformly distributed and $\pi_i=i$ for a investor indexed by $i \in [0, 1]$.

With an additional intermediate date, the investors will have one more chance to consider their investments. Therefore, assume that all the loans only last for one period. At $t=0$, based on their expected payoff, the investors will be endogenously separated into buyers (or, borrowers) and sellers (or, lenders), and the equilibrium is characterized by the asset price P_0 and the boundary investor i_0^*. The borrowers get their loans from the lenders, using their assets as collateral. When it comes to $t=0.5$, conditional on the signal they receive, the investors have to adjust their expectation on $t=1$ payoff and reconsider their holdings of risky asset, i.e., the borrowers may want to increase or have to deplete their asset stocks, the lenders may want to liquidate the collateral or roll over their loans into the next period (we will explain the details later). The equilibrium depends on the observed signal: asset price $P_{0.5,S}$ and the boundary investor $i_{0.5,S}^*$ under signal $S \in \{U, D\}$.

In the current three-date model, the investors are more optimistic at $t=0$ than in the baseline model, since the investor i's subjective probability of having a low return R_D is $(1-i)^2<1-i$. Therefore, similar to the comparative analysis of the last section, the equilibrium price P_0 and the boundary investor i_0^* are connected by $[1-(1-i_0^*)^2]R_U+(1-i_0^*)^2R_D=P_0$. As is argued before, the equilibrium price P_0 tends to be higher than the baseline model, given that the investors are more optimistic.

The difference here is the buyer's borrowing capacity. Note that all the loans are short term so that for the loans made at $t=0$, the collateral value is the value from liquidating the risky asset at $t=0.5$, i.e., the asset price $P_{0.5,S}$ which further depends on the signal observed at $t=0.5$. When $S=U$, it is easily seen that

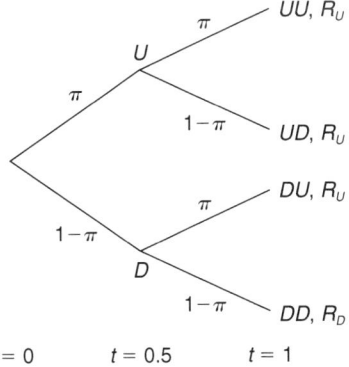

Figure 5.9 The three-date extension.

$P_{0.5,U}=R_U$ because R_U will be realized at $t=1$ with certainty; when $S=D$, $P_{0.5,D}$ is yet to be determined, but should be above R_D because there is still a positive probability of ending up with DU at $t=1$. In the end, the buyers' total borrowing capacity at $t=0$ should be larger than that in the baseline model. As is argued before, the equilibrium price P_0 tends to be higher, along with the buyers' higher borrowing capacity.

Suppose that with equilibrium P_0 and i_0^* the time goes on from $t=0$ to $t=0.5$, when the first signal gets revealed. If $S=U$, the high return R_U is guaranteed with certainty, and the asset price will be bid up to R_U. The economy booms before the high return is materialized.

In contrast, if $S=D$, the economy incurs a crash. To make it worse, the downward spiral will be fueled by the general equilibrium effect. To see this, note that when signal D is observed,

1 For investor i the probability of having a low return becomes $1-i>(1-i)^2$, i.e., the investors become more pessimistic, implying a lower asset price $P_{0.5,D}$.
2 Therefore the initial buyers at $t=0$ go bankrupt as Figure 5.10 shows, and all their asset holdings as collateral are seized by the initial sellers.
3 Now only the less optimistic investors $i\in[0, i_0^*)$ are still in the market. Given that all the investors are more pessimistic, the equilibrium price of the risky assets $P_{0.5,D}$ has to fall even further.
4 With a sufficiently low $P_{0.5,D}$, the investors on the top of $[0, i_0^*)$ are willing to buy the asset. However, the collateral value is only R_D in this case, implying that the borrowing capacity has been also contracted. Such deleveraging imposes more downside pressure on $P_{0.5,D}$.

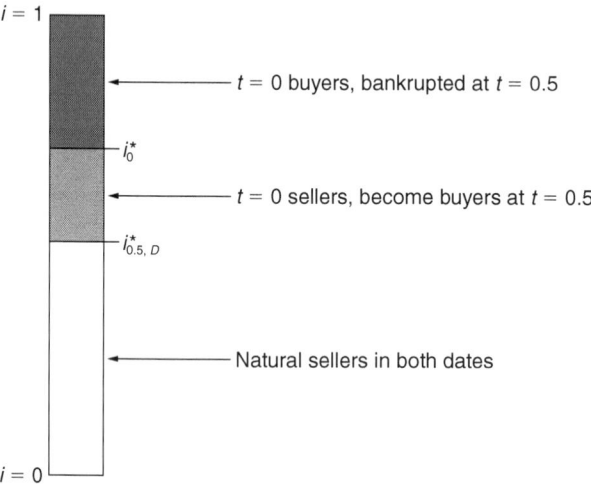

Figure 5.10 The leverage cycle and the marginal buyer.

In the end, the equilibrium ends up with a low $P_{0.5,D}$, and the boundary investor $i^*_{0.5,D}$ for the surviving investors.

Such vicious spiral makes a perfectly analogy to fire sale, and the key mechanism in the model explains how economic downturn triggers the disastrous fire sale. In contrast to the standard models with representative investors, i.e., all the investors are (at least *ex ante*) homogeneous in all dimensions, here the investors are from the beginning heterogeneous in their subjective expectation of the future payoff from holding risky asset. Thus, by the simple "buy low, sell high" principle, the investors are endogenously separated into natural buyers and sellers: those more optimistic investors hold the asset, which they buy from the pessimistic ones using the funds borrowed from the sellers. Since the borrowers need to post their asset as collateral, their leverage ratio is endogenously determined in equilibrium, too. Certainly the asset price in equilibrium is determined by the law of demand and supply; however, what becomes more important here is who serves as a buyer or a seller when the shock gets revealed. When the market becomes more optimistic about the fundamentals, the asset price is bid up, and the trend is then dampened by the leverage of the economy. But when a negative shock hits and the market becomes more pessimistic, after the first wave of asset price decline caused by the deteriorating fundamentals, the initial natural buyers, or the optimistic investors, get bankrupted and driven out of the market. This further aggravates the market outcome: now the buyers are less optimistic and their willingness to pay is low, and their borrowing capacity gets contracted because of the deterioration in the fundamentals. These two factors jointly depress the asset price even further into a full collapse, and the effect is amplified by deleveraging. Finally, it is not surprising that asset has to be sold at the fire sale price – simply because the optimal buyers are all gone.

The endogenous leverage cycle through general equilibrium sheds much light on many asset price puzzles both in the economic boom and in the financial crisis. However, even in the current simplest model with only one dimension heterogeneity, the equilibrium is hard to compute and it is often not obvious to make comparative statics analysis. This may limit the model's applicability. But, on the other hand, with powerful computers getting universally available, it becomes easier to allow for more heterogeneities and agents at play. A more agent based, computer aided, general equilibrium framework seems promising to help us find out more equilibrium patterns which are missed by the homogeneous, representative agent models.

6 Micro fragility and macro stability

> For those who work in banking and finance it will, perhaps, come as a surprise that the blame for the crisis has been widely attributed to modern macroeconomic theory rather than their own industry. Most people in banking and finance work with theories they regard as very different from those of modern macroeconomics, whilst most modern macroeconomic theories largely ignore banking and give only a cursory role to financial markets. Macroeconomics has been heavily criticized for assuming that financial markets are efficient and expectations are rational despite both being centre-pieces of modern finance theory.
>
> (Wickens, 2010)

The Great Moderation in the past decade also marks the heyday of modern macroeconomics. It once seems that we know much about macroeconomics that Wicksell and Fisher did not and every shock to the economy can be well under control. However, the eruption of current financial crisis simply reminds us economists that there is actually a lot of macroeconomics that Wicksell and Fisher already knew but we have long forgotten.

Although it is unfair to blame macroeconomists for not being able to forecast or prevent the financial crisis – just as we cannot attribute the crash of any aircraft to the failure of physics – there is still something extremely relevant to macro economy but systematically missing in modern macroeconomics. For long time macroeconomics and finance have been much isolated fields. Financial economists usually don't look at the impact of financial market on macro economy, and macroeconomics models seldom have an explicit role for finance. Macroeconomics in practice, now often criticized for being incompetent for predicting, preventing, and handling the financial crises, is widely based on the dynamic stochastic general equilibrium (DSGE) framework which focuses on price and labor frictions and does not have any role for financial intermediaries and financial market. But the reality greatly differs from the world in the models. As is once more revealed in the crisis, the healthy financial market provides a lifeline for the non-financial firms to get funding, directing the resources in the economy to the place where they are best used, while the financial market in trouble freezes borrowing and lending, bringing the real economy into a nuclear winter.

Of course macroeconomists are fully aware of the importance of financial sector; there are both practical and technical reasons why there is seldom a role for finance in the workhorse models of modern macroeconomics. The DSGE models are largely developed out of the central banks' desire to maintain price stability and employment, while financial stability has not been the stipulated mandate for the central banks in the developed economies. Therefore, to capture the transmission mechanism of monetary policy and to model the friction in the labor market are among the highest priorities. And there are also technical difficulties to integrate financial sector in the standard and already complicated DSGE paradigm. The representative (homogeneous) agent approach makes it fairly difficult to capture the typical mismatch of time preferences, or liquidity problems; the desire for convergence makes it difficult to consider the discontinuities in payoffs, for example, bank runs; the local stability analysis using linear approximation misses the chance to capture any non-linear effect in the financial crisis, and so on. If one wants to stay with DSGE models, some techniques and tricks need to be designed to capture the financial frictions in a tractable way.

One of the modeling strategies successfully applied in many dynamic macroeconomics models is the "financial accelerator," to be discussed in Section 6.1, that comes from the credit constraint from the borrower side. The agents in the economy are heterogeneous in productivity; therefore, some of them become natural lenders who want their endowments best used by the agents – the natural borrowers – who are more efficient in production. However, because of the costly state verification problem, the borrowers have the incentive to lie on their realized returns and get some private rent. The lenders can only get the true information if they invest in a costly auditing technology, and the equilibrium thus must be incentive compatible such that the borrowers always tell the truth. When there is a boom, the borrower's net worth increases and this makes the borrowing constraint less binding. The result is a lower probability of auditing, and there are more resources used for production; on the contrary, in the downturn the borrower has to rely more on outside funding and this increases the probability of being audited. In the end, there is less resource invested on production. The financial friction "accelerates" the productivity shock on the economy.

In the standard financial accelerator framework, the borrowers are exogenously differentiated by their productivity so that in equilibrium there are projects with various productivities at work and financial accelerator works through moving the threshold of the productivity. In Section 6.2, we relax this assumption by allowing the borrowers to endogenously choose among the projects with different productivities and degrees of agency problems. Again, the borrower's net worth plays a pivotal role here, but now the borrower has to balance between its borrowing constraint (depending on the severity of the agency problem) and the profitability of investment (depending on the productivity of the projects). Therefore, along the path of convergence, the interaction between these two constraints may force the borrowers to jump between different projects, generating very rich patterns of growth paths which correspond to different impacts of financial friction on macro economy.

Although the DSGE approach is heavily criticized for not taking into sufficient account the role of financial sector, it is by no means that researchers should discard the entire framework. Having been used as the workhorse in most central banks for a decade, people have accumulated a great deal of knowledge about the mechanism at work, the algorithm to tackle the complicated dynamic problems, as well as the econometric tools for forecasting. It would be a huge value added if the impact of financial frictions is captured in the framework through a proper way. Now researchers worldwide are making a huge effort for this purpose, while most of the outputs are still in the stage of working papers. In Section 6.3, we will briefly present some recent work which explicitly models the financial intermediaries in the dynamic macroeconomic framework.

6.1 The agency problem and financial accelerator

The financial accelerator, first explored by Bernanke and Gertler (1989), is among the pioneer ideas that integrate the financial frictions in the standard dynamic macroeconomics models. The credit constraint comes from the agency problem that the borrowers have the incentive to seek for private rent and the lenders have to implement a costly auditing technology to monitor the borrowers. A borrower's net worth thus reflects her borrowing capacity, hence the plausible resource for value creation.

6.1.1 Model setup

The agents, preferences, and technology

Consider a Samuelson–Diamond type economy in discrete time $t = 0, 1, \ldots$ populated by overlapping generations. The population of each generation is constant with one unit mass. A new generation is born at each period t – call it generation t – who work to earn labor income at t when they are young using their labor endowment (normalized to be one), and save for future consumption after they retire at $t+1$. In each generation the population is exogenously divided into two groups of agents when they are born:

1 A fraction η are entrepreneurs who own the production technology (will be explained later). The entrepreneurs are heterogeneous in the cost of production ω, which is uniformly distributed with support [0, 1]. In the rest of this section, the entrepreneurs are ranked by their ω. The entrepreneurs don't consume when they are young, but consume their lifetime income when old.
2 A fraction $1-\eta$ are investors. The investors consume in both periods, and the utility function of one representative generation t investor is

$$U_t = u(c_t^y) + \beta u(c_{t+1}^o).$$

$c_t^y(c_{t+1}^o)$ is her consumption at $t(t+1)$ when she is young (old), and β is the discount factor. $u(\cdot)$ is strictly concave and twice differentiable.

There are two goods in the economy:

1   Consumption good, which is the output from the production. It can be consumed, or used as input of capital production (will be explained later) which convert the consumption good to capital in the next period. Consumption good can also be stored, with gross return rate $r \geq 1$ for one period.
2   Capital good, which is not consumable, but is used as input for producing consumption good. In each period the depreciation rate of capital is 100 percent.

Technologies. There are technologies for producing consumption good and capital, respectively:

1   Consumption good is produced via a neoclassical technology, with labor and capital as inputs, $Y_t = \tilde{\theta}_t F(K_t, L_t)$ in which Y_t is the aggregate output in period t, K_t the aggregate capital stock, and L_t the labor supply. $\tilde{\theta}_t$ represents the random exogenous technological shock which is i.i.d. overtime with mean θ. The production function is homogeneous of degree 1 so that it can be written in per capita form

$$y_t = \tilde{\theta}_t f(k_t).$$

2   Capital good is produced through the entrepreneurs' projects. Each entrepreneur has one unit of project, which transfers y units of consumption good into k units of capital, to be used as the next period's capital input for producing consumption good. For an entrepreneur with type ω, such technology is featured by

$$k = \begin{cases} 0 & if \ y < x(\omega), \\ \kappa_i & if \ y \geq x(\omega) \end{cases}$$

That is, each project has to incur a fixed cost $x(\omega)$, which is an increasing function of ω, and the marginal product of the project is zero if the input exceeds such threshold. κ_i can take two values: with probability π the output is κ_H, and with probability $1-\pi$ the output is $\kappa_L < \kappa_H$. Denote the expected value of κ_i as κ.

The agency problem

Because of costly state verification problem (its micro foundation is provided by Townsend (1979) and Gale and Hellwig (1985)), the exact output of the project is private information for the entrepreneur it belongs to and cannot be directly verified by the outsiders. Therefore, the entrepreneur can misreport κ_H as κ_L and pockets the difference $\kappa_H - \kappa_L$ as private benefit. The other agents can learn the output only by employing auditing, which costs γ units of capital goods and makes the output as public information. Therefore, for any period t with i_t projects deployed and a share of h_t audited, the expected capital intensity for $t+1$ is

$$k_{t+1} = (\kappa - h_t \gamma) i_t. \tag{6.1}$$

6.1.2 Market equilibrium with no asymmetric information

As a reference, we first analyze the market equilibrium with perfect information, i.e., there is no auditing cost to learn the true output of one project, $\gamma = 0$. For any period t, denote the next period price of capital as q_{t+1}, then the expected return of a project invested at t is $q_{t+1}\kappa$, and the opportunity cost of investing on project instead of storage is $rx(\omega)$. The profitability constraint for entrepreneur ω – call it $(PC-\omega)$ – is

$$q_{t+1}\kappa \geq rx(\omega). \ (PC-\omega) \tag{6.2}$$

And

$$\bar{\omega} = x^{-1}\left(\frac{q_{t+1}\kappa}{r}\right)$$

is the cut-off value separating the entrepreneurs: those with $\omega \leq \bar{\omega}$ make the investment, while those with $\omega > \bar{\omega}$ make the storage. To focus on the interesting case, assume that the aggregate saving in the economy is large enough to finance the entrepreneurs' projects, i.e.,

$$\underbrace{\eta w_t}_{(A)} + \underbrace{(1-\eta)(w_t - c_t^y)}_{(B)} > \int_0^{\bar{\omega}} x(\omega) d\omega .$$

Part (A) in the left hand side is the aggregate wage income of the entrepreneurs, and part (B) is the investors' net income after consumption.

Out of all the entrepreneurs – whose measure is η – only a share of $\bar{\omega}$ carry out the projects, therefore, the total number of the projects at t is

$$i_t = \bar{\omega}\eta. \tag{6.3}$$

With $\gamma = 0$ the expected capital intensity for $t+1$ is

$$k_{t+1} = \kappa i_t = \kappa \bar{\omega}\eta. \tag{6.4}$$

Combine (6.4) with (6.2), the equilibrium capital price is

$$q_{t+1} = \frac{r}{\kappa} x\left(\frac{k_{t+1}}{\kappa\eta}\right). \tag{6.5}$$

This defines the entrepreneurs' willingness to invest on projects producing capital, or the supply curve (S) of capital as Figure 6.1 shows. The supply curve is upward sloping since

$$\frac{\partial q_{t+1}}{\partial k_{t+1}} = \frac{r}{\kappa^2 \eta} x' \left(\frac{k_{t+1}}{\kappa \eta} \right) > 0.$$

On the other hand, in the competitive capital market, the capital price q_{t+1} is determined by the expected marginal product of capital, i.e.,

$$q_{t+1} = E_t [\tilde{\theta}_{t+1}] f'(k_{t+1}) = \theta f'(k_{t+1}). \tag{6.6}$$

This defines the demand of capital, curve (D) in Figure 6.1, which is downward sloping since

$$\frac{\partial q_{t+1}}{\partial k_{t+1}} = \theta f''(k_{t+1}) < 0.$$

The equilibrium capital price and intensity are jointly determined by (6.5) and (6.6). Since all the other parameters are constant, in equilibrium, q and k will be constant over time. The economy builds up its capital stock from any initial capital intensity k_0, just as the standard overlapping generation model does.

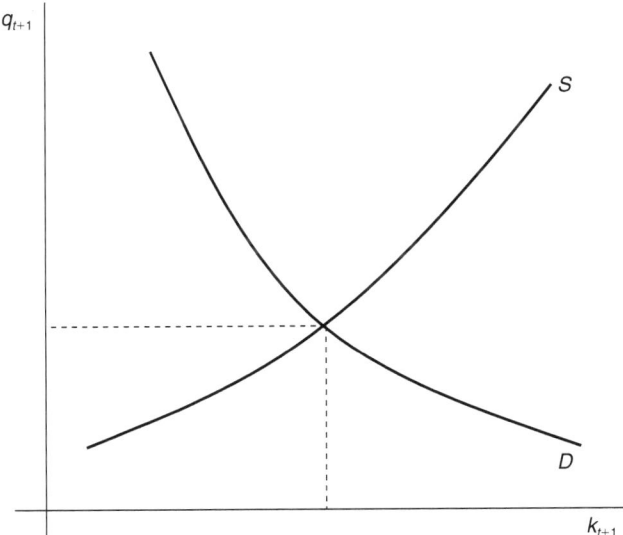

Figure 6.1 Capital demand and supply.

6.1.3 *Market equilibrium with asymmetric information*

Now suppose that because of costly state verification problem the outsiders have to incur an auditing cost to learn the true output of the projects. This will make difference for those entrepreneurs who need to borrow, i.e., those with small ω – the project's net present value is positive – while the financing cost exceeds the wage income, or the saving made in the first period of life, $x(\omega) > w_t$.

The optimal contract for the borrowers is defined by the revelation principle (the general theorem is investigated in Mas-Colell *et al.*, 1995, Chapter 23), which is featured by

1   participation constraint for investors $(PC-i)$: the expected return from lending must exceed the return from storage;
2   the incentive compatibility, or truth telling constraint (IC): entrepreneurs do not lie about the projects' outcomes;
3   limited liability (LL): entrepreneurs only have limited liability.

To find the optimal contract, notice that the entrepreneur only gets private benefit if she announces her project's outcome as κ_L while the true one is κ_H. Therefore, there is no need for auditing if one entrepreneur's announcement is κ_H. It is only necessary to audit if the announcement is κ_L.

Suppose a representative generation t entrepreneur's consumption is c_t^i if she announces κ_i, $i \in \{H, L\}$. When she announces κ_L, there is a probability $p_t \in [0, 1]$ that she is audited. After auditing, the consumption is c_t^a if she tells the truth, c_t^l if she lies. The optimal contract for the entrepreneur is to find

$$\{p_t, c_t^H, c_t^L, c_t^a, c_t^l\} = \arg\max(1 - \pi)[p_t c_t^a + (1 - p_t)c_t^L] + \pi c_t^H, \tag{6.7}$$

$$\begin{aligned} s.t. \, (1 - \pi)[q_{t+1}\kappa_L - p_t(c_t^a + q_{t+1}\gamma) - (1 - p_t)c_t^L] + \\ \pi(q_{t+1}\kappa_H - c_t^H) \geq r[x(\omega) - w_t], \, (PC-i) \end{aligned} \tag{6.8}$$

$$c_t^H \geq (1 - p_t)[q_{t+1}(\kappa_H - \kappa_L) + c_t^L] + p_t c_t^l, \, (IC) \tag{6.9}$$

$$c_t^L \geq 0, \, (LL-1) \tag{6.10}$$

$$c_t^a \geq 0, \, (LL-2) \tag{6.11}$$

First of all, the optimal c_t^l to meet (IC) is to maximize the punishment for lying, i.e., $c_t^l = 0$. Given that the entrepreneur always tells the truth, $(PC-i)$ says that the expected return of the entrepreneur's project must be sufficient to repay the investors, with the expected capital price being q_{t+1}. Further, expected consumption maximization as in object function (6.7) implies that $(PC-i)$ is always binding. (IC) means that when κ_H is realized, the expected consumption from telling the truth must exceed that from telling a lie. $(LL-1)$ and $(LL-2)$ mean that the entrepreneur has limited liability in the bad state, even after being audited.

The optimal contract depends on the value of the entrepreneur's project. The best scenario is that the value always exceeds the entrepreneur's liability to the investors, even in the bad state. In this case, there is no need to audit, and the entrepreneur never defaults, i.e.,

$$q_{t+1}\kappa_L \geq r[x(\omega) - w_t] \text{ with } p_t = 0.$$

With given q_{t+1}, $x(\omega)$, the minimum income level with which the entrepreneur is able to borrow without being audited is

$$w_t^* = x(\omega) - \frac{q_{t+1}\kappa_L}{r}. \tag{6.12}$$

With $p_t = 0$, (PC−i) implies that with optimal contract

$$(1-\pi)[q_{t+1}\kappa_L - c_t^L] + \pi(q_{t+1}\kappa_H - c_t^H) = r[x(\omega) - w_t],$$

$$E[c_t] = q_{t+1}\kappa - r[x(\omega) - w_t]. \tag{6.13}$$

The expected consumption of the entrepreneur is her profit from capital production.

However, the problem gets complicated if $q_{t+1}\kappa_L < r[x(\omega) - w_t]$. In this scenario, the value of the entrepreneur's project cannot meet the entrepreneur's liability to the investors in the bad state, and the entrepreneur has to default. Should there be no auditing, the entrepreneur would always have the incentive to misreport κ_H as κ_L and pocket the difference $\kappa_H - \kappa_L$ as private benefit, making the loan contract break down. Therefore, in equilibrium, the probability of auditing, p_t, must be positive to deter such moral hazard problem. The object function (6.7) implies that the constraint (6.8)–(6.11) are all binding, through which the equilibrium p_t can be solved as

$$p_t = \frac{r[x(\omega) - w_t] - q_{t+1}\kappa_L}{\pi q_{t+1}(\kappa_H - \kappa_L) - (1-\pi)q_{t+1}\gamma} \tag{6.14}$$

As long as the gain from deterring misreporting, $\pi q_{t+1}(\kappa_H - \kappa_L)$, exceeds the cost of auditing, $(1-\pi)q_{t+1}\gamma$, the probability of auditing, p_t, is always positive. One can further infer from (6.14) that p_t decreases with the entrepreneur's own saving, w_t, which is fairly intuitive: the higher stake the entrepreneur holds in her investment, the less she has to borrow and, hence, the less private benefit she can get from misreporting, or, the less severe the moral hazard problem is.

Applying (6.14) in (PC−i), the expected consumption of the entrepreneur is

$$E[c_t] = \frac{\pi q_{t+1}(\kappa_H - \kappa_L)}{\pi q_{t+1}(\kappa_H - \kappa_L) - (1-\pi)q_{t+1}\gamma} \{q_{t+1}\kappa - r[x(\omega) - w_t] - (1-\pi)q_{t+1}\gamma\} \tag{6.15}$$

Return to (6.13) where there is no agency problem,

$$\frac{\partial E[c_t]}{\partial w_t} = r.$$

This is because one additional unit of saving will become an additional unit of investment on the project, returning her the market rate of investment. In contrast, here we have

$$\frac{\partial E[c_t]}{\partial w_t} = \frac{\pi q_{t+1}(\kappa_H - \kappa_L)}{\pi q_{t+1}(\kappa_H - \kappa_L) - (1-\pi)q_{t+1}\gamma} r > r.$$

Having one additional unit of saving for the entrepreneur who suffers from the costly state verification problem has two effects: first, same as before it returns r from the capital market; second, by having one unit more "inside" funding from her own pocket, the entrepreneur can have one unit less "outside" funding from borrowing, or, less agency cost; this gives her more resource for consumption.

Now for an arbitrary entrepreneur ω, whether she is successful in carrying out her project depends on its expected profit, or the difference between the expected return of the project and its opportunity cost less the auditing cost, $E_t[R_{t+1}(\omega)] = q_{t+1}\kappa - rx(\omega) - p(1-\pi)q_{t+1}\gamma$, which further depends on her character ω and the probability of being audited. There are several generic cases:

1   She is never able to start the project because the expected profit of the project is negative, even when there is no auditing cost with $p=0$, $E_t[R_{t+1}(\omega)] = q_{t+1}\kappa - rx(\omega) < 0$, or

$$\omega > \bar{\omega} = x^{-1}\left(\frac{q_{t+1}\kappa}{r}\right).$$

2   She is always able to start the project because the expected profit of the project is always positive, even when there is the maximum auditing cost with $p=1$, $E_t[R_{t+1}(\omega)] = q_{t+1}\kappa - rx(\omega) - (1-\pi)q_{t+1}\gamma > 0$, or

$$0 \le \omega < \underline{\omega} = x^{-1}\left(\frac{q_{t+1}\kappa - (1-\pi)q_{t+1}\gamma}{r}\right).$$

3   When $\underline{\omega} < \omega < \bar{\omega}$, whether she is successful depends on the auditing probability p.

Those in case (1) will become investors, lending their income to the successful entrepreneurs instead of running the projects by themselves; those in case (1) are certainly successful entrepreneurs, but whether their projects will be audited or not depends on their income – there is no auditing only if the wage income exceeds w_t^* so that the project is fully collateralized as (6.13) shows. Those in case (3) are ambiguous, call them "swinging entrepreneurs": as (6.14) shows, the auditing probability p is negatively correlated with w_i; therefore, when w_i is lower than p, hence the auditing cost is so high to make $E_t[R_{t+1}(\omega)] = q_{t+1}\kappa - rx(\omega) - (1-\pi)q_{t+1}\gamma < 0$, the entrepreneur will be barred from running her project. However, when w_i is high enough to make $E_t[R_{t+1}(\omega)] > 0$, the entrepreneur will carry out the project.

In contrast to the market equilibrium without financial friction where q and k are constant over time, here the agency problem generates both short-term (intra-period) and long-term fluctuations through the supply curve of capital, although the demand curve remains the same as before.

In Figure 6.2, first of all, notice that the supply curve of capital with financial friction (the gray curves) is always above the supply curve without financial friction (the black curve) as Figure 6.2 shows, since the agency problem implies a dead weight loss in capital production. In the short run, notice that the supply of capital k_{t+1} depends on the number of the entrepreneurs who participate the capital production at t, and this depends on the entrepreneurs' income w_t. The neoclassical production function $y_t = \tilde{\theta}_t f(k_t)$ implies that $w_t = \tilde{\theta}_t[f(k_t) - kf'(k_t)]$, which depends on the technological shock $\tilde{\theta}_t$. When the realized $\tilde{\theta}_t$ is high, the entrepreneurs' wage income increases, too. This increases the net worth of the projects from the successful entrepreneurs, making them more likely to face lower probability of being audited, or even completely collateralized so that there is no need for auditing at all. As a result, the agency cost is lower and there

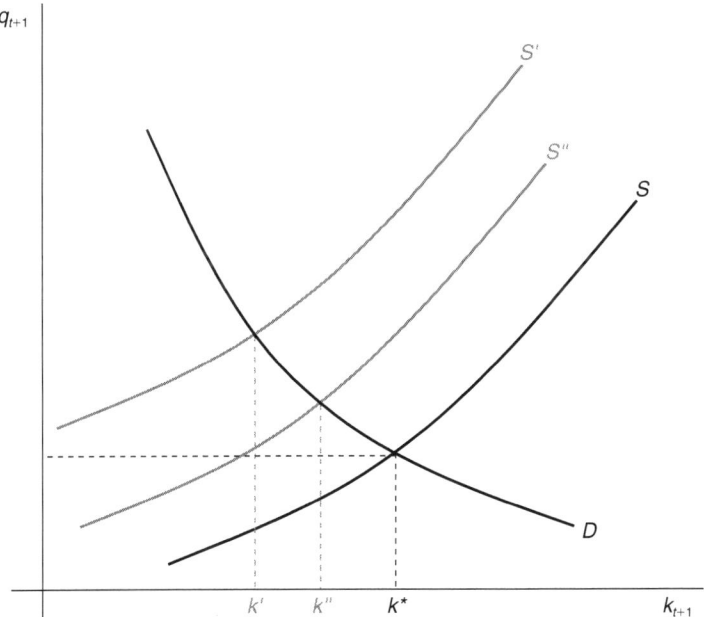

Figure 6.2 Capital supply with financial friction.

will be more resources devoted to capital production. Further, the increase in the entrepreneurs' income makes the swinging entrepreneurs more likely to break even, i.e., $E_t[R_{t+1}(\omega)] = q_{t+1}\kappa - rx(\omega) - p(1-\pi)q_{t+1}\gamma > 0$ because of the falling auditing probability p. Therefore, more entrepreneurs will become successful ones, carrying out more projects. These two effects jointly shift the capital supply curve S'' closer to the frictionless equilibrium supply curve S, leading to a higher level of capital production k'', as Figure 6.2 shows. The interesting feature here is that the economic boom does not only increase the net worth of the projects which enables the entrepreneurs to expand their balance sheets, but also make more entrepreneurs accessible to outside funding which further increases the capital output – exhibiting a financial accelerator effect.

On the contrary, when the realized $\tilde{\theta}_t$ is low, the entrepreneurs' wage income declines. The fall in the projects' net worth both increases the auditing costs for the successful entrepreneurs and drives some of the swinging entrepreneurs out of the successful ones. These two effects jointly shift the capital supply curve S' away from the frictionless equilibrium supply curve S, leading to a lower level of capital production k', as Figure 6.2 shows.

Such short-run fluctuations also ripple into the long-run future. A positive technological shock $\tilde{\theta}_t$ leads to higher capital output from period t projects, or, higher capital input k_{t+1} for period $t+1$ production. This makes the economy more resilient in the next period, i.e., when there is a negative technological shock $\tilde{\theta}_{t+1}$ the wage income w_{t+1} won't decline as long as the shock is small, so that there is even a persistent economic growth in the mid-term.

The long-run implication for such financial accelerator effect is not straightforward. Suppose that an economy starts with very low initial capital intensity k_0, or high marginal product of capital $\tilde{\theta}_0 f'(k_0)$. The high productivity of capital may outweigh the possible negative technological shock, and the economy starts accumulating capital although the growth path is stochastic due to the random shocks $\tilde{\theta}_t$ coming in each period. However, with time going on, the marginal product of capital diminishes when k_t gets higher, a negative shock $\tilde{\theta}_t$ now may sharply decrease the labor income. With the presence of the financial accelerator, this suffocates many candidate projects and highly raises the auditing cost; the economic growth may be completely reversed. And, to make it worse, such economic downturn will persist for some periods. Without further restrictions on the parameter values, the economic growth is hardly determinate. Matsuyama (2008) shows that the model has a rich variety of growth patterns. We will see this in the next section.

The financial accelerator is a powerful modeling strategy for introducing the financial friction in the standard macroeconomic model in a tractable way. The idea is heavily explored to uncover the impact of credit constraints on macro economy. A very recent example is Korinek (2011), in which endogenous systemic risk arises from the feedback between incomplete financial markets and the real economy. Adverse shocks tighten individuals' credit constraints, triggering the contraction of economic activities. This depresses the prices of productive assets, hence the net worth of their owners, and worsens their credit constraints. The financial accelerator amplifies negative shocks to the economy, giving rise to externalities: atomistic agents take the level of asset prices in the economy as given. In their demand for productive assets, they do not internalize the externalities that arise when aggregate shocks lead to aggregate fluctuations. So decentralized agents undervalue social benefits of having stronger buffers when financial constraints are binding, taking on too much systemic risk in their investment strategies.

6.2 Financial friction and credit cycle

In the standard financial accelerator model, the borrowers are rather "passive" in the sense that they have to stick to their predetermined productivity. Matsuyama (2008) relaxes this restriction by having the borrowers free to choose among different investment opportunities. In the following, we will see how this small change generates very rich patterns for the impacts of financial friction on the macro economy.

6.2.1 Model setup

Consider a similar Samuelson–Diamond type economy in discrete time $t=0$, $1,\ldots$, as in Section 6.1.1, populated by overlapping generations with no population growth. Each agent is endowed with a unit of labor when she is born. Assume that each agent works *only* when she is young and consumes *only* when she is old. The timing of events for a representative agent in generation t is shown as Figure 6.3.

1   After she is born at t, she first works to earn wage w_t, which comes from the
     output of consumption good production Y_t, then she chooses to be

   a   an entrepreneur, who builds up a project producing both capital and
        consumption goods (to be explained later); or
   b   an investor, who lends her wage income to an entrepreneur as her invest-
        ment on the project, and will get repaid at $t+1$ with gross interest rate r_{t+1}.

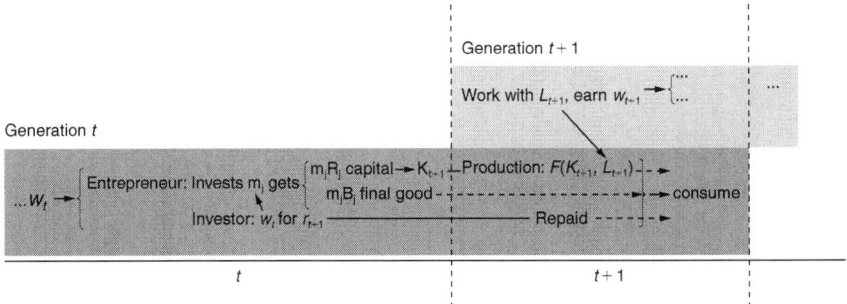

Figure 6.3 Timing of the model.

2   Then at $t+1$ the entrepreneur employs the labor force from generation $t+1$, plus the capital good as another input, for producing consumption good Y_{t+1}. The labor is paid by the competitive wage w_{t+1}, the generation t investors get paid, and all the agents of generation t consume. Then everyone in the young generation chooses her role, and the entire procedure repeats.

The entrepreneurs have expertise on two technologies:

1   The project technology, which transfers m_j units of input at t into $m_j R_j$ units of capital and $m_j B_j$ units of consumption good at $t+1$. There are J indivisible projects which are heterogeneous in the fixed cost m_j and productivities R_j and B_j, $j \in \{1, \ldots, J\}$. Each entrepreneur is only able to choose one project.
2   The neoclassical production technology, which transfers capital and labor inputs into consumption good, $Y_t = F(K_t, L_t)$, or $y_t = f(k_t)$ as per capita form. With competitive factor market, the rental rate of capital ρ_t and the wage w_t are defined by the marginal product of capital and labor respectively, i.e., $\rho_t = f'(k_t)$ and $w_t = f(k_t) - k_t f'(k_t)$.

The agency problem is introduced in a slightly different way. Assume that the entrepreneur can only commit to forward a share λ_j of project j's capital return and a share μ_j of project j's consumption good return to the investor. This assumption can be motivated by many reasons, for example, the hold-up problem we discussed in Section 3.1 such that the investor can only recover a share λ_j of the project j's value of capital and a share μ_j of the project j's value of consumption good if she takes over the project from the entrepreneur. Therefore, the investor can only pledge a fraction λ_j of the project j's return of capital as well as a fraction μ_j of the project j's return of consumption good.

6.2.2 Market equilibrium: the general conditions

The payoff of a generation t entrepreneur with project j who needs to borrow $m_j - w_t$ is

$$c_t^j = m_j R_j \rho_{t+1} + m_j B_j - r_{t+1}(m_j - w_t).$$ (6.16)

The payoff of a generation t investor is

$$c_t^o = r_{t+1} w_t.$$ (6.17)

One is willing to become an entrepreneur running project j only the profitability constraint $(PC-j)$ holds, $c_t^j \geq c_t^o$. Combine (6.16) and (6.17), and notice that in market equilibrium $\rho_t = f'(k_t)$, this constraint is equivalent to

$$R_j f'(k_{t+1}) + B_j \geq r_{t+1}. \; (PC-j).$$ (6.18)

Because of the agency problem, the entrepreneur can only borrow up to the pledgeable value of her project, implying the borrowing constraint $(BC-j)$

$$\lambda_j m_j R_j f'(k_{t+1}) + \mu_j m_j B_j \geq r_{t+1}(m_j - w_t). \ (BC-j) \tag{6.19}$$

Therefore, the market interest rate r_{t+1} is restricted by both constraints

$$\frac{1}{r_{t+1}} \leq \max \left\{ \frac{1 - \dfrac{w_t}{m_j}}{\lambda_j R_j f'(k_{t+1}) + \mu_j B_j}, \frac{1}{R_j f'(k_{t+1}) + B_j} \right\}.$$

Its upper bound is depicted as the solid line in Figure 6.4.

Suppose that the measure of type j projects is n_j, then the market equilibrium is featured by

1   resource constraint in investment: the aggregate investment on the projects cannot exceed the total wage income of generation t,

$$w_t \geq \sum_{j=1}^{N} m_j n_j;$$

2   resource constraint in capital input:

$$k_{t+1} \leq \sum_{j=1}^{N} m_j R_j n_j;$$

3   $(PC-j)$ and $(BC-j)$,

$$\frac{1}{r_{t+1}} \leq \max \left\{ \frac{1 - \dfrac{w_t}{m_j}}{\lambda_j R_j f'(k_{t+1}) + \mu_j B_j}, \frac{1}{R_j f'(k_{t+1}) + B_j} \right\}.$$

And all the constraints are binding in the equilibrium.

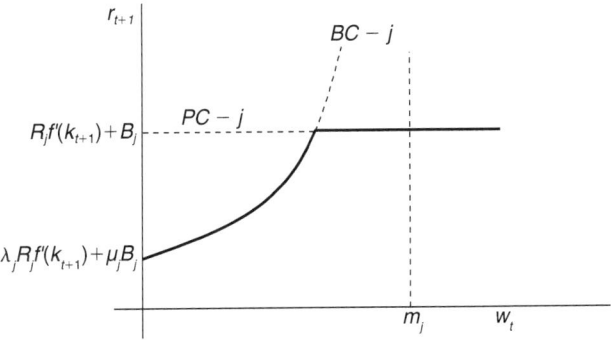

Figure 6.4 The determination of market interest rate r_{t+1}.

6.2.3 *Market equilibrium with homogeneous projects*

When the projects are homogeneous, i.e., $j=1$, the market equilibrium degenerates to

1   resource constraint in investment: $w_t = mn$;
2   resource constraint in capital input: $k_{t+1} = mRn = Rw_t$;
3   $(PC-j)$ and $(BC-j)$:

$$\frac{1}{r_{t+1}} = \max\left\{ \frac{1-\dfrac{w_t}{m_j}}{\lambda Rf'(k_{t+1}) + \mu B}, \frac{1}{Rf'(k_{t+1}) + B} \right\}.$$

In addition, like standard overlapping generation models, some regularity conditions are necessary for steady state equilibrium:

1   decreasing marginal return:

$$\frac{\partial\left(\dfrac{w_t}{k_t}\right)}{k_t} < 0;$$

2   Inada conditions:

$$\lim_{k_t \to 0} \frac{w_t}{k_t} = +\infty, \text{ and } \lim_{k_t \to +\infty} \frac{w_t}{k_t} = 0.$$

Since there is only one technology devoted to capital production, the equilibrium growth path for the baseline case is no different from the standard overlapping generation model. As Figure 6.5 shows, starting from an arbitrary initial capital intensity k_0, the economy converges to the equilibrium capital stock k^*.

6.2.4 *Market equilibrium with endogenous investment decisions*

Now we take into account the heterogeneity in the productivity of capital generation, but temporarily neglect the difference in the output of consumption good, i.e., assume that there are J types of projects while $B_j = 0$, $\forall j \in \{1,\ldots, J\}$. The market equilibrium is therefore featured by

1   resource constraint in investment:

$$w_t = \sum_{j=1}^{N} m_j n_j;$$

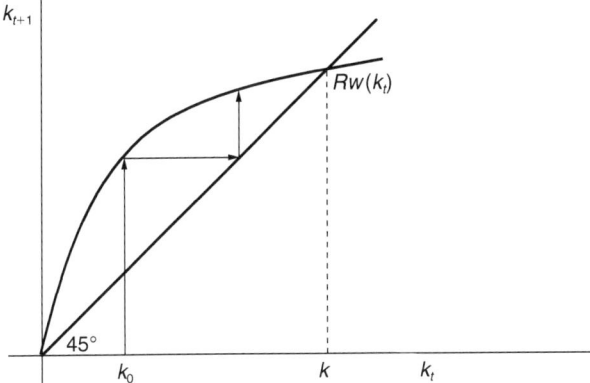

Figure 6.5 The converging path with homogeneous projects.

2   resource constraint in capital input:

$$k_{t+1} = \sum_{j=1}^{N} m_j R_j n_j;$$

3    $(PC-j)$ and $(BC-j)$,

$$\frac{f'(k_{t+1})}{r_{t+1}} = \frac{1}{R_j} \max\left\{ \frac{1-\dfrac{w_t}{m_j}}{\lambda_j}, 1 \right\}.$$

The solid black line in Figure 6.6 shows the equilibrium

$$\frac{r_{t+1}}{f'(k_{t+1})}$$

as a function of w_t, which is the upper bound of $(PC-j)$ and $(BC-j)$ constraints.

To see clearly the dynamic in the investment decision, let us focus on a simple case with only two types of projects, $J=2$. Type 1 is the "riskless" type, with lower productivity but less severe agency problem; type 2 is the "high-tech" type, with higher productivity but more severe agency problem as well. This corresponds to $R_2 > R_1 > \lambda_1 R_1 > \lambda_2 R_2$.

Figure 6.7 presents the $(PC-j)$ and $(BC-j)$ constraints for both types of projects. In equilibrium, since investors of generation t are maximizing their utility by choosing the entrepreneurs with higher r_{t+1}, the entrepreneurs will always pick up the projects offering higher profit. Therefore, the equilibrium

$$\frac{r_{t+1}}{f'(k_{t+1})}$$

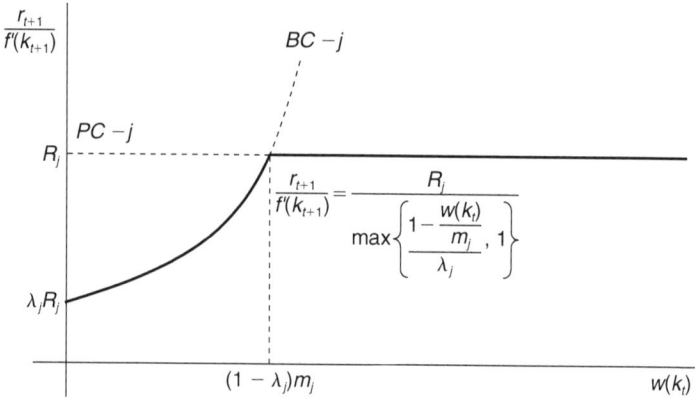

Figure 6.6 The equilibrium market interest rate.

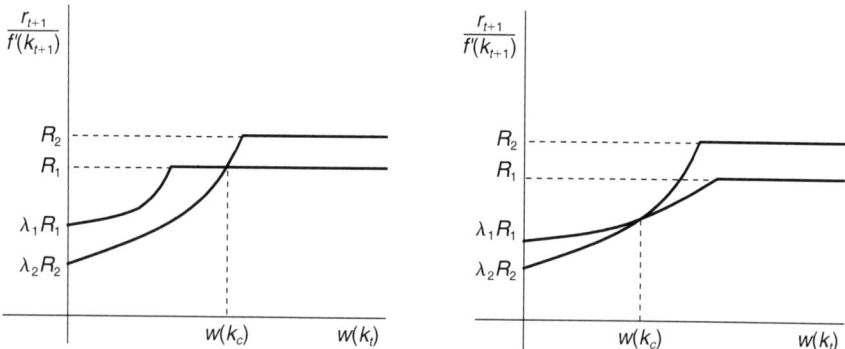

Figure 6.7 The market interest rate under heterogeneous capital productivity I.

is featured by the higher of the two constraints for every w_t. There are two generic cases regarding the intersection $w(k_c)$, in each case, all the entrepreneurs choose type 1 projects when $k < w^{-1}(k_c)$, and type 2 projects when $k_t > w^{-1}(k_c)$.

Such endogenous investment choice generates very rich patterns of growth path. The generic patterns are presented in Figure 6.8. In each graph, the higher $k_{t+1}(k_t)$ corresponds to the growth path with type 2 projects, and the lower one with type 1 projects. The dynamic of the system therefore depends on the intersection k_c and the initial value of k_t. In case (a), the economy follows a lower growth path initially. But when the capital intensity reaches k_t, the entrepreneurs switch to the high-tech projects, leading the economy to a higher growth path. In case (b), the economy is featured by multiple equilibria, two stable and one unstable. Therefore, if the economy starts with a capital intensity lower than k_c, it will end up with a low stable equilibrium k^*. In case (c), the economy starts with a high growth path initially, with $k_t > k_c$. However, the high path is not sus-

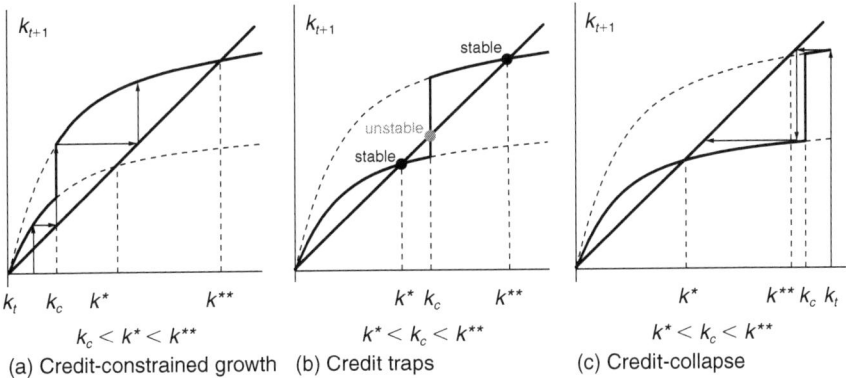

Figure 6.8 The growth path under heterogeneous capital productivity I.

tainable and will collapse over time, marching toward a low growth path with the low stable equilibrium k^*.

Note that the intersection k_c comes from the entrepreneurs' decision on the investment, which hinges on the rate of return of projects. The feedback between the projects' rate of return and the resource-credit constraints drives the dynamic of the economy.

Now let's come to another case with different setup for the agency problem. Suppose that type 1 project is the "agricultural" type, with lower productivity and more severe agency problem; type 2 is the "industrial" type, with higher productivity and less severe agency problem. This corresponds to $R_2 > R_1 > \lambda_2 R_2 > \lambda_1 R_1$.

Figure 6.9 presents the $(PC–j)$ and $(BC–j)$ constraints for both types of projects. Similar as before, all the entrepreneurs choose type 2 projects when

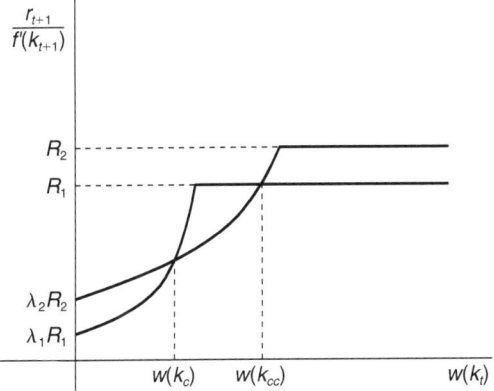

Figure 6.9 The market interest rate under heterogeneous capital productivity II.

$k_t < w^{-1}(k_c)$, but switch to type 1 projects when $w^{-1}(k_c) < k_t < w^{-1}(k_{cc})$, and come back to type 2 projects when $k_t > w^{-1}(k_{cc})$.

Since the entrepreneur can go back and forth between two types of projects, the growth path is likely to be more volatile. As in Figure 6.10, case (a) shows that the entire growth path can get around the low productivity type 1 projects and stay with the fast lane; however, case (b) means that the only steady state is the one with low capital intensity k_c, and the economy fluctuates between two types of projects. In case (c), there are two stable steady states, one with low capital intensity k_c and the other with high capital intensity k^{**}, as well as an unstable steady state k_{cc}. However, if the economy starts with a low capital intensity, it is trapped by the low steady state.

Now we take one step further, adding the heterogeneity in the output of consumption good, i.e., assume that there are two types of projects with $R_1 = R$, $R_2 = 0$, $B_1 = 0$, $B_2 = B > 0$. Obviously these two projects have different effects on growth: type 1 projects generate positive output of capital and raise the capital stock for the future, while type 2 ones have no impact for the future but only contribute to consumption of current generation. The market equilibrium is therefore featured by

1   resource constraint in investment:

$$w_t = m_1 n_1 + m_2 n_2;$$

2   resource constraint in capital input:

$$k_{t+1} = m_1 R n_1;$$

3    $(PC-j)$ and $(BC-j)$,

$$f'(k_{t+1}) = \frac{B \max \left\{ \dfrac{1 - \dfrac{w_t}{m_1}}{\lambda_1}, 1 \right\}}{R \max \left\{ \dfrac{1 - \dfrac{w_t}{m_2}}{\mu_2}, 1 \right\}}$$

when $n_2 > 0$; $k_{t+1} = R w_t$ when $n_2 = 0$.

To understand the impact of financial friction, let's start with the simplest case and relax the assumptions step by step. First, assume that there is no financial friction such that $\lambda_1 = \mu_2 = 1$. There is no more borrowing constraint and the model degenerates to Figure 6.11. The growth in capital stock is only upper-bounded by the opportunity cost of investing on capital production. The entrepreneurs cease to invest on more type 1 projects when the marginal return from capital production is equal the productivity of type 2 projects.

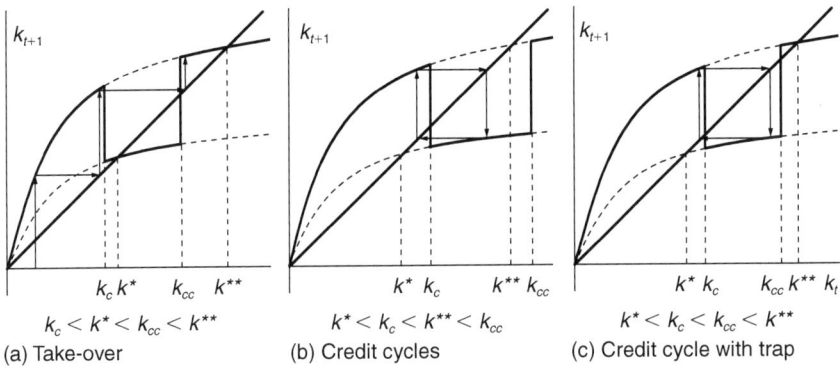

Figure 6.10 The growth path under heterogeneous capital productivity II.

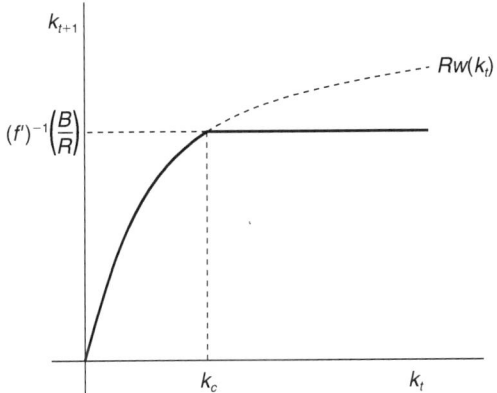

Figure 6.11 Capital accumulation under heterogeneous good productivity.

The growth path, as Figure 6.12 shows, depends on the productivity of type 2 projects, or, B. When B is large, the entrepreneurs will start investing on type 2 projects when k exceeds k_c; while when B is small, the entrepreneurs will never invest on type 2 projects in the steady state.

Now we introduce the friction in type 1 projects, i.e., $\lambda_1 < 1$ while $\mu_2 = 1$. As Figure 6.13 shows, the relevant constraints are $k_{t+1} = Rw_t$ with $(PC-1)$ and $(BC-1)$, or

$$Rf'(k_{t+1}) = B \max \left\{ \frac{1 - \dfrac{w_t}{m_1}}{\lambda_1}, \ 1 \right\} \geq B.$$

The friction in capital production projects adds much hysteresis in macro economy, as the generic cases in Figure 6.14 shows. Because of the agency

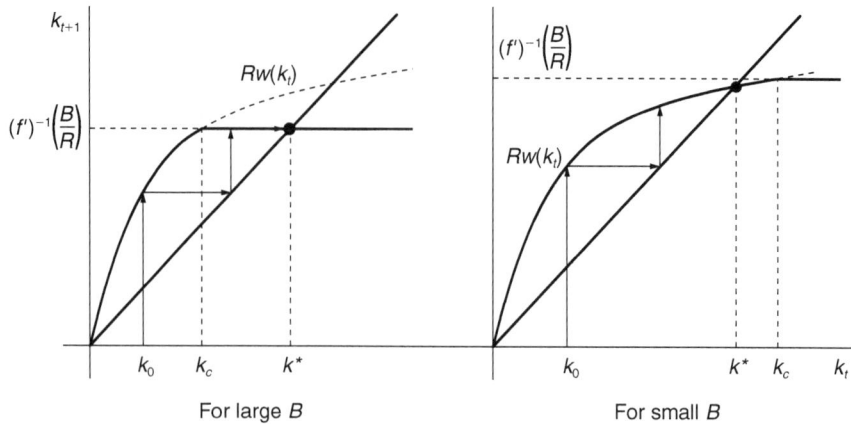

For large B For small B

Figure 6.12 The growth path under heterogeneous good productivity.

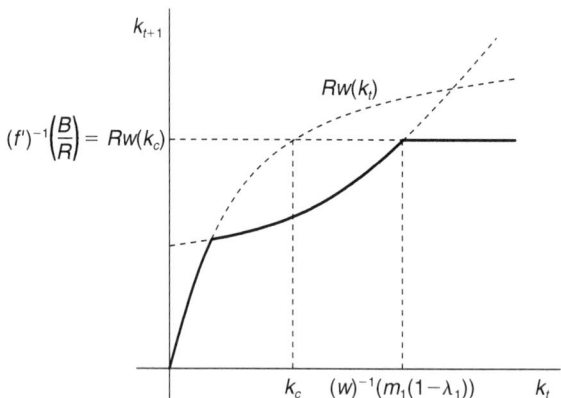

Figure 6.13 Capital accumulation under heterogeneous good productivity and agency problem I.

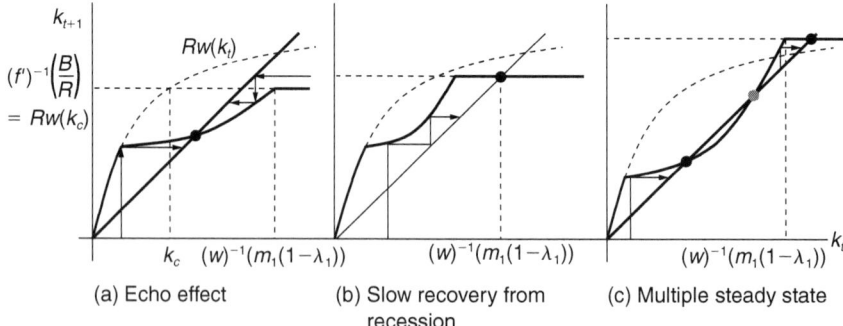

(a) Echo effect   (b) Slow recovery from recession   (c) Multiple steady state

Figure 6.14 The growth path under heterogeneous good productivity and agency problem I.

problem in generating new capital, if the economy starts from a low level of capital stock, the financial friction restricts the borrower's capacity of increasing investments on capital production, leading to a much staggering growth path.

Finally, if there is friction in type 2 projects, i.e., $\lambda_1 = 1$ while $\mu_2 < 1$, as Figure 6.15 shows, the relevant constraints are $k_{t+1} = Rw_t$ with $(PC-2)$ and $(BC-2)$, or

$$
B = Rf'(k_{t+1}) \max \left\{ \frac{1 - \dfrac{w_t}{m_2}}{\mu_2}, \ 1 \right\} \geq Rf'(k_{t+1}).
$$

The friction in type 2 projects leads to the over-investments on type 1 projects. However, such over-investment changes the capital stock in the economy, generating a long-run impact. Indeed, the result in macro dynamics exhibits higher volatility as the generic cases in Figure 6.16 shows. The system may end up in oscillation, or even chaos.

6.3 Financial intermediaries in the macro framework

Financial accelerator modeling is a very concise, technically tractable way to capture some of the financial imperfections in the dynamic macroeconomics framework. Its implications have been widely studied, and the concept has been extended in many DSGE models for policy analysis, such as Bernanke *et al.* (1999). However, in most of the DSGE models with financial accelerator, the role of financial friction rarely goes beyond enhancing the persistence of technological or monetary shocks. The highly non-linear part of the business cycle fueled by the bubbles and crashes from the financial market is by far almost absent.

Besides the borrowing constraints motivated by the agency problem, in financial market there are still many important features which have strong impact on

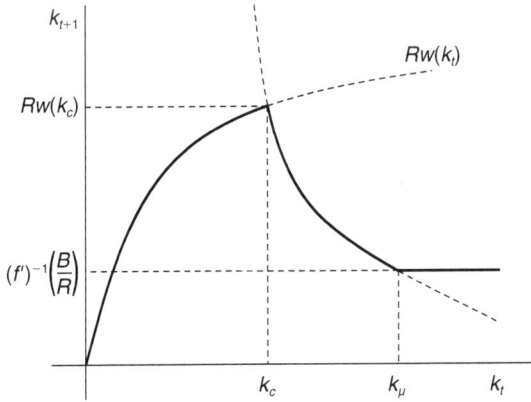

Figure 6.15 Capital accumulation under heterogeneous good productivity and agency problem II.

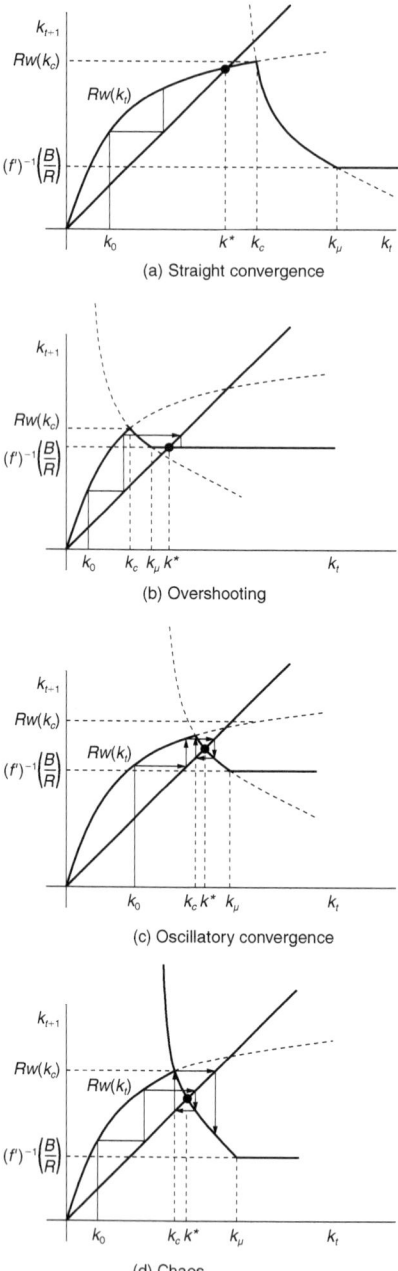

(a) Straight convergence

(b) Overshooting

(c) Oscillatory convergence

(d) Chaos

Figure 6.16 The growth path under heterogeneous good productivity and agency problem II.

macro economy but have not yet shown up in most of existing macroeconomics analysis. One of the key lessons we learned from the financial crisis is that macroeconomists can no longer neglect the role of financial intermediaries. It was the financial intermediaries who fabricated the structured financial products, which later turned to be the weapons of mass destruction on the macro economy.

Unfortunately it is not easy to explicitly have financial intermediaries in the dynamic macroeconomics models, which are already complicated. There is some early success in such practice, but most of the research projects are still in their infant stages. One of the approaches is to create internal heterogeneity in a representative agent framework, as adopted by Gertler *et al.* (2011) and Gertler and Kiyotaki (2010), and financial intermediaries finance their activities via leverage. In the rest of this section, we present their modeling strategy, with focus on the mechanism at work.

In general, the infinitely lived economy with discrete time, $t=0, 1, \ldots$, consists of two sectors, the production sector with firms and the households. To focus on the role of financial intermediaries, the model here abstracts from the standard DSGE framework with sticky prices arising from monopolistic competition and rigidities in price adjustments. There are two types of firms:

1   The goods producers, using Cobb-Douglas technology transforming capital and labor inputs into consumption goods. The capital is financed by the loans from the banks, and the producers commit to pay all their future profits to the banks.
2   The capital producers, using a linear technology transforming capital stock of period t into capital input of period $t+1$. When the capital producers integrate the new investment into the capital stock, they have to incur the adjustment cost. The capital production is subject to an exogenous technological shock, which triggers the fluctuation in asset prices and generates the source of financial crisis.

On the household side, the individual household is modeled as the utility maximizer. This preserves the representative agent approach in dynamic macroeconomic models. However, there is heterogeneity inside the household, some of the household members are workers earning their wages from their labor supply, and the rest are bankers intermediating the households' investments with the goods producers. In each period a household member of one type can become another type with a positive probability. To generate some persistence, the household has some habit or inertia in consumption so that its utility of each period t is a function of both consumption level of t and $t-1$.

In each period, the representative household has several options for making investments. It can invest on government bonds or short-term non-contingent demand deposit in the bank, both being regarded as riskless. It can also invest on the banks' equity and receive the dividend. One bank's equity can come from the households' investments, the "outside" equity, or from the retained profit of the bank, the "inside" equity.

The financial friction is introduced via the agency problem. Since the dividend payment on the equity depends on the bank's performance which is not verifiable, a banker has an incentive to steal some of the yields of the assets. The agency problem gets worse when the share of outside equity in the bank's capital is higher. Knowing this, the households are only willing to invest on the bank's equity up to some level. This gives the funding constraint of the bank.

However, the households' willingness to invest on the outside equity also depends on the dividend they can get. When the bank gets higher profit from its loans to the firms, the households can achieve higher dividend and are therefore more willing to invest on the bank's equity, and vice versa. The value of the bank's inside equity is the bank's net worth; therefore, the ratio of the bank's total loan value to its net worth defines the bank's leverage ratio.

The feedback between the financial sector and macro economy works through the interaction between the bank's inside and outside equity. When there is an economic downturn, i.e., an unexpected negative shock on the capital productivity in this model, the next period aggregate capital input for the goods producers declines, hence the output of consumption goods as well as the profit for the bank. This reduces the bank's net worth and makes the bank's funding constraint tighter. The bank's outside equity therefore has to decrease, or, the bank has to deleverage. As a result, the bank has to cut back its new loans to the firms, and the firms have to downsize its investments. This makes the goods production contract even more, and further deteriorating the bank's net worth. The initial technological shock thus propagates into a vicious cycle. The bank's leverage exhibits strong procyclicality.

The model clearly shows how moral hazard brings funding constraints to the banks, leading to the banks' expanding balance sheets in the boom while a credit crunch in the bust. Therefore, the central bank can play its role as the lender of last resort to ease the banks' credit constraint during the crisis, although there is a time inconsistency problem which aggravates the banks' moral hazard. In an extended version, Gertler and Karadi (2011), the feedback between the financial sector, monetary policy, and macro economy is captured by a cashless economy, in which nominal rigidity is introduced by having additional monopolistically competitive retail firms whose price adjustment process is sticky.

The key driving force in this strand of research is the interaction between the bank's inside and outside equity, and the impact on real economy through the bank lending channel. The similar mechanism is also explored in Brunnermeier and Sannikov (2011), while in a completely different framework. Instead of staying with the standard DSGE paradigm, Brunnermeier and Sannikov (2011) focus on the moral hazard problem in a dynamic contracting framework. In the boom, the banks get leveraged up, ignoring the fact that their fire sales in the downturn depress asset prices and hence impose a negative externality on the other banks. In the crisis, the plummeting asset prices in the fire sales deteriorate a bank's net worth. With the bank's funding constraint being binding, the similar vicious cycle emerges.

Part II
Topics in macroprudential regulation

7 From microprudential to macroprudential regulation

Now it is much clear that one of the biggest challenges to contemporary financial regulation is to accommodate the systemic risks. As is studied in the first part of this book, systemic risk arises from various channels, such as the coordinative failure of creditors, the banks' collective engagement in excess risk taking, and the bank failure spilled over across the web of claims. They are originated from the externalities one bank's behavior imposed on the others, or the network effect which makes one bank's trouble contagious. The systemic risk is hardly fixed by the pure market mechanism, since the atomistic financial institutions do not take such externalities and network effect into account when they make their investment decisions.

The framework for banking regulation before the crisis is now heavily criticized for failing to address the systemic risks, since the framework was largely based on the microprudential philosophy that treats the financial stability as a natural outcome of maintaining the stability of each individual bank. However, the increasingly threatening systemic risk in the financial market calls for a more macroprudential approach in banking regulation. In contrast to the microprudential structure, the macroprudential framework refers to, as defined by the Bank of International Settlements (Clement, 2010), "the use of prudential tools with the explicit objective of promoting the stability of the financial system as a whole, not necessarily of the individual institutions within it." Especially,

> the distinction between the micro- and macro-prudential dimensions of financial stability is best drawn in terms of the objective of the tasks and the conception of the mechanisms influencing economic outcomes. It has less to do with the instruments used in the pursuit of those objectives.

Microprudential policies focus on the stability of institutions in isolation; therefore, the risks that one financial firm is likely to face are mostly taken as exogenously given. One example is the widely used Value-at-Risk (*VaR*) approach in risk management as discussed in Section 5.1. There the banks' adjustment to their balance sheets is rather a mechanical response to the changing exogenous market environment, rarely taking into account the impact they make on the rest of the system. However, the stability of financial system is not automatically guaranteed by stabilizing each individual bank. The factors that put the entire market under threat are those beyond the reach of one single bank's risk management, as we emphasized in the first part of the book, these are rather the risks endogenized from the banks' interactions within the system. Further, another lesson we have learned from the past regulatory practice is that the banks make strategic response to the rules, known as regulatory arbitrage, to get rid of the regulation. Therefore, regulators have to go beyond the traditional atomistic, static view on financial regulation and establish a systemic, dynamic, and macroprudential framework.

There is no doubt that macroprudential framework will become the basis of the future banking regulation, and its global standard Basel III is in development. This chapter is not designed as a full coverage of the framework in progress, but rather a review of some of the indicators and instruments specialized for managing the systemic risks.

The macroprudential policy is based on the credible measures of systemic risks. In practice, systemic risks can hardly be directly measured because the risks are endogenous from the financial institutions' collective behavior. Therefore, indirect indicators or proxies are necessary for estimating the systemic risks. Section 7.1 presents some of these indicators and proxies.

Although the distinction between micro- and macroprudential policies is on the objective rather than the instruments, there are several instruments that have been proposed to empower the macroprudential regulators' toolbox. Section 7.2 provides a review on several macroprudential tools.

7.1 Indicators of systemic risk

7.1.1 Systemic importance

The systemic importance of one financial institution contains twofold meanings. The first is related to its role during a financial crisis, for example, during the crisis the collapse of a systemically important dealer bank, such as Lehman Brothers, may bring a meltdown to the entire financial system; the second is related to its role in triggering the financial crisis – sometimes ripples from a less well known bank ends up with a financial tsunami. For one specific bank these two meanings may overlap, but are not equivalent. The first one is more determined by the bank's intrinsic role in the system – e.g., "the bank is systemically important because it is the clearing bank of the economy" – while the second one is more determined by the characteristics of the financial system, – e.g., "the bank's failure triggers a systemic collapse because the banks are too heavily exposed to each other." Most of the indicators proposed by the recent literature measure one of these two features. Using the terms coined by Drehmann and Tarashev (2011), there are "top-down" measures which "first derive systemic (i.e., system-wide) risk and then allocate it to individual institutions," and "bottom-up" measures which first assume "distress in a particular institution" and then evaluate "the level of system-wide risk associated with that event." In the following we discuss several measures of systemic importance that have been recently proposed.

CoVaR

Adrian and Brunnermeier (2010) proposed a *VaR* based indicator of one bank's systemic importance, conditional on the events from the bank. The Conditional, or Contributing Value-at-Risk, $CoVaR_{\alpha}^{j|i}$, defines the value-at-risk, or *VaR* of financial institution j conditional on some event $C(X^i)$ of institution i, i.e.,

$$Prob\ (X^j \leq CoVaR_{\alpha}^{j|C(X^i)}\ |\ C(X^i)) \geq \alpha.$$

Suppose the event $C(X^i)$ is the failure of bank i, then $CoVaR_{\alpha}^{j|C(X_i)}$ measures the bank j's Value-at-Risk coming from this event with confidence level α. If we define j as the rest of the financial system, $CoVaR_{\alpha}^{j|C(X_i)}$ gives the measure on the stress of the financial market coming from bank i's failure.

A more practical measure is the difference between $CoVaR_{\alpha}^{j|i}$ under some extreme event – for example, bankruptcy – and $CoVaR_{\alpha}^{j|i}$ in the orderly time. This gives the additional pressure the event brings, or the bank i's contribution to j:

$$\Delta CoVaR_{\alpha}^{j|i} = CoVaR_{\alpha}^{j|X^i=VaR_{\alpha}^i} - CoVaR_{\alpha}^{j|X^i=median^i}$$

Again, if we define j as the rest of the financial system, $\Delta CoVaR_{\alpha}^{j|i}$ gives the additional stress of the financial system in terms of *VaR* when bank i incurs a predefined loss, comparing the *VaR* of the system under the "median" state of bank i or bank i's orderly time. Obviously, in this case $\Delta CoVaR_{\alpha}^{j|i}$ captures the systemic risk bank i contributes to the rest of the market.

Systemic expected shortfall (SES)

Acharya *et al.* (2010b) proposes that a financial institution's contribution to the systemic risk can be measured by its systemic expected shortfall (*SES*).

Note that the *VaR* of a financial institution at confidence level α, denoted by VaR_{α}, means that the event that the realized loss L exceeds VaR_{α} happens at a probability no higher than $1 - \alpha$, i.e.,

$$Prob\ (L > VaR_{\alpha}) \leq 1 - \alpha.$$

The expected shortfall of a financial institution at confidence level α, denoted by ES_{α}, is thus the conditional expected loss when the loss L exceeds VaR_{α}, i.e.,

$$ES_{\alpha} = E[L\ |\ L > VaR_{\alpha}].$$

Further, one can examine the components of as well as their contributions to ES_{α}. Suppose that there are I sources for the bank's loss, the loss from each source $i \in \{1,\ldots, I\}$, whose weight in the bank's entire portfolio is y_i, is denoted by l_i. Then ES_α can be rewritten as

$$ES_\alpha = \sum_{i=1}^{I} y_i E[l_i \mid L > VaR_\alpha].$$

The contribution of source i to the bank's overall loss, or the marginal expected shortfall of source i at confidence level α denoted by MES_α^i, is

$$MES_\alpha^i = \frac{\partial ES_\alpha}{\partial y_i} = E[l_i \mid L > VaR_\alpha].$$

One can extend such idea and use the similar notion to analyze one financial institution's contribution to the aggregate risk in the financial system, or the systemic risk. As an analogy, the entire financial system can be viewed as one single bank, and when the financial system is in distress, the "marginal expected shortfall" of the system with respect to any individual bank i exactly captures the impact of the bank's failure on the systemic stability.

However, there are several concerns about generalizing the idea of *MES* for the financial system. First, a measure of one financial institution's contribution to the systemic risk should not only focus on the absolute value of loss, but, rather, on its systemic impact, i.e., to what extent this bank's failure puts the other banks in trouble. Therefore, a proper measure is more likely an indicator of the externality of a bank's failure. Second, in practice *MES* for a bank is usually estimated from the historical data, which is sufficiently informative for an institution's performance. But as people learned from the financial crisis, historical data is hardly able to exhaust all the tail events, leaving the estimation inevitably biased. Third, as a practical issue, the indicator should be easy to compute and informative for both regulators and banking practitioners.

The systemic expected shortfall (*SES*) is defined as the bank i's shortage in capital when the entire financial system is in distress and undercapitalized, i.e.,

$$SES^i = E[w^* - w^i \mid W < W^*],$$

where $w^* - w^i$ is the difference between the bank's equity w^i and the required level w^*, conditional on the systemic undercapitalization such that the aggregate capital in the banks, W, is below the target W^*.

As is discussed in Section 5.1, the notion of *VaR* provides an anchor for the banks to actively adjust their balance sheets, via managing equity and/or assets holding, and ES_α presents the expected loss when such threshold is reached. *SES* captures the similar idea in another way. Here the threshold of the systemic event is defined by the adequate level of capitalization. During the financial crisis, an individual bank's capital ratio falls below the adequate level, along with the other banks in the financial system. The higher *SES^i* corresponds to the higher loss in the bank's asset holding, and the higher *SES^i* is, the more likely that the bank downsizes its balance sheet through entering fire sales, imposing a downward pressure on the asset price, creating an externality on the other banks. Therefore, SES^i serves both as an indicator of the individual bank's loss and as a proxy of the externality the bank imposes on the financial system.

Other measures

Segoviano and Goodhart (2009) takes a similar notion by viewing the financial system as a portfolio of banks. There they focus on the interdependent feature of banks in distress, especially on the fact that such interdependence changes along with the banks' probabilities of distress. By examining the banking system's multivariate density that characterizes both the individual and joint asset value movement of the banks in the portfolio, the authors establish the banking stability measures which quantify the distress dependence among the banks.

Alessandri *et al.* (2009) interpret the systemic risk as the echo between macroeconomic shock and banking network. They explicitly take the banks' balance sheets into account, in order to identify each bank's exposure to the rest of the banking network and estimate how bank failure propagates via contagion across the web of the claims. The macroeconomic shock first leads to losses in the banks' investment, bringing both market and funding liquidity shortages, and then bank failure emerges. Via mutual exposure in the banking network, the bank failure spreads and drags the overall banking system into distress. The bank lending contraction as a result further aggravates the economic downturn, widens the banks' losses, and fuels more negative feedback into the network. Based on the banks' balance sheets data and the network structure, after feeding an exogenous shock into the system, the equilibrium outcome can be easily illustrated and simulated.

Instead of looking into the banks' balance sheet information, Huang *et al.* (2009) proposes a "market" measure of systemic risk, which is interpreted as a series of simultaneous defaults of systemically important financial institutions. They take credit default swaps (CDS) spreads of the banks, as a proxy of the banks' default probabilities from the market's view, and get the asset return correlations from the co-movements of the banks' equity returns. The former predicts the likelihood of a systemic distress, and the latter estimates how vulnerable a bank is during a systemic event. The high frequency data from the market makes it possible for real-time analysis on financial stability.

Drehmann and Tarashev (2011) compare the measures from both "top-down" and "bottom-up" approaches. The measures in the former category are different versions of expected shortfall (*ES*) measures, while those in the latter are based on a reversed $ES - \tilde{ES}_\alpha = E[L|l_i > VaR^i_\alpha]$ – the conditional expected shortfall of the financial system when bank *i* is in distress. The authors also take simple indicators, such as the bank size, interbank lending, and interbank borrowing, as references to the bank's systemic importance. Regarding the banks in the sample, they find that the rankings of the banks' systemic importance do not coincide under the measures from different approaches, implying that regulators do need to take both views of systemic importance into account. Further, the authors find that the simple indicators in the reference, especially bank size, are good proxies of a bank's systemic importance, no matter which view is taken. However, those sophisticated model based measures such as *SES* contain more systemic level information, which is useful for the regulators to get a complete picture about the financial stability.

7.1.2 Real estate price and asset bubbles

As has been for long observed, financial crises are often heralded by real estate booms, and followed by collapses in the housing market. The housing price in the US skyrocketed in one decade before the current crisis by any standard (normalized by year 1980 price index), as Figure 7.1 shows. Figure 7.2 compares the trends of housing prices in three of the hardest hit countries. The patterns are quite similar: they all experienced strong housing market prosperity before the crisis and free falls in real estate prices since the advent of the crisis.

The real estate market played a key role in the current crisis. In the decade before the crisis, the "saving glut" and global imbalance provided huge amount of cheap credit for the financial institutions in the developed economies, encouraging the banks to chase for yield. At the same time, the banks chose to rely more on the short-term repo funding, which created a huge demand for collaterals. This stimulated the rapid growth in securitization, producing highly rated securities for collateral purpose out of the mortgage pools. The lending standard had been thus continuously lowered to contain more mortgage loans for the alchemy of securitization. This reversely increases the demand for real estate and the housing price, which further fuels the credit boom. Once the subprime bor-

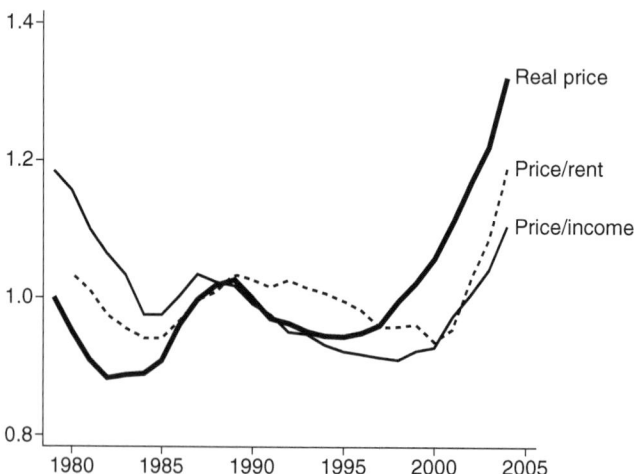

Figure 7.1 Real US house price index, price-to-rent, and price-to-income ratios (source: Himmelberg *et al.*, 2005).

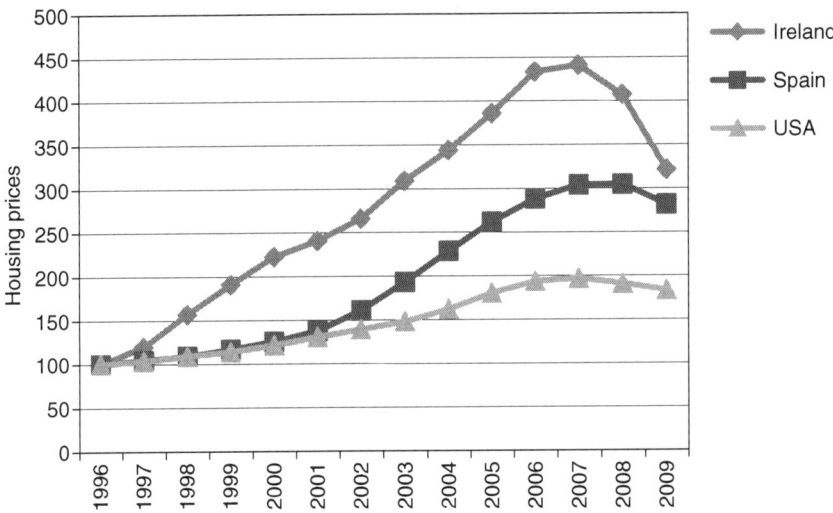

Figure 7.2 Housing prices in Ireland, Spain, and the US (source: Allen and Carletti, 2011).

rowers were no longer able to repay their loans and the housing price staggered, the financial market came into trouble. Therefore, the housing price may be a good indicator predicting bubbles and crashes.

The dramatic increase in housing price is likely to be a sign of bubble, and the bubble collapses when it cannot sustain itself. As defined by Brunnermeier (2008), bubbles "refer to asset prices that exceed an asset's fundamental value because current owners believe that they can resell the asset at an even higher price in the future." The reasons why financial bubbles emerge have been intensively studied; one of the excellent surveys on this topic is Brunnermeier (2001). Bubbles are more likely to arise in real estate market since it is subject to severe principle–agent problems: the exact credit worthiness of mortgage borrowers is largely private information; the originate-to-distribute securitization model makes the outsiders less informed of the quality of the loans; the financial institutions lose track of risks along the complex intermediation chain, and so on. As Glaeser *et al.* (2008) indentified, housing price exhibits strong positive serial correlation. This encourages the investors to speculate and ride on the upward trend, leading to a self-fulfilling growth of real estate bubble.

Therefore, the real estate price is an important proxy for systemic risk. However, such proxy is quite imperfect, i.e., the growing housing price per se does not necessarily mean there is a bubble, since rising real estate price can also be driven by fundamental reasons, for example, the strong residential demand, instead of speculations from the investors. Himmelberg *et al.* (2005) is an example of how difficult it is to make a separation between these two forces. Indeed, as shown in Allen and Carletti (2011) these two factors can coexist in the equilibrium and even reinforce each other. This is especially true in the current institutional setup where the banks' losses are covered by deposit insurance. Although whether there was a real estate bubble becomes clearer after a crisis breaks up, it had been always a big question mark when the price was on the rise.

Although it is premature to directly relate rising housing price to financial bubble, it is not impossible to use real estate price as an indicator for systemic risk. The prosperity in housing market is usually accompanied by the fast expansion of credit, rapid growth of households' indebtedness, the "race-to-the-bottom" lending standard in issuing new mortgages, and these side effects are those factors that make the mortgage-related funding unsustainable and the rest of the financial system vulnerable to the volatilities in real estate market. Therefore, the systemic risk associated with a real estate boom is best estimated by the other market indicators together with the housing price.

Since real estate market has been the origin for many financial market turbulences and real estate takes a large share of the households' wealth, it is crucial for the regulators to monitor its stability. Although there is little doubt that housing market needs better regulation, there are still many questions about what the regulators can do, especially at the time when a bubble is emerging and threatening financial stability.

One debate on this question is whether the central bank should respond to real estate bubbles by tightening monetary policy, or whether central bank should use interest rate tool to prick the bubble. The current crisis presented a rather negative answer: the short-term interest rate seems to be better suited for inflation targeting, and it is not obvious that the inflation in asset prices is translated into the inflation in consumer prices. There came the dilemma for the monetary authority: before the crisis the central banks saw no need for a more stringent monetary policy, given the one-handed instrument of short-term interest rate. The low interest rate then fueled the expansion in the credit market, and further created property bubbles in the US and several European countries.

Furthermore, such "one-size-fit-all" tools for taming real estate bubbles, as monetary policy, may be much less effective for a highly heterogeneous housing market such as US or China, where the bubbles mainly conglomerate in certain regions and the fundamental part of property prices is highly diverse across the country. In this case, the more direct and localized policies, such as cap for loan-to-value ratio or tax surcharges, may work better.

7.1.3 Leverage

In the traditional regulatory practice, the leverage ratio of the regulated financial institutions does not seem to be a much informative measure on systemic risk. The banks have to meet a fixed, non-negotiatable ratio for capital holdings; therefore, the leverage ratio is more or less fixed as well.

However, as is demonstrated in the recent crisis, the devastating procyclical leverage–deleverage cycle arises from the shadow banking system, which has been for long outside the regulators' radar. To better understand the systemic risk, a macroprudential regulator has to put a wider range of leverage measures under its scrutiny (although whether the scope of financial regulation should cover the entire shadow banking system is another question).

In contrast to the regulated commercial banks, the leverage ratio in the shadow banking sector is highly procyclical, as documented by Adrian and Shin (2010). As shown in Chapter 5, the rising asset price improves the financial institutions' net worth, and their response is to increase the capacity of debts and expand the balance sheets. As a result, the leverage rises, too. This corresponds to the low haircut – another sign of high leverage – in the repo market, and the market is abundant with liquidity. Although this does not automatically mean that the financial institutions are taking more risks, the rising leverage itself contains systemic risk. The reason is that the excess leverage the banks take does not internalize the negative externalities on asset prices when they deleverage in the downside, and this makes the deleveraging in the crisis even more damaging. Therefore, the leverage ratios for both regulated and non-regulated financial institutions should be taken as crucial systemic risk indicators in the macroprudential regulatory framework.

7.2 Tools for macroprudential regulation

7.2.1 Interest rate

In the past decades maintaining price stability became almost the only mandate for the central banks of the developed economies (although in history central banks were initially created to achieve financial stability). Such stance was repeatedly stressed by several central banks even in the beginning of the current crisis that the central banks should avoid too much intervention of financial market but rather concentrate on battling with inflation. In most of the central banks' workhorse framework for monetary policy, there is not much explicit role for financial sector. The price level is well under control by using interest rate tools, and the financial intermediaries can be almost abstracted away from the policy concerns.

Such view is much challenged after the crisis. Obviously interest rate policy affects the real economy through the lending channel offered by the financial intermediaries, but it has been clearly seen that such channel is not frictionless. The policy rate affects the banks' borrowing cost, which directs them to expand or contract their lending scales. This is amplified through the intermediation chain, increasing the systemic risk. One example is the Fed's interest rate policy before the crisis. It is widely accepted that it was Fed keeping its rate too low for too long time that encouraged the banks' excess risk taking, led to the explosive growth in subprime products, and sowed the seeds for the crisis.

There has been much literature on the transmission mechanism of monetary policy, especially on how interest rate policy affects the banks' lending, but much less work on the impact of monetary policy on financial stability, or the "risk taking channel." The notable recent study among them is Altunbas *et al.* (2010), in which the authors argue that monetary policy, especially short-term interest rate, affects the banks' risk taking in two ways. One is that the borrowing cost varies with interest rate, which changes the banks' own measure of risk; the other one is that low nominal rate pushes down the riskless return, so that the "search for yields" incentive drives the banks toward riskier investments. The empirical evidence much supports these hypotheses, and this suggests a role for interest rate policy in stabilizing the financial system. In a theoretical framework, Stein (2011) demonstrates that financial market is inefficient in creating liquidity so that active monetary policy helps restore the first best allocation.

However, how to implement interest rate policy as a regulatory instrument is still not very clear. One of the policy debates is whether central bank should use interest rate tool to "prick the bubble" when the soaring asset price – especially the real estate price – starts to show the sign of becoming a destabilizing factor (the poetry version of this debate is whether the central bank should "lean against the wind" when the asset price deviates from the fundamentals). So far there are more questions than agreements on this issue. One general argument is that the interest rate response needed to prick the bubble is so big that the cost of such recessionary policy is too high. Bank of England (2009) suggests that the impact of short-term interest rate on asset prices is not yet certain and using interest rate as a financial stabilizing tool detriments the economic agents' inflation expectation, damaging the role of interest rate policy in price and output stabilization. Adrian and Shin (2009) argue that interest rate policy has a stronger influence on market liquidity and financial institution's risk appetite, since the leveraged financial firms are more sensitive to the borrowing cost and the change of just a few basis points may completely reverse a bank's financing decision. Therefore, the interest rate policy response to systemic risk can be far less brutal.

Of course it is hardly possible to achieve two goals – price stability and financial stability – using one single instrument, the interest rate tool, the regulator needs to combine with the other macro- and microprudential policies. Another caveat of taking interest rate instrument in macroprudential regulation is the time inconsistency problem, just as what has been seen before the crisis. During the crisis the central bank needs to lower the interest rate to ease the stress in the market, and has to raise the rate again when the economy starts to recover. However, at the point when recovery starts, it is always *ex post* optimal to postpone lifting the rate since in short run this hurts the banks' profit and temporarily hinders the economic growth – although stepwise raising interest rate is necessary for long run stability. Knowing this, the banks will take excess risk and make the central bank more reluctant to restore the policy rate. As a result, the low interest rate will be kept too low for too long time, allowing more risk taken by the banks and sowing the seeds for the next crisis. Farhi and Tirole (2011) discuss the likelihood of such scenario.

7.2.2 Surcharges

As has been analyzed, systemic risk arising from financial market comes from the externalities each financial institution imposes on the other banks and non-financial sector, as well as the amplification effect of financial risks emerging from the highly interconnected banking network. Therefore, an effective stabilization instrument to combat systemic risk is to raise surcharges on financial firms and/or non-financial firms. The role of regulatory surcharges is twofold:

1   Aligning incentives. Systemic risk comes from negative externalities that the financial institutions don't internalize in their decisions so that they coordinate to engage in riskier investments, increasing the overall risk level in the entire financial system. Therefore, as a classical solution to externalities, the Pigouvian tax type of financial surcharge proportional to the externalities serves to induce the right incentives of financial institutions and eliminate the collective risk taking.
2   Providing better cushions. This type of surcharge works for the defense in depth, i.e., when one financial firm faces market stress, such surcharge comes in as a "bail in" mechanism, minimizing the risks for the counter parties, insulating the trouble, and preventing the contagion through the financial network. This type of surcharge is different from the standard existing liquidity and capital buffers held by the banks, given that the existing regulatory liquidity and capital requirements mostly focus on the survival of individual firms. The surcharge here is on top of the existing buffers, mainly reflecting the need to contain the spillover of one bank's failure to the rest of the financial system. In principle, it is proportional to the bank's importance in the financial system.

These two types of surcharges may overlap. Although the idea of regulatory surcharges is not yet widely adopted in policy practice (by the time the book is written, Switzerland is one of the countries where the surcharge rules have been undergoing the legislation process), there are several surcharges that may be considered in the macroprudential regulation for the future.

The first is the Pigouvian tax charged on one bank's business. Although the principle has been quite well understood that the behavior generating negative externalities can be deterred by tax surcharge and similar policies have been widely taken on issues such as environmental protection, the taxation design on banking can be far more challenging since the banking business contains a wide variety of transactions in different types so that the inherent externalities are extremely difficult to measure. One possible solution is to reduce the complexity by focusing on the generic channels that have been well understood. For example, one well identified mechanism is the feedback mechanism between credit growth and risk taking, such that the banks hold excess illiquid assets to reap the profit in the boom since they neglect the negative externality of their fire sale in the downside. Therefore, a tax on bank lending may reduce the aggregate risk taking and improve the social welfare. The design of tax is discussed by Jeanne and Korinek (2010, 2011) in slightly different contexts.

The tax revenue can be also used as insurance, or an additional buffer to ease the systemic stress. Cao (2010) has a discussion on such solution. The idea is to use tax surcharge to reduce the aggregate risk taking, and the tax revenue as a safety fund to cushion against the liquidity shock. The details will be presented in Chapter 9, and it is shown there that such scheme helps restore the first best allocation. However, there are also problems – mainly political economy problems – to get the scheme to work. Typically the tax authority is a different institution from the regulatory agency, and the conflict of interest makes the scheme hardly possible to be implemented. Especially, when the crisis hits at the time when the accumulated fund is still insufficient, public debt needs to be raised to cover the gap. This is beyond the regulator's scope and politically costly; the lengthy political process makes the fund hardly possible as a resource for prompt intervention.

Besides the Pigouvian approach, surcharges can also be levied on capital and liquidity to keep the shocks to the systemically important institutions on the leash. Depending on its role in the financial system, one bank may be required to hold extra capital buffer and/or liquid assets in order to prevent its failure spilled over to the other banks. Again, such buffer should be installed on top of the existing ones, i.e., the liquidity regulation (to be discussed in Chapter 8) and the equity requirements (to be discussed in Chapter 9), since it is designed to maintain the systemic stability. In practice the measure of systemic importance discussed in Section 7.1.1 may shed some light on determining the necessary size of the capital and liquidity surcharges. For instance, *CoVaR* (Adrian and Brunnermeier, 2010) captures the Value-at-Risk of the financial system conditional on some institutions being under distress, and one institution's contribution to systemic risk is measured by the *CoVaR* of the institution in distress minus the *CoVaR* of the institution in orderly time. These indicators can be used by the regulator as guidelines for determining the surcharges.

Of course whether surcharge should be set on liquidity buffer or capital requirement is still a question, since each approach corresponds to different cost to individual institution and the economy. There is still much research to be done on discovering the benefit and cost of different surcharges.

Another form of surcharge is an additional capital/liquidity insurance. As suggested by Kashyap *et al.* (2008), because capital surcharge is costly for the banks, it would be better if the banks can attend an insurance scheme that they obtain additional capital only when the risk of insolvency gets materialized. In addition, during the crisis, many countries provided full insurance guarantee for bank deposits. However, the insurance surcharge introduces other problems. It may encourage the banks' moral hazard in excess risk taking. Further, as is shown in Section 1.3, the fragile structure of banking also serves as a useful commitment device to discipline the banks' behavior. Therefore, perfect insurance against the structural fragility may destroy such mechanism and result in excessive rents in the banking industry, eventually making the investors rather worse off.

7.2.3 Complexity control

Financial innovation and the complexity in financial intermediation it brings out are widely blamed to be responsible for the recent crisis, and there have been cries from the public to ban some of the financial innovation, standardize the financial products, and reduce the complexity. In contrast, such view is not well supported in research. Complicated intermediation structure together with financial innovation help make the bank assets more liquid, improving market efficiency. For example, Albertazzi *et al.* (2011) find that the banks tend to be much aware of the information problems in the complex securitization process and hence take precautionary measures to defend their lending standard. Evidence from Norden and Wagner (2008) shows that financial innovation like credit default swaps (CDS) reduces the loan spreads and makes the banks more resilient than otherwise during the financial turbulence.

As argued in Chapter 4, systemic risk does not come out of financial innovation and intermediary complexity per se, but, rather, it is caused by the information problem associated with computational complexity and agency problem. The welfare loss from the investors also arises from the banks abusing their market power. From the regulator's point of view, supervisory and regulatory agencies usually lack the human resources on closely scrutinizing all the transactions of all financial institutions; therefore, generally the priorities in regulating the financial complexity are actually to fix the informational inefficiencies and to restricting the market power for consumer protection. Only if it is too costly to achieve these aims, should the regulator take the direct control on financial products and intermediation structure.

One solution to dealing with the information loss in the long intermediation chain is to standardize the products. As is demonstrated in theory by Allen and Gale (1999), as long as information acquisition is costly, product standardization lowers the frictions in sophisticated markets. As suggested by Brunnermeier and Oehmke (2009), the "risk characteristics, potential benefits and potential pitfalls of a financial security" are assessed by the regulatory authority, following the very similar lengthy and extremely cautious approval procedure of the US Food and Drug Administration (FDA), and financial contracts are made standardized. This much reduces the murkiness in the financial products and helps both banks and investors correctly price the risks. However, the authors also acknowledge that such process is likely to be highly subjective, since there is no objective guideline on how to justify the "safety" of the financial products. The information problem is thus hardly got around through product standardization.

It is also hard to restrict the banks' market power, for consumer protection purpose, by cutting down the product and intermediation complexity. In this case, it may be more effective to improve the information disclosure rules. The banks should be obliged to offer the investors *ex ante* a concise summary of the features, mechanisms, and the risks of their products, and the investors need more assistance to get the necessary information on the products they purchase, as well as the assistance to get access to legal remedies when any fraud has been detected.

As a concluding remark, the information and incentive problems associated with financial complexity are hardly solved by curbing the complexity. Besides the rules directly dealing with these problems, the precautionary policy setups such as liquidity and capital buffers are necessary complements to defend financial stability.

8 Liquidity regulation and the lender of last resort policy

Bear Stearns never ran short of capital. It just could not meet its obligations. At least that is the view from Washington, where regulators never stepped in to force the investment bank to reduce its high leverage even after it became clear Bear was struggling last summer. Instead, the regulators issued repeated reassurances that all was well. Does it sound a little like a doctor emerging from a funeral to proclaim that he did an excellent job of treating the late patient?

(Floyd Norris, *New York Times*, April 4, 2008)

The provision of large liquidity facilities penalizes those financial institutions that sat out the dance, encourages herd behavior and increases the intensity of future crises.

(Mervyn King, *Financial Times*, September 12, 2007)

Moral hazard fundamentalists misunderstand the insurance analogy.

(Lawrence Summers, *Financial Times*, September 24 2007)

Although financial crises can be triggered by many reasons, the propagation of a crisis often follows the liquidity channel. In the downturn, the financial intermediaries, or the banks, whose business model is featured by investing on the high yield and risky long assets funded by the short-term debts, immediately feels the stress from liquidity, i.e., the difficulty in raising short-term funds to roll over their long-term investments. As argued in Chapter 3, liquidity is the key to understanding financial crises. But also it may play a pivotal role in the rules preventing the market crunch.

To cushion the market shocks and cut off the propagation of crisis, in banking regulation the most straightforward solution is to have some obligatory liquidity buffer in the banking sector. The buffer should be thick enough to meet the demand shocks; the interbank market should be resilient enough for the banks to borrow and lend even when the market is under stress; and the buffer should be "liquid" enough so that it can be easily converted to fulfill the banks' instantaneous demand for cash without losing much value in the conversion.

The level of regulatory liquidity requirement certainly depends on the liquidity risk. The safest case is to require all the banks to hold so much liquid assets that they are able to meet the demand in all contingencies. Of course this eliminates all the liquidity crises, but is not optimal since holding liquid assets implies giving up the high yields from the illiquid assets. The investors will be better off if the banks are allowed to take some risk under certain contingencies.

However, allowing the banks to take risks implies that they may fail in some states of the world. The bank failure is obviously costly and should be avoided; therefore, the optimal liquidity regulation needs to be companioned by the active intervention of the regulator – usually the central bank. The central bank in this case plays a role as the lender of last resort facilitating the liquidity provision to ease the market stress, known as "the Bagehot principle" such that in the crisis the central bank should lend freely – at penalty interest rates, though – to anyone who could offer good assets as collateral.

But the central bank intervention opens another source of trouble, since the regulated banks actively respond to regulation and undo the regulatory policies. Because bank failure is costly, when there is a pure liquidity problem it is always optimal to bail out all the banks *ex post* even if some of them do not follow the liquidity requirement *ex ante*. Anticipating such "Greenspan put," the banks will coordinate on excess risk taking without observing any of the liquidity requirements. The moral hazard thus endogenously arises as the banks' response to regulation.

The episodes from the current crisis shed much light on this issue. For quite some time before the crisis started in mid-2007, at least a few market participants had the feeling that financial markets have been susceptible to excessive risk taking, encouraged by extremely low risk spreads. There was the notion of abundant liquidity, stimulated by a "savings glut", by an "investment drought," or by central banks running too-loose monetary policies. In that context, some brave economists warned against the rising risk of a liquidity squeeze which might force central banks to ease policy again (compare, for example, "A fluid concept," *The Economist*, February 2007). Frequently it was argued that it was exactly the anticipation of such a central bank reaction which encouraged further excessive risk taking: the belief in "abundant" provision of aggregate liquidity might have resulted in overinvestment in activities creating systemic risk.

Afterwards, following the turmoil on financial markets, there has been a strong debate about the adequate policy response. Some have warned that central bank actions may encourage dangerous moral hazard behavior of market participants in the future. Others instead criticized central banks for responding far too cautiously. The most prominent voice has been Willem Buiter, who – jointly with Ann Sibert – right from the beginning of the crisis in August 2007 strongly pushed the idea that in times of crises, central banks should act as market maker of last resort (see Buiter and Sibert 2007). As an adaptation of the Bagehot principles to modern times with globally integrated financial systems, central banks should actively purchase and sell illiquid private-sector securities and so play a key role in assessing and pricing credit risk. In his *Financial Times* blog "Maverecon," Willem Buiter stated the intellectual arguments behind such a policy very clearly on December 13, 2007:

Liquidity is a public good. It can be managed privately (by hoarding inherently liquid assets), but it would be socially inefficient for private banks and other financial institutions to hold liquid assets on their balance sheets in amounts sufficient to tide them over when markets become disorderly. They are meant to intermediate short maturity liabilities into long maturity assets and (normally) liquid liabilities into illiquid assets. Since central banks can create unquestioned liquidity at the drop of a hat, in any amount and at zero cost, they should be the liquidity providers of last resort, both as lender of last resort and as market maker of last resort. There is no moral hazard as long as central banks provide the liquidity against properly priced collateral, which is in addition subject to the usual "liquidity haircuts" on this fair valuation. The private provision of the public good of emergency liquidity is wasteful. It's as simple as that.

Buiter's statement represents the prevailing mainstream view that there is no moral hazard risk as long as the Bagehot principles are followed as best practice in liquidity management.

According to Goodfriend and King (1988), a lender-of-last-resort policy should target liquidity provision to the market, but not to specific banks. Central banks should "lend freely at a high rate against good collateral." This way, public liquidity support is supposed to be targeted toward solvent yet illiquid institutions, since insolvent financial institutions should be unable to provide adequate collateral to secure lending. In the following, Section 8.1, we will challenge the view that a policy following the Bagehot principle does not create moral hazard.

The key argument is that this view neglects the endogeneity of aggregate liquidity risk. Starting with Allen and Gale (1998) and Holmström and Tirole (1998), there have been quite a few models recently analyzing private and public provision of liquidity. But in most of these models, exposure to aggregate systemic risk is assumed to be exogenous.

In Holmström and Tirole (1998), for instance, liquidity shortages arise when financial institutions and industrial companies scramble for and cannot find the cash required to meet their most urgent needs or undertake their most valuable projects. They show that credit lines from financial intermediaries are sufficient for implementing the socially optimal (second-best) allocation, as long as there is no aggregate uncertainty. In the case of aggregate uncertainty, however, the private sector cannot satisfy its own liquidity needs, so the existence of liquidity shortages vindicates the injection of liquidity by the government. In their model, the government can provide (outside) liquidity by committing future tax income to back up the reimbursements.

In Holmström and Tirole's model, the lender of last resort indeed provides a free lunch: public provision of liquidity in the presence of aggregate shocks is a pure public good, with no moral hazard involved. The reason is that the probability for being hit by an aggregate shock is not affected by the amount of investment in liquid assets carried out by the private sector. The same holds in Allen and Gale (1998), even though they analyze a quite different mechanism for public provision of liquidity: the adjustment of the price level in an economy with nominal contracts. In Section 8.1 we adopt Allen and Gale's mechanism, but we endogenize the exposure of financial intermediaries to aggregate (systemic) liquidity risk. Such endogeneity allows us to capture the feedback from liquidity provision to risk taking incentives of financial intermediaries. We will show that the share invested in illiquid projects rises endogenously with central bank liquidity provision: the anticipation of unconditional central bank liquidity provision encourages excessive risk taking (moral hazard). It turns out that in the absence of liquidity requirements, there will be overinvestment in risky activities, creating excessive exposure to systemic risk.

In contrast to what the Bagehot principle suggests, unconditional provision of liquidity to the market (lending of central banks against good collateral) is exactly the wrong policy: it distorts incentives of banks to provide sufficient private liquidity, thus reducing investors' payoff. In Section 8.1, we concentrate on pure illiquidity risk: there will never be insolvency unless triggered by illiquidity (by a bank run). Illiquid projects promise a higher, yet possibly delayed, return. Relying on sufficient liquidity provided by the market (or by the central bank), financial intermediaries are inclined to invest more heavily in high-yielding, but illiquid, long-term projects. A central bank's liquidity provision, helping to prevent bank runs with inefficient early liquidation, encourages banks to invest more in illiquid assets. At first sight, this seems to work fine, even if systemic risk increases: after all, public insurance against aggregate risks should allow agents to undertake more profitable activities with higher social return. As long as public insurance is a free lunch, there is nothing wrong with providing such a public good.

However, as is shown in Section 8.1, the incentive of financial intermediaries to free-ride on liquidity in good states results in excessively low liquidity in bad states. Even worse, as long as they do not suffer runs, free-riding banks can always offer more attractive collateral in bad states – so they are able to outbid prudent banks in a liquidity crisis. For that reason, the Bagehot principle, rather than providing correct incentives, is the wrong medicine in modern times with a shadow banking system relying on liquidity being provided by other institutions.

To fix such moral hazard problem, the solution for the pure illiquidity risk case, as proposed in Section 8.2, is to have *ex ante* liquidity requirement as an entry condition for banking business together with *ex post* conditional bailout.

However, as is argued in Section 4.3, the highly complicated financial products make it hardly possible to distinguish between illiquidity and insolvency problems. When a financial institution falls into liquidity stress, there is a probability that some of the assets are toxic instead of purely illiquid. In this case, as is shown in Section 8.3, pure liquidity requirement is not sufficient to avoid bank failures. Because the central bank doesn't have superior knowledge to that of market participants, i.e., it isn't able to distinguish between illiquidity and insolvency risks, the value of the banks' collateral in the bad state cannot be as high as that in the good state. Therefore, the banks cannot get sufficient liquidity from the central bank in the bad state even if they do observe the *ex ante* liquidity requirement. A costly bank run is, thus, not avoided any more. The *ex post* optimal unconventional policy only creates moral hazard.

This finding suggests that the additional insolvency risk implies an extra cost for stabilizing the financial system, i.e., the regulator needs extra resources to fight against the insolvency risk. Therefore, a counter-cyclical taxation or deposit insurance mechanism proposed in Section 8.3.3 will work. The proposal is as follows: the banks have to be taxed away part of their revenue in the good state and the taxation revenue can be used to cover the cost in central bank's liquidity provision in the bad state. It is shown that the constrained efficiency can be restored under such taxation/insurance scheme. However, there will be many difficulties in implementing the rule, especially for reasons of political economy.

8.1 Nominal contracts and the lender of last resort policy

First of all, to introduce liquidity regulation and motivate the role of central bank as the lender of last resort, we have to go beyond the banking models with real contract. In the following, we reconstruct the baseline banking model in Section 3.1, allowing for nominal financial contracts.

Many positive theories of financial regulation in the existing literature are based on the real models, in which there is no role for money and all the financial contracts are made in real terms. This approach much simplifies the modeling, making it easier for people to focus on the market outcome without dealing with price effects. However, when it comes to liquidity policy, the models with real contracts may miss the impact of money, underestimate the central bank's role as lender of last resort, and neglect the risk taking channel from monetary policy (see Borio and Zhu, 2008) to the banks' behavior. In a world of nominal contracts, the market equilibrium and the effectiveness of regulatory policy can be quite different.

In the financial market with nominal contracts, the liquidity regulation and liquidity policy in the crisis have implicit distributional effects. Such effects may work through different channels. In the financial crisis, the central bank's credible role as the lender of last resort eases the liquidity stress of banks and their counter parties, so that the borrowing and lending in the financial market can still go on. The production sector can thus maintain the output level instead of going bankrupt and default, which further stabilizes the financial sector. The lender of last resort policy restores efficiency through such "financial multiplier" channel. On the other hand, the liquidity injection during the crisis serves to keep asset prices afloat, via creating an implicit inflation in the economy. This "price channel" mechanism is in fact equivalent to a transfer from the healthy financial institutions to those in trouble, penalizing "those financial institutions that sat out the dance." Anticipating to be bailed out *ex post* by somebody else's money, the banks will coordinate *ex ante* on taking more risks, sowing the seeds for the next crisis. The lender of last resort policy actually has a feedback on the banks' risk taking behavior, creating the moral hazard and increasing the systemic risk.

8.1.1 *Model setup*

In the following, we explore such feedback mechanism by extending the baseline real model in Section 3.1 with nominal contracts and liquidity regulation. A lender of last resort, usually the central bank, cannot create real liquidity in period 1 when the banks in trouble need bailout, neither has it the authority of taxation to directly mobilize the resources among different sectors in the economy. But a central bank can add nominal liquidity at the stroke of a pen. Following Allen and Gale (1998) and Diamond and Rajan (2006), assume from now on that deposit contracts are arranged in nominal terms.

Timing

Keeping most of the settings the same as in Section 3.1, here is the timing of the nominal model, as Figure 8.1 shows:

1   At $t=0$, the banks provide nominal deposit contracts to investors, promising a fixed nominal payment d_0 at $t=1$. The central bank announces a minimum level $\underline{\alpha}$ of investment on safe projects, and only those banks that meet the requirement will be eligible for liquidity support in the time of a crisis.
2   At $t=0.5$, the banks decide whether to borrow liquidity from the central bank. If yes, the central bank will provide liquidity for the banks, provided they fulfill the requirement α.
3   At $t=1$, the liquidity injection with the banks' illiquid assets as collateral is carried out so that the banks are able to honor their nominal contracts, which reduces the real value of deposits just to the amount of real resources available at that date.
4   At $t=2$, the banks repay the central bank using the returns from the late projects, with gross nominal interest rate r^M agreed at $t=1$.

As a new element in this extended model, we allow the central bank to impose minimal liquidity holdings in addition to lender of last resort policy as a way to implement the allocation maximizing the investors' payoff.

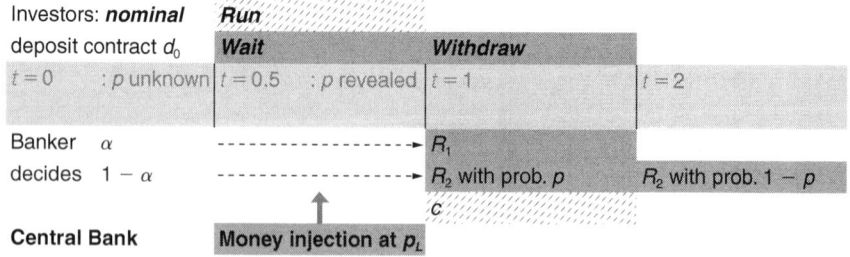

Figure 8.1 A banking model with central bank.

Money-in-the-market pricing

We capture the distributional effect of the lender of last resort policy through the price channel. For simplicity we assume that one unit of money is of equal value to one unit real good in payment. And the price level is determined by *cash-in-the-market principle* (Allen and Gale, 2005), i.e., the ratio of amount of liquidity (the sum of money and real goods) in the market to amount of real goods. In our model, when the central bank provides liquidity in the form of fiat money in the market during the downturn, i.e., the time when the real intermediate return is low, the liquidity injection raises the price level for the real good while still keeps the troubled banks solvent in nominal terms. Since the fiat money and the real good have the same purchasing power, the investors from the troubled banks with more money and less real good in their repayments actually enjoy the same real consumption as the ones from the healthy banks whose repayments consist of more real good. Therefore, there is an implicit transfer from the healthy banks to the ones in trouble. Later we will see this has a profound implication to the banks' behavior in equilibrium.

8.1.2 Liquidity regulation and lender-of-last-resort policy

With nominal contracts, the central bank's optimal policy as lender of last resort can be summarized in the following proposition.

Proposition 8.1 With nominal contracts, the central bank can act as lender of last resort. The central bank's optimal policy that maximizes the investors' return is as follows:

1 set $\underline{\alpha} = \alpha_H$ for all $\pi \in [\bar{\pi}_2', 1]$, where

$$\bar{\pi}_2' = \frac{\gamma E[R_L] - \kappa}{\gamma E[R_H] - \kappa} < \pi_2$$

and $\kappa = \alpha_H R_1 + (1 - \alpha_H) p_L R_2$;
2 set $\underline{\alpha} = \alpha_L$ for all $\pi \in [0, \bar{\pi}_2')$;
3 set $r^M = 1$.

What's more, under such a policy bank runs are eliminated for the eligible banks; i.e., the eligible banks will not experience runs when p_L is revealed.

Proof: see Appendix 8.4.1.

The investors' return is maximized when the banks get liquidity injection at the lowest cost, the central bank setting $r^M = 1$. With liquidity injection, bank runs are prevented when the bad state (with low payoffs at $t = 1$) occurs. Essentially, nominal deposits allow the central bank to implement state-contingent payoffs, and such a policy replicates the optimal allocation in the central planner's problem.

Such constraint efficient result is also supported by Allen *et al.* (2011). In a quite different setting, Allen *et al.* focuses on a monetary economy with nominal contracts and prices, instead of introducing money only through lender of last resort policy. Similar to the standard Diamond–Dybvig model (see Section 1.1), the banks finance their long assets via demand deposits from the investors, whose liquidity preference gets revealed in the intermediate date. The economy is complete nominal in the sense that money is the medium for all the transactions: the banks borrow money from the central bank, then make loans to firms with short-term or long-term projects, the investors sell their endowment to the firms and deposit the revenue in the banks. The authors then examine wide varieties of uncertainties, such as aggregate shocks to the returns of projects, both aggregate and idiosyncratic liquidity shocks. It is shown that if a central bank, which serves as a Bagehot-type lender of last resort, is always willing to inject liquidity to the banks distressed by liquidity, it is able to eliminate the banking crises caused by pure liquidity problems and restore the first best allocation.

8.1.3   Time inconsistency problem and risk taking channel

Such constraint efficient result seems to confirm the view that the lender of last resort can indeed provide a free lunch, delivering a public good at no cost. It turns out, however, that the anticipation of these actions has an adverse impact on the amount of aggregate liquidity provided by the private sector, affecting endogenously the exposure to systemic risk.

Proposition 8.2 Assume that a market equilibrium exists, i.e., $\pi p_H R_2 + (1 - \pi)$ $p_L R_2 \geq 1$. If the central bank is willing to provide liquidity to the entire market in times of crisis, all banks have an incentive to free-ride, choosing $\alpha = 0$, and investors are made worse off.

Proof: see Appendix 8.4.2.

The reason for this surprising result is the following: if the central bank targets liquidity provision to the market instead of to specific banks, the optimal policy as stated by Proposition 8.1 is not enforceable. Since we concentrate on the case of pure illiquidity risk, in our model all projects will certainly be realized at $t = 2$. So there is no doubt about solvency of the projects, unless insolvency is triggered by illiquidity. If the central bank follows the Bagehot principle and creates artificial liquidity at the drop of a hat – against allegedly good collateral – all private incentives to care about *ex ante* liquidity provision will be destroyed, exacerbating the moral hazard problem: the free-riding banks, investing all their funds in the projects with higher returns, can always get liquidity support and thus are able to offer more attractive terms to investors at $t = 0$. This drives out all the prudent banks and leaves the investors worse off. The lender-of-last-resort policy actually increases systemic risk through such risk taking channel.

8.2 Optimal liquidity regulation under pure illiquidity risk

So what policy options should be taken? One might argue that a central bank should provide liquidity support only to prudent banks (conditional on banks having invested sufficiently in liquid assets). But such a commitment is simply not credible: as emphasized by Cao and Illing (2008), there is a serious problem of dynamic consistency since it is always optimal to bail out those free-riding banks *ex post* even if they are not eligible by the rule *ex ante* – knowing this, no one will choose to be prudent in the first place.

Rather than relying on an implausible commitment mechanism, the obvious solution is a mix of two instruments: *ex ante* liquidity regulation combined with *ex post* lender-of-last-resort policy. The second-best outcome from the investors' point of view needs to be implemented by the following policy: in a first step, a banking regulator has to impose *ex ante* liquidity requirements. Requesting minimum investment in liquid type 1 assets of at least α_L for all $\pi < \overline{\pi}_2'$ and α_H for $\pi \geq \overline{\pi}_2'$ would give investors the highest expected payoff, as characterized in Figure 8.2. When banks are not allowed to operate with insufficiently low liquidity holdings, there are no incentives for free-riding. For high values $\pi \geq \overline{\pi}_2'$, the central bank acts as lender of last resort in the bad state, eliminating costly bank runs. This raises the expected payoff for investors, even though it increases the range of parameter values with systemic risk.

The lesson we learn here is that the *ex ante* liquidity regulation should be an entry condition for the banking industry, instead of an option that the banks are free to choose. Otherwise the regulatory authority will certainly suffer from the time inconsistency problem and has to bail out all the free-riding banks *ex post*, with its credibility severely damaged, creating the origin for the next crisis.

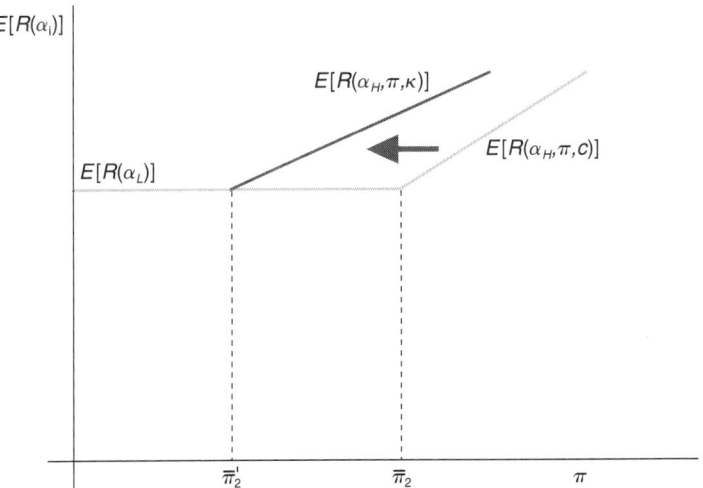

Figure 8.2 Investors' real expected return $E[R(\alpha_H, \pi, c)]$ for the case of *ex ante* liquidity regulation combined with *ex post* lender-of-last-resort policy for high π, in comparison with the market equilibrium, $E[R(\alpha_H, \pi, c)]$.

This result has been also emphasized in Rochet (2004), in a completely different setup. In a framework where the banks explicitly engage in moral hazard in operating investment projects, the market discipline fails to deter the banks seeking for private rents; this motivates the regulator's role in fixing the market failure. The optimal policy is that the central bank has to commit to only bailing out the banks that do not get involved in moral hazard and take too much risk. In order to achieve this, the central bank should be independent from the pressure of politicians and stick to the exclusive mandates on price stability and financial stability. However, in our model where the moral hazard emerges endogenously, even the independent central bank is no longer free from the temptation of bailing out the free-riding banks altogether since in a liquidity crisis it is always optimal *ex post* to prevent bank failure to maintain financial stability. Therefore, the moral hazard incentive has to be deterred *ex ante* and the liquidity requirement has to be strictly imposed as the entry condition.

In another quite different setting, using a framework with asymmetric information, Farhi and Tirole (2011) derive related results. They show that monetary policy (with the real interest rate as policy variable) faces a commitment problem. They also derive a role for a minimum liquidity ratio. Our setup shows that the key challenge for regulators and the central bank is to cope with incentives for financial intermediaries to free-ride on liquidity provision. Furthermore, it allows us to compare liquidity regulation with alternative mechanism designs.

One might expect that imposing equity requirements is sufficient to provide a cushion against liquidity shocks. As another alternative, one might impose narrow banking in the sense that banks are required to hold sufficient liquid funds so as to pay out in all contingencies. As shown later in Section 9.2.2, these options turn out to be strictly worse than imposing minimum liquidity standards *ex ante* combined with lender-of-last-resort policy, as long as illiquidity is the only problem.

8.3 Liquidity regulation under financial complexity

As is argued in Chapter 4, the market structure and financial products are getting extremely complex in modern finance. As a positive concern, it is necessary to know whether the optimal policy we derived in a simple model is robust under a more complicated setup, or whether *ex ante* liquidity regulation combined with *ex post* lender-of-last-resort policy is still optimal if we lift some of the assumptions. In this section, we will try to answer this question in a setup with the elements capturing financial complexities, which is the framework from Section 4.3.

8.3.1 Central bank and insolvency risk

In a similar way to Section 4.3, we introduce nominal contract and the role for central bank as the lender of last resort into the real framework we developed in Section 8.1. Suppose that from now on the banks are required to invest a minimum level $\underline{\alpha}$ on the safe projects, and only those who observe the requirement will be offered the lifeboat when there's liquidity shortage. Usually such lender of last resort is the central bank, which is able to create fiat money at no cost. The model with central bank and insolvency risk is similar to Section 8.1, with the timing being summarized in Figure 8.3.

In the presence of nominal contracts as well as the central bank as the lender of last resort, as Section 8.1.2 argues, the optimal policy is to restore the efficient allocation as that of Proposition 8.1. Therefore, the liquidity requirement $\underline{\alpha} = \alpha_L$ for $0 \leq \pi \leq \overline{\pi}_2$ and $\underline{\alpha} = \alpha_H$ for $\overline{\pi}_2 < \pi \leq 1$. Moreover, the troubled banks should get liquidity injection at the lowest cost, i.e., $r^M = 1$.

With $\underline{\alpha} = \alpha_L$ as a requirement for entry, the inefficient mixed strategy equilibrium is completely eliminated and the constrained efficiency is restored for $0 \leq \pi \leq \overline{\pi}_2$. For $\overline{\pi}_2 < \pi \leq 1$, with $\underline{\alpha} = \alpha_H$ the banks can meet the deposit contract with their real return at $t=1$ if $(p \cdot \eta)_H$ is revealed

$$d_0 = \alpha_H \gamma R_1 + (1 - \alpha_H) \gamma E[R_2 \mid (p \cdot \eta)_H] = d_{0|(p \cdot \eta)_H}.$$

If $(p \cdot \eta)_L$ is revealed, the banks need liquidity injection to meet the nominal contracts. However, since r^M is bounded by one, the central bank can only inject liquidity up to the expected return of the risky assets. Therefore, the maximum nominal payoff the depositors can get is

$$d_{0|(p \cdot \eta)_L} = \alpha_H \gamma R_1 + (1 - \alpha_H) \gamma E[R_2 \mid (p \cdot \eta)_L] < d_0.$$

The banks will still experience run even if they obtain the promised lifeboat from the central bank, and the outcome is no different from that in the market equilibrium. The scheme fails to eliminate the inefficient bank runs for $\overline{\pi}_2 < \pi \leq 1$.

With both illiquidity and insolvency risks, the value of the risky assets is depressed when the bad state is revealed, which makes the banks unable to get as much liquidity as they may need. Therefore, in contrast to the models with pure illiquidity risk such as in Section 8.2, the pure liquidity regulation with conditional bailout is no longer sufficient to eliminate the costly bank runs.

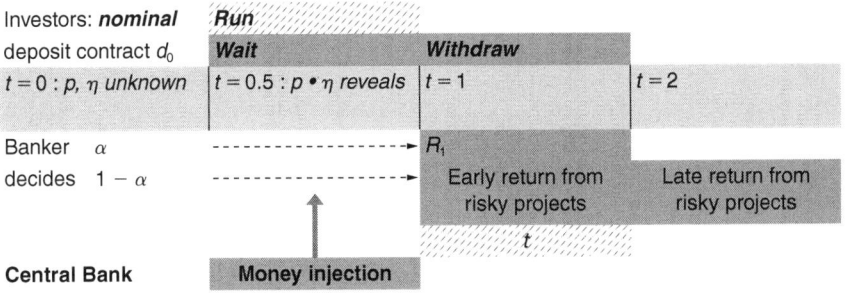

Figure 8.3 Nominal contracts with insolvency risk.

8.3.2 Unconventional policy and moral hazard

However, in the financial crisis, the central bank may take non-conventional monetary policy measures and go beyond the $r^M = 1$ lower bound, in order to mitigate the liquidity stress and stabilize the financial system at a cost through some emergency lending facilities. The notable example is, after the collapse of Lehman Brothers, the European Central Bank (ECB) immediately broadened its collateral framework and started accepting virtually any assets (though with the official rating threshold as BBB–) as collateral, in order to provide the stressed banks sufficient liquidity. As of Reuters (May 2, 2011), the value of collateral banks put forward for use in ECB's lending operations remained at the record €2 trillion, with the toxic asset-backed accounting for almost a quarter of all assets. This is equivalent to offering the banks so much liquidity they need while accepting all the assets as collateral in our model. Given that the expected return of the toxic assets is lower than their face value, the effective rate r^M is below one. The policy is intrinsically subsidizing liquidity provision.

Of course such non-conventional monetary policy is *ex post* optimal, in the sense that it stabilizes the market and prevents the costly bank failure, although the cost in liquidity subsidy has to be paid from somewhere else in the economy, most likely by the taxpayers. However, the bigger problem here again is the moral hazard the policy creates, the similar problem as the previous section demonstrates: as a time inconsistency problem, it is always *ex post* optimal to bail out the banks no matter whether there is a minimum liquidity requirement *ex ante*. Knowing this, the banks will coordinate on excess risk taking, and the prudent banks are driven out of the market. This result is much in line with Repullo (2005), which shows in a model with asymmetric information that the banks opt for a smaller liquidity buffer if the anticipated lender-of-last-resort interest rate is low. Furthermore, the optimality of pure liquidity regulation with conditional bailout ceases to hold even if the minimum liquidity requirement is imposed as an entry condition, as long as the collateral value is below the banks' demand for liquidity when the crisis hits.

8.3.3 Conditional liquidity injection with procyclical taxation

The failure of pure liquidity regulation comes from the fact that the potential insolvency risk adds an extra cost to stabilizing the financial system. This implies that the regulator needs to find a second instrument for covering such cost, for example, an additional banking tax: in addition to the scheme in Section 8.3.1, a tax has to be paid at $t=1$ if $(p \cdot \eta)_H$ is observed, and the troubled banks will be bailed out with liquidity injection plus such the tax revenue if $(p \cdot \eta)_L$ is observed.

Such augmented scheme works as follows. At $t=0$, a minimum liquidity requirement α_T is imposed on all banks and at $t=1$ the banks are taxed away a fixed amount $T_H \geq 0$ out of their revenue if $(p \cdot \eta)_H$ is observed. The banks are bailed out with liquidity injection plus the tax revenue if $(p \cdot \eta)_L$ is observed, and in this case the banks pay no tax, $T_L = 0$.

To find the optimal policy, first consider the high values of π. To eliminate the bank runs, T_H should be so high that the central bank has just sufficient resource to cover the gap left by liquidity injection, i.e.,

$$
\begin{aligned}
&\underline{\alpha}_T \gamma R_1 + (1-\underline{\alpha}_T)\gamma E[R_2 \mid (p \cdot \eta)_H] - T_H = \\
&\underline{\alpha}_T R_1 + (1-\underline{\alpha}_T)(p \cdot \eta)_H R_2 - T_H = d_{0,T},
\end{aligned}
\tag{8.1}
$$

as well as

$$
\begin{aligned}
&\underline{\alpha}_T \gamma R_1 + (1-\underline{\alpha}_T)\gamma E[R_2 \mid (p \cdot \eta)_H] - T_H = \\
&\underline{\alpha}_T \gamma R_1 + (1-\underline{\alpha}_T)\gamma E[R_2 \mid (p \cdot \eta)_L] + T_H \frac{\pi}{1-\pi}.
\end{aligned}
\tag{8.2}
$$

Equation (8.1) is no different from the social planner's problem for high π, therefore, the liquidity requirement $\underline{\alpha}_T = \alpha_H$ when π is high. Equation (8.2) says that the tax revenue should be just sufficient to fill in the gap in the liquidity bailout,

$$
T_H = (1-\pi)\gamma(1-\alpha_H)E[R_2 \mid (p \cdot \eta)_H] - E[R_2 \mid (p \cdot \eta)_L].
$$

The depositors' real return in the bad state is

$$
\alpha_H R_1 + (1-\alpha_H)(p \cdot \eta)_L R_2 + T_H \frac{\pi}{1-\pi}.
$$

When π gets lower, it would be costly to stay with α_H. The regulator should switch to $\underline{\alpha}_T = \alpha_L$ when

$$
\gamma E[R_L] > \pi\{\alpha_H \gamma R_1 + (1-\alpha_H)\gamma E[R_2 \mid (p \cdot \eta)_H] - T_H\} +
$$

$$
(1-\pi)\left[\alpha_H R_1 + (1-\alpha_H)(p \cdot \eta)_L R_2 + T_H \frac{\pi}{1-\pi}\right] = \pi\gamma E[R_H] + (1-\pi)\kappa,
$$

$$
\pi < \frac{\gamma E[R_L] - \kappa}{\gamma E[R_H] - \kappa} = \bar{\pi}'_{2T}.
$$

The effectiveness of the scheme is summarized in the following proposition:

Proposition 8.3 With liquidity regulation complemented by the procyclical banking tax, the bank runs are completely eliminated. Moreover,

1 For $\pi \in [0, \bar{\pi}'_{2T}]$, banks are required to invest a share of $\underline{\alpha}_T = \alpha_L$ on the safe assets, and no banking tax is necessary. The investors' expected real return is lower than the central planner's constrained efficient solution.

2 For $\pi \in (\bar{\pi}'_{2T}, 1]$ banks are required to invest a share of $\underline{\alpha}_T = \alpha_H$ on the safe assets. The banking tax T_H is charged at $t=1$ when $(p \cdot \eta)_H$ is revealed, and the investors' expected real return is the same as the central planner's constrained efficient solution.

Proof: see Appendix 8.4.3.

However, in practice such safety funds via procyclical taxation are certainly subject to implementation difficulties. The funds have to be accumulated to a sufficient amount before they are in need, i.e., when a crisis hits. Otherwise, when a crisis comes before the funds are fully established, the government must face a public deficit which can only be covered by the future taxation revenue. Usually raising public deficits implies political debates and compromises, substantially restricting the effectiveness of such scheme. In this sense, a "self-sufficient" solution such as equity holding may be superior, which is to be studied in the next chapter.

8.4 Appendix

8.4.1 Proof of Proposition 8.1

The central bank's optimal policy is to restore the constrained efficiency, as stated in Proposition 8.1. Therefore, the optimal liquidity requirement, which is captured by α, should be exactly the same as α_H (α_L) for high (low) π. So is it with r^M.

In addition, any bank that observes α will get bailed out whenever necessary. This only happens when a bank follows $\underline{\alpha} = \alpha_H$ but p_L is revealed. In this case, the investors will get $\kappa = \alpha_H R_1 + (1 - \alpha_H)p_L R_2$ real return plus $d_0 - \kappa$ fiat money if they do not run on the bank at $t = 0.5$. In contrast, the investors will only get the liquidated value $c < 1 < \kappa$ as the real return if they run on the bank. Of course, they will wait instead of run.

8.4.2 Proof of Proposition 8.2

Suppose that a representative bank chooses to be prudent with $\alpha_i = \underline{\alpha}$, and promises a nominal deposit contract $d^i_0 = \gamma[\alpha R_1 + (1 - \underline{\alpha})R_2]$ in order to maximize its investors' return. Then when the bad state with high liquidity needs is realized, the central bank has to inject enough liquidity into the market to keep the interest rate at $r = 1$ in order to ensure bank i's survival. However, given $r = 1$, a free-riding bank j can always profit from setting $\alpha_j = 0$, promising the nominal return $d^j_0 = \gamma R_2 > d^i_0$ to its investors. Thus, surely the banks prefer to free-ride.

For those parameter values such that $\pi p_H R_2 + (1 - \pi)p_L R_2 < 1$, there exists no equilibrium with liquidity injection. The reason is the following:

1   Any symmetric strategic profile cannot be equilibrium, because

    a   if there is no trade under such strategic profile – i.e., α is so small that the real return is less than one – one bank can deviate by setting $\alpha = 1$ and trading with investors;

b   if there is trade under such strategic profile – i.e., $\alpha > 0$ for all the banks
    – then one bank can deviate by setting $\alpha = 0$ and getting higher nominal
    return than the other banks.

2   Any asymmetric strategic profile, or profile of mixed strategies, cannot be
    equilibrium, because

a   if there is no trade under such strategic profile, then the argument of
    (1a) applies here;

b   if there is trade under such strategic profile, then one bank can deviate
    by choosing a pure strategy, $\alpha = 0$, and get better off – there is no reason
    to mix with the other dominated strategies.

8.4.3 Proof of Proposition 8.3

For $\pi \in (\bar{\pi}'_{2T}, 1]$, equation (8.1) implies that the depositors' expected return is the
same in both states, therefore, bank runs are completely eliminated. Since $\kappa > c$,
$\bar{\pi}'_{2T} < \bar{\pi}_2$, which means $[0, \bar{\pi}'_{2T}]$ is a subset of $[0, \bar{\pi}_2]$ where α_L maximizes the
depositors' expected return in the market equilibrium.

   Equation (8.1) is exactly the same as $E[R(\alpha_H)]$ in Figure 4.8, implying that
the investors' expected real return is the same as the central planner's constrained efficient solution for $\pi \in (\bar{\pi}'_{2T}, 1]$.

9 Capital requirements and equity buffer

> If you have to continue to hold an asset to meet a requirement, it is not liquid. What is needed is a buffer, not a minimum requirement. There is a story of a traveler arriving at a station late at night, who is overjoyed to see one taxi remaining. She hails it, only for the taxi driver to respond that he cannot help her, since local bye-laws require one taxi to be present at the station at all times!
>
> (Charles Goodhart, in Turner *et al.*, 2010, pp. 175)

Besides holding sufficient liquid assets to meet the demand shocks, the banks can also hold some capital buffer in order to absorb the losses. It has been well recognized during the current crisis that the lightly regulated, highly leveraged shadow banking system collapsed quickly because the capital buffer there is too thin to sustain any stress. But even the regulated banks, which were regarded as well capitalized before the crisis (as Flannery and Rangan (2008) documented, the banks' capital holding was significantly much higher than the regulatory requirement), did not find themselves better protected, either. Of course it is likely that the banks' capital ratio, although well above the lower bound of regulatory level, was still below the optimal – although there is by far no consensus on the socially optimal level of capital holding, or the shock was beyond anyone's expectation so that no bank got prepared enough. But the reason why the banks' capital buffer failed to work in the crisis may also be partially attributed to the flaws in the regulatory policy. As Repullo and Suarez (2009) argue, since the regulatory rule only stipulated the minimum level of capital holding, the banks have to build up the capital buffer beyond this level that is rescalable for loss absorption. However, since raising capital holding reduces the banks' profit from lending, the equilibrium capital buffer is still lower than what is necessary to tame the economy-wide shocks.

Capital requirement has been adopted in banking regulation for long time, and is still stimulating new debates. There are several excellent surveys on this issue, such as French *et al.* (2010, Chapter 5). This chapter is not intended to be an intensive survey of current research on capital regulation, but rather focuses on several questions.

First, we want to better understand the benefit and cost of capital requirement. Since equity is the most common form for the banks' capital holding, in the following we regard "equity" and "capital" as interchangeable terms. Capital requirement is designed to stabilize the financial system via using the banks' own resources, but this comes with a cost since holding equity is costly for the banks. In Section 9.2 we model the cost and benefit in a banking model, and compare the effectiveness of capital requirement with liquidity regulation which is subject to the moral hazard problem.

Second, we want to discuss the efficiency of banking regulation, using combined regulatory tools. As shown in Section 8.3.2, in a complex financial system with illiquidity and insolvency uncertainty, the regulator faces a dilemma between creating moral hazard and bank bailout. Pure equity requirement solves this problem, as proved in Section 9.3.1, but the capital buffer needs to be higher to cover the regulatory cost arising from the imperfect information. By combining the liquidity regulation with capital requirement, the regulatory cost can be reduced.

Third, we want to analyze the banks' response to the capital holding rules in Section 9.4 through an example. The regulatory policy delivers the right incentive structure only if the regulator understands how the banks react to the rules, but as many authors argue, such as Repullo and Saurina (2011), Allen *et al.* (2011), that regulators often neglect such feedback that may effectively undo the policy. As an example, we take contingent convertible debt which has many appealing features and been proposed as a next generation regulatory tool. It is shown that many complementary rules have to be worked out to address the potential incentive problems.

9.1 The role of equity in banking regulation

To see the benefit and cost of capital regulation, let us now introduce equity requirements into the model we developed in Section 3.1. The banks are now required to hold some equity as a share of their assets. Instead of pure fixed deposit contracts, the banks now issue a mixture of deposit contracts and equity for attracting funds from the investors (Diamond and Rajan 2000, 2005, 2006). Equity can reduce the fragility by providing a cushion against negative shocks. This, however, comes at a cost, since it allows the bank manager to capture a rent. So the regulator needs to strike a balance between benefit and cost.

Being a renegotiable claim, in contrast to deposits, equity is subject to the hold-up problem, i.e., equity holders will only get a share ζ ($\zeta \in [0, 1]$) of the surplus, the bank manager extracting the remaining part $1 - \zeta$ as rent from his or her superior collection skills. Without changing the nature of the problem, in the following we simply assume that

$$\zeta = \frac{1}{2}.$$

With

$$\zeta = \frac{1}{2},$$

the bank manager and equity holders share the surplus over deposits equally. So the equity value of a bank not suffering from a run is

$$\frac{\gamma E[R_s] - d_0}{2}$$

in state s with expected return $\gamma E[R_s]$ and deposit claims d_0. Assume that some equity requirement k is imposed – that is, the share of equity to bank assets is k, with

$$k = \frac{\dfrac{\gamma E[R_s] - d_0}{2}}{\dfrac{\gamma E[R_s] - d_0}{2} + d_0}.$$

Solving for d_0 gives the return to depositors as

$$d_0 = \frac{1 - \kappa}{1 + \kappa} \gamma E[R_s],$$

with equity holders receiving

$$\frac{\kappa}{1 + \kappa} \gamma E[R_s].$$

Thus investors providing funds both in the form of deposits and equity to the banks will receive the payoff

$$\frac{1}{1 + \kappa} \gamma E[R_s] < \gamma E[R_s] \text{ at } t = 1.$$

In the absence of aggregate risk, introducing equity requirements is a pure cost, reducing the investors' payoff. Somewhat counterintuitively, without aggregate risk, equity requirements even reduce the share α invested in safe projects. The reason is that with equity financing bank managers get the rent

$$\frac{\gamma E[R_s] - d_0}{2},$$

extracting part of the surplus over deposits from equity holders. Since the return at $t=2$ is higher than at $t=1$, bank managers are willing to consume late, so the amount of resources needed at $t=1$ is lower in the presence of equity. Consequently, the share α will be reduced. Obviously, banks holding no equity provide more attractive conditions for investors, so equity could not survive. This seemingly counterintuitive result simply demonstrates that there is no role (or rather only a payoff-reducing role) for costly equity in the absence of aggregate risk.

The benefit of equity comes in when there is aggregate risk: equity helps to absorb aggregate shocks and avoid the costly bank runs. In the simple two-state setup, equity holdings need to be just sufficient to cushion the bad state. With sufficient equity, the bank can choose $\alpha = \alpha_H$, profiting from the high return in the good state and still staying solvent in the bad state. In that case, it just needs to be able to pay out the fixed claims of investors, wiping out all equity.

Therefore, the effective equity requirement should include two parts: the inflexible minimum equity holding, plus the equity buffer that can be used to absorb losses. The latter is crucial for maintaining financial stability, without it the equity requirement is just the useless taxi kept in the station (although the context of the quote from Charles Goodhart in the front of this chapter is about liquidity buffer, the principle is quite the same). Here we neglect the role of equity as medium of control right or monitoring device; therefore, the inflexible minimum equity holding requirement is normalized to be zero.

With equity k and investment $\alpha = \alpha_H$, the total amount that can be pledged to investors providing funds both as depositors and equity holders is

$$\frac{1}{1+\kappa}\gamma E[R_s]$$

in the good state, with claims of depositors being $d_0 = \alpha_H R_1 + (1-\alpha_H)p_L R_2$ and return on equity

$$\frac{\kappa}{1+\kappa}\gamma E[R_s].$$

In the bad state, a marginally solvent bank is able to pay out $d_0 = \alpha_H R_1 + (1-\alpha_H)$ $p_L R_2$ to depositors. So the minimum k^* to prevent bank runs is determined by the condition

$$\frac{1-k^*}{1+k^*}\gamma E[R_H] = \alpha_H R_1 + (1-\alpha_H)p_L R_2,$$

and we solve to get

$$k^* = \frac{\gamma E[R_H]-d_0}{\gamma E[R_H]+d_0} \tag{9.1}$$

It can be seen that k^* is decreasing in p_L: the higher p_L, the lower the cushion k^* which is needed to stay solvent in the bad state.

Condition (9.1) determines the minimum equity requirement k^* a regulator needs to impose in order to eliminate the risk of costly bank runs. Setting k lower ($k < k^*$) would not help to prevent bank runs; setting k too high ($k > k^*$) would just raise the cost of holding equity without additional benefit. Thus from now on we can concentrate on the level k^* without loss of generality. In the following, we compare the investors' payoff in an economy subject to equity requirements with the payoff in the absence of any regulation and then with the case of liquidity requirements, combined with the central bank acting as lender of last resort.

9.2 The efficiency of equity requirements

9.2.1 Equity requirements versus market equilibrium

We first ask whether equity requirements can improve the investors' allocation in this economy, relative to the payoff they get in the market equilibrium we characterized in Proposition 3.3. As shown in Section 3.3.2, the investors' payoff depends on the probability π of the good state. If π is low enough, banks choose the safe strategy α_L. For high π, they pick α_H, with payoff increasing in π. In an intermediate range, free-riding banks drive down investors' return relative to what they could earn from investment in the safe strategy α_L. The overall payoff as a function of π is shown by the gray lines in Figure 9.1. Let us call this function $\Pi(\pi)$. It seems natural to expect that equity requirements are superior at least for the intermediate range. As we will show, this intuition does not hold.

In Figure 9.1, the solid black lines show the investors' expected return

$$\Pi_e(\pi) = d_0 + \frac{\Pi}{2}\pi$$

for the case of equity requirements. With equity requirements, the investors' expected return is uniformly increasing in π. The equity requirement k^* is chosen such that deposits will always be paid out fully, even in the bad state. Thus, the fixed deposit payment d_0 is independent of π. In contrast, the return on equity

$$\frac{\Pi}{2}$$

is paid out only in the good state. The more likely the good state (the higher π), the higher is the expected return on equity. Its value is determined by

$$\frac{\Pi}{2} = \frac{\gamma E[R_H] - d_0}{2} = \frac{\gamma E[R_H] - \frac{1-k}{1+k}\gamma E[R_H]}{2} = \frac{k}{1+k}\gamma E[R_H].$$

Under what conditions will a banking system with equity requirements outperform the investors' return in the market equilibrium? Intuition suggests that relative performance depends on parameter values. Actually, equity requirements

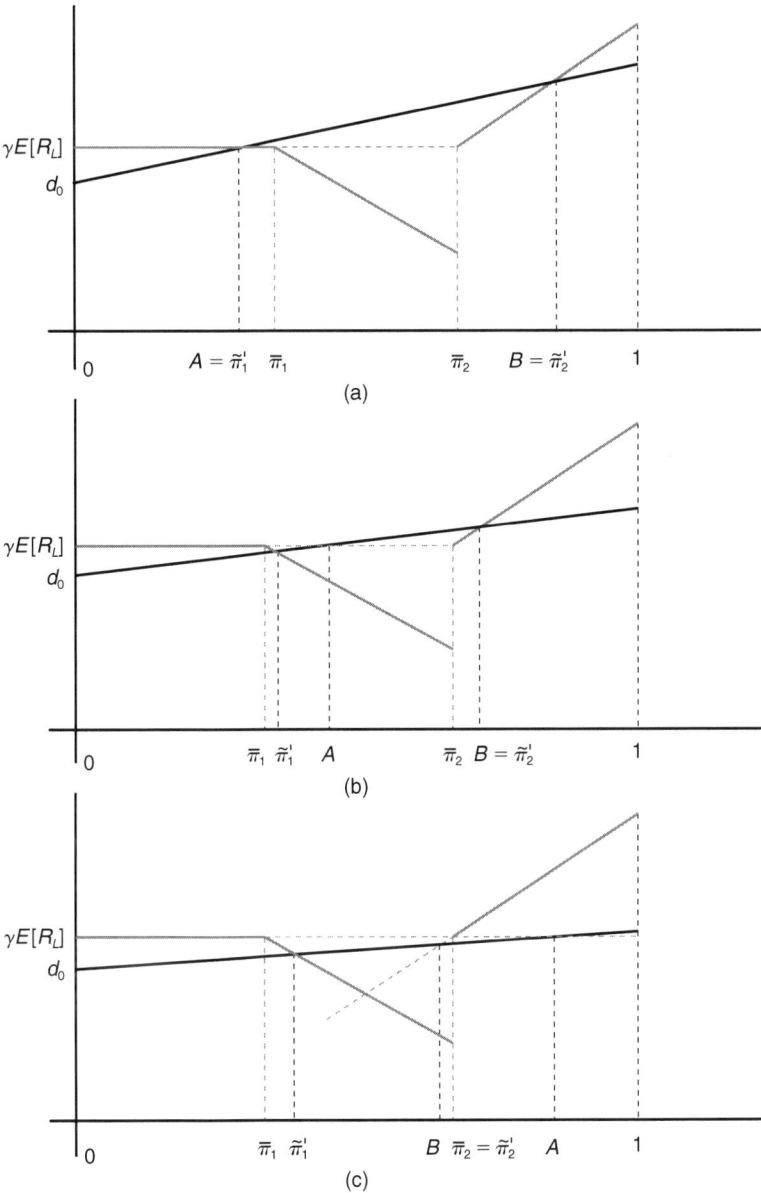

Figure 9.1 Investors' expected return in the market equilibrium (solid gray lines)/under equity requirements (solid black lines). In each of the three cases, the range where the equity regulation regime dominates the market equilibrium is denoted by the interval $(\bar{\pi}'_1, \bar{\pi}'_2)$.

can never dominate the market outcome uniformly. It is straightforward to compare the investors' payoff under equity requirements with the market equilibrium with free-riding for the extreme values $\pi=0$ and $\pi=1$.

When $\pi=0$,

$$\Pi_e(\pi) = d_0 + \frac{\Pi}{2} \cdot 0 = \alpha_H R_1 + (1-\alpha_H)p_L R_2 < \alpha_L R_1 + (1-\alpha_L)p_L R_2 = \gamma E[R_L].$$

When $\pi=1$,

$$\Pi_e(\pi) = d_0 + \frac{\Pi}{2} = \frac{\alpha_H R_1 + (1-\alpha_H)p_L R_2 + \alpha_H R_1 + (1-\alpha_H)p_H R_2}{2} <$$

$$\alpha_H R_1 + (1-\alpha_H)p_H R_2 = \gamma E[R_H.]$$

The intuition of such comparison is straightforward: since there is no uncertainty when $\pi=0$ or $\pi=1$, it is inferior to hold costly equities as explained above. Figure 9.1 suggests, however, that equity requirements might uniformly improve the investor's expected return for the range of parameter values resulting in the mixed-strategy equilibrium with free-riding banks. Unfortunately, Proposition 9.1 shows that this need not be the case. The equity regulation regime may even be sometimes dominated by the market equilibrium with free-riding, as summarized in Proposition 9.1.

Proposition 9.1 Imposing the equity requirement k^* may make investors better off than the mixed-strategy equilibrium with free-riding banks for some range of parameter values. But the costs of imposing equity requirements may be so high that the equity regulation regime may be dominated even by the market equilibrium with free-riding. There are three possible cases:

1   The equity regulation regime dominates the market equilibrium in the case of free-riding – that is, for $\bar{\pi}_1 \leq \pi \leq \bar{\pi}_2$.
2   In the range $\bar{\pi}_1 \leq \pi \leq \bar{\pi}_2$, the equity regulation regime dominates for high values of π, whereas the market equilibrium with free-riding dominates for low values. In addition, the equity regulation regime dominates the market equilibrium for the low values of π in the range $\bar{\pi}_2 \leq \pi \leq 1$.
3   In the range $\bar{\pi}_1 \leq \pi \leq \bar{\pi}_2$, the equity regulation regime dominates for high values of π, whereas the market equilibrium with free-riding dominates for low values. In addition, the equity regulation regime is uniformly dominated by the market equilibrium in the range $\bar{\pi}_2 \leq \pi \leq 1$.

Proof: see Appendix 9.5.1.

The three possible cases are characterized in Figures 9.1a, b, and c, respectively. Numerical examples illustrating these cases are presented in Figure 9.2a, b, and c. Proposition 9.1 says that the effectiveness of imposing equity requirements is

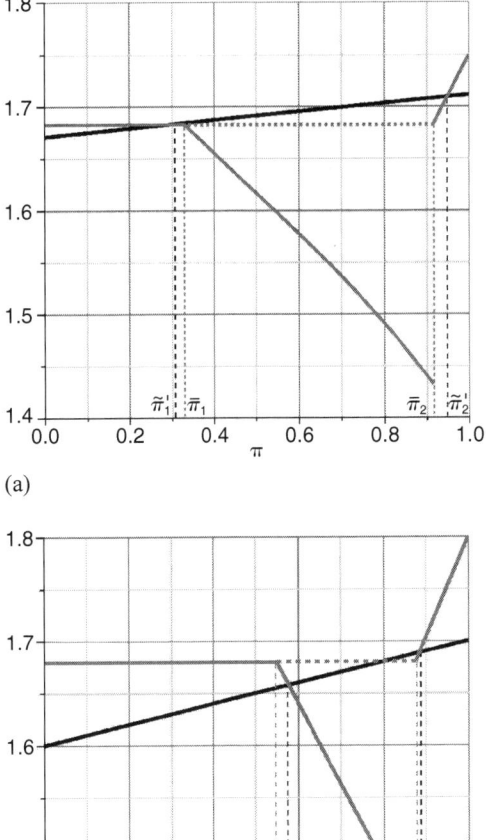

(a)

(b)

Figure 9.2 Investors' expected return in the market equilibrium (solid gray lines)/ under equity requirements (solid black lines).

Note

Parameter values: (a) $p_H=0.3$, $p_L=0.25$, $\gamma=0.6$, $R_1=1.8$, $R_2=5.5$, and $c=0.9$; (b) $p_H=0.4$, $p_L=0.3$, $\gamma=0.6$, $R_1=2$, $R_2=4$, and $c=0.8$; (c) $p_H=0.5$, $p_L=0.25$, $\gamma=0.7$, $R_1=1.8$, $R_2=2.5$, and $c=0$.

continued

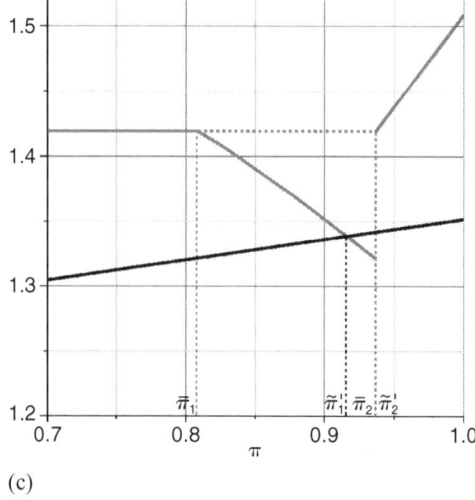

(c)

Figure 9.2 Continued

dubious. Equity requirements may give investors a higher payoff than the mixed-strategy equilibrium with free-riding banks for all parameter values with mixed-strategy equilibrium $\overline{\pi}_1 \leq \pi \leq \overline{\pi}_2$. This case is captured as case (A) in Figure 9.1a (as Proposition 9.1(1)). Since free-riding partly destroys the value of assets held by prudent banks (forcing them to hold a riskier portfolio), it might seem that imposing equity requirements will always dominate the market equilibrium outcome with mixed strategies. But according to Proposition 9.1, it is quite likely that equity requirements result in inferior payoffs for some range of parameter values (for example, when c is not very low and p_H is close to γ, i.e., the bank run cost is not very high), as shown in case (B) in Figure 9.1b (when $A \in (\overline{\pi}_1, \overline{\pi}_2)$, as Proposition 9.1(2), equity requirements result in inferior payoffs to mixed-strategy equilibrium for $(\overline{\pi}_1, \tilde{\pi}'_1)$, but superior to market equilibrium for some high values of $(\overline{\pi}_2, \tilde{\pi}'_2)$. It might be that imposing equity requirements makes investors even worse off, as in Figure 9.1c, representing case (C) (when $A > \overline{\pi}_2$), as Proposition 9.1(3), equity requirements result in inferior payoffs to mixed-strategy equilibrium for $(\overline{\pi}_1, \tilde{\pi}'_1)$ and inferior payoffs for all $\pi \in [\overline{\pi}_2, 1]$.

The intuition behind this result is that holding equity can be quite costly; if so, it may be superior to accept the fact that systemic risk is a price to be paid for higher returns on average.

9.2.2 Equity requirements versus conditional lender-of-last-resort policy

As just shown, there is no clear ranking between market equilibrium without regulation and a regime with equity requirements. In contrast, the mix of *ex ante* liquidity requirements with *ex post* lender-of-last-resort policy is always domi-nating equity requirements: see Figure 9.3. The reason is as follows: consider that the banks are required to hold $\alpha = \alpha_H$ when π is high. Then when p_H is revealed, the investors' real return is $\gamma E[R_H]$; and when p_L is revealed, the inves-tors' real return is $\alpha_H R_1 + (1 - \alpha_H)p_L R_2$. Therefore the investors' overall expected return turns out to be

$$\Pi_m = \gamma E[R_H]\pi + (1 - \pi)[\alpha_H R_1 + (1 - \alpha_H)p_L R_2],$$

which is linear in π, as the chain line of Figure 9.3 shows. Note that when $\pi = 1$,

$$\Pi_m = \gamma E[R_H] > d_0 + \frac{\Pi}{2};$$

and when $\pi = 0$, $\Pi_m = \alpha_H R_1 + (1 - \alpha_H)p_L R_2 = d_0$. Therefore, Π_m line is above

$$d_0 + \frac{\Pi}{2}\pi, \forall \pi \in (0, 1);$$

i.e., the mix of liquidity requirements with lender-of-last-resort policy is always dominating equity requirements when aggregate uncertainty exists.

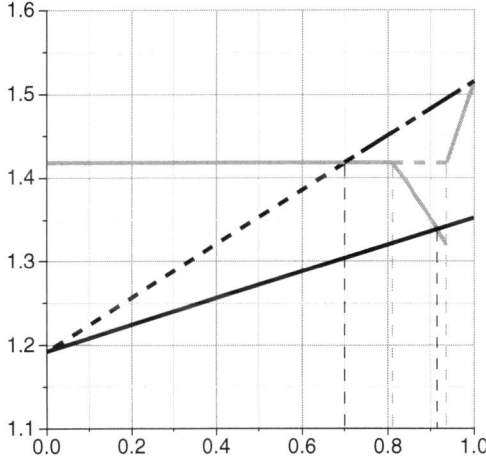

Figure 9.3 Real expected return with credible liquidity injections (black chain line), comparing to investors' expected return in the market equilibrium (solid gray lines)/under equity requirements (solid black lines).

Note
Parameter values are taken from Figure 9.2(c).

9.2.3 *Equity requirements and narrow banking*

In times of crises, frequently there are calls to go back to narrow banking in order to avoid the risk of runs. Under narrow banking, institutions with deposits would be required to hold as assets only the most liquid instruments so as to be always able to meet any deposit withdrawal by selling their assets. Obviously, narrow banking can be extremely costly. In our model, banks would be required to hold sufficient liquid funds to pay out in all contingencies: $\alpha \geq \alpha_l$. As Figure 9.4 illustrates, under narrow banking an investor's payoff (the solid gray line) can be much lower for high π compared with *ex ante* liquidity regulation combined with *ex post* lender-of-last-resort policy (the solid black line). Just as with equity requirements, narrow banking (imposing the requirement that banks hold sufficient equity so as to be able to pay out demand deposits in all states of the world) can be quite inferior: if the bad state is a rare probability event, it simply makes no sense to dispense with all the efficiency gains from investing in high-yielding illiquid assets despite its impact on systemic risk.

9.3 Equity requirement under insolvency uncertainty

As seen in Section 8.3, with the coexistence of both illiquidity and insolvency risks, the scheme of liquidity requirement with conditional bailout only works if an additional cost is introduced. Such cost can be either "external," for example, establishing safety funds via taxation as the past section suggested, or "internal," for example, covering the cost with equity holdings.

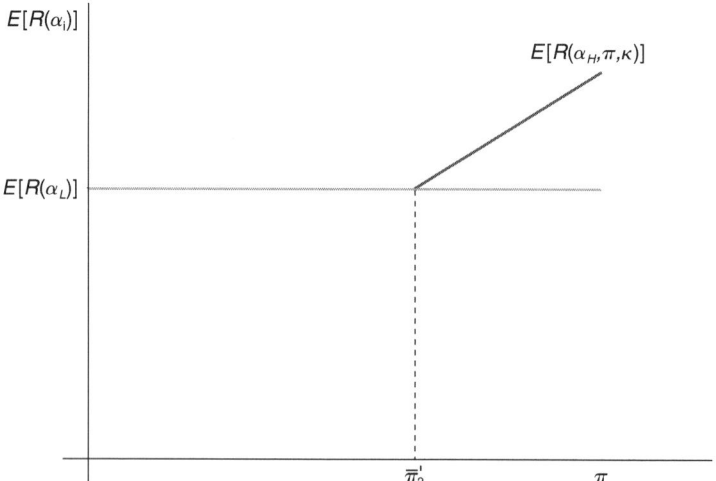

Figure 9.4 Real expected return with narrow banking compared with *ex ante* liquidity regulation.

9.3.1 Pure equity requirement

Now suppose an equity requirement is imposed to stabilize financial system in a way that all the losses will be absorbed by equity holders. Like Section 9.1, equity is introduced *à la* Diamond and Rajan (2005) such that the banks issue a mixture of deposit contract and equity for the investors. Assume that the equity holders (investors) and the bank managers equally share the profit, i.e., in the good time the level of equity k is defined as the ratio of a bank's capital to its assets

$$k = \frac{\dfrac{\gamma E[R_H] - d_{0,E}}{2}}{\dfrac{\gamma E[R_H] - d_{0,E}}{2} + d_{0,E}}, \text{ i.e. } d_{0,E} = \frac{1-k}{1+k} \gamma E[R_H],$$

in which $d_{0,E}$ denotes the investors' return from deposits under equity requirements.

The minimum equity requirement k should make the banks just able to survive without bank runs in the bad state, i.e., all the equity is wiped out when $(p \cdot \eta)_L$ is observed,

$$\frac{1-k}{1+k} \gamma E[R_H] = \underbrace{\alpha_H R_1 + (1-\alpha_H)(p \cdot \eta)_L R_2}_{\kappa} = d_{0,E}, \tag{9.2}$$

or

$$k = \frac{\gamma E[R_H] - d_{0,E}}{\gamma E[R_H] + d_{0,E}}.$$

Since

$$\frac{\partial k}{\partial (p \cdot \eta)_L} < 0$$

by equation (9.2), banks need higher equity ratio to survive in the bad state when both (or either) of the two plagues get(s) more severe, implying a higher regulatory cost.

Now the investors' real expected return is the sum of the deposit return and the dividend from equity holding

$$\frac{1-k}{1+k} \gamma E[R_H] \pi + (1-\pi)\kappa + \frac{\gamma E[R_H] - d_{0,E}}{2} \pi = \kappa + = \frac{\gamma E[R_H] - d_{0,E}}{2} \pi. \tag{9.3}$$

Figure 9.5 visualizes the results by numerical simulation. Again, as Section 9.1 shows, holding equity is costly when π is high (i.e., less funds are available for the relatively safe, high yields risky assets, although the costly bank runs are

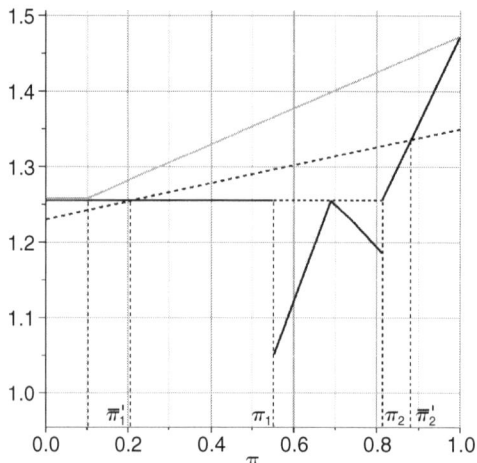

Figure 9.5 Investors' expected return in equilibrium: market economy (solid black line) versus economy with (1) equity requirement (black dash line) (2) conditional liquidity injection and procyclical taxation (solid gray line).

Note
Parameter values: $(p \cdot \eta)_H = 0.36$, $(p \cdot \eta)_L = 0.24$, $\gamma = 0.6$, $R_1 = 1.5$, $R_2 = 4$, $c = 0.3$, $\bar{\eta} = 0.8$, $\eta_H = 0.9$, $\eta_L = 0.6$, $\bar{p} = 0.4$, $p_H = 0.45$, $p_L = 0.3$, $\sigma = 0.5$, $\zeta = 0.5$. The outcome under equity requirement is superior to that of market economy for $\pi \in [\pi_1', \pi_2']$.

completely eliminated). Holding equity may be superior to the mixed strategy equilibrium depending on parameter values, but is inferior to conditional liquidity injection with procyclical taxation – because taxation revenue is entirely returned to investors as bailout funds, while in the current scheme part of the profits goes to bank managers as dividends. However, concerning the implementation difficulties of imposing an extra tax, this may be a necessary cost for both investors and regulators.

9.3.2 Combining equity requirement with liquidity regulation

Liquidity requirements with conditional liquidity injections work best with pure illiquidity risk, but the scheme fails when there's additional insolvency risk. On the other hand, pure equity requirements are able to stabilize the system under both settings at a relatively high cost. Now the question is: is it possible to design a regulatory scheme that combines the advantages of these two at a lower cost?

Consider the right hand side of equation (9.2). If the banks are required to maintain the financial stability in a self-sufficient way, in all contingencies the depositors can only receive the same expected return as in the bad state. However, since there's a positive probability that the risky assets are simply illiquid, the expected future return from the risky assets can be higher, i.e., the "fair" value of the risky assets is higher. Therefore, liquidity injection from the central bank may enable the banks to pledge for bailout funds up to the fair value of their late risky assets. And the banks only need equity to cover the gap left over by liquidity injection; it'll be much less costly for the banks to carry equity.

The proposed regulatory scheme is as follows. First, all the banks are required to invest $\underline{\alpha_E} = \alpha_H$ of their funds on safe assets at $t=0$ for high π, and $\underline{\alpha_E} = \alpha_L$ for low π (the cutoff value of π is different from $\bar{\pi}_2$, and we'll compute it later); second, all the banks are required to meet a minimum equity ratio k' for high π. The banks are bailed out by liquidity injection in the form of fiat money provision when the time is bad. In this case, the regulator only needs to set k' to fill in the gap after a liquidity injection when $(p \cdot \eta)_L$ is observed, i.e.,

$$\frac{1-k'}{1+k'}\gamma E[R_H] = \alpha_H \gamma R_1 + (1-\alpha_H)\gamma E[R_2 \mid (p \cdot \eta)_L] = \gamma E[R_{H|L}] = d'_{0,E}, \qquad (9.4)$$

in which $k' < k$ since the right hand side of (9.4) is higher than that of (9.2), and $\alpha_H R_1 + (1-\alpha_H)E[R_2|(p \cdot \eta)_L]$ is denoted by $E[R_{H|L}]$. The investors' deposit return is now $d'_{0,E}$. Then when $(p \cdot \eta)_H$ is observed, the investors' real expected return is

$$\frac{1-k'}{1+k'}\gamma E[R_H].$$

However, when $(p \cdot \eta)_L$ is observed, the investors' real expected return is κ (the right hand side of (9.2)) and the liquidity is injected for the banks to meet the nominal deposit contract. Therefore, the investors' real expected return is the sum of the deposit return and the dividend from equity holding

$$\frac{1-k'}{1+k'}\gamma E[R_H]\pi + (1-\pi)\kappa + \frac{\gamma E[R_H] - d'_{0,E}}{2}\pi = \qquad (9.5)$$

$$\pi\gamma E[R_{H|L}] + (1-\pi)\kappa + \frac{E[R_H] - E[R_{H|L}]}{2}\gamma\pi.$$

For sufficiently low π the banks are required to hold $\underline{\alpha_E} = \alpha_L$, and the investors' expected return is $\gamma E[R_L]$. It pays off for the banks to choose α_L instead of α_H only if they get higher expected real return than (9.5), i.e., when

$$\gamma E[R_L] > \pi\gamma E[R_{H|L}] + (1-\pi)\kappa + \frac{E[R_H] - E[R_{H|L}]}{2}\gamma\pi. \qquad (9.6)$$

The solution gives the cutoff value $\bar{\pi}_2''$, which can be solved from (9.6) when it holds with equality

$$\bar{\pi}_2'' = \frac{\gamma E[R_L] - \kappa}{\gamma\dfrac{E[R_H] + E[R_{H|L}]}{2} - \kappa}.$$

The effectiveness of the scheme is summarized in the following proposition:

Proposition 9.2 With liquidity regulation complemented by equity requirements, the bank runs are completely eliminated. The investors' expected real return is higher than that under pure equity requirements, but lower than that under liquidity regulation complemented by the procyclical banking tax.

Proof: see Appendix 9.5.2.

Figure 9.6 visualizes the results by numerical simulation. Such hybrid scheme indeed effectively reduces regulatory costs in comparison to pure equity requirement, since the banks do not have to hold that much equity to stabilize the system, i.e., regulator needs two instruments to deal with two troubles.

Figure 9.6 compares the investors' returns under all schemes. Again, the outcome under conditional liquidity injection with procyclical taxation is superior to all the others, since all the profits that are levied as the safety tax will be entirely returned to the investors. However, when the political cost is too high to impose an extra tax and raise public deficit, combining the advantages of liquidity regulation and equity requirement is the best self-sufficient scheme.

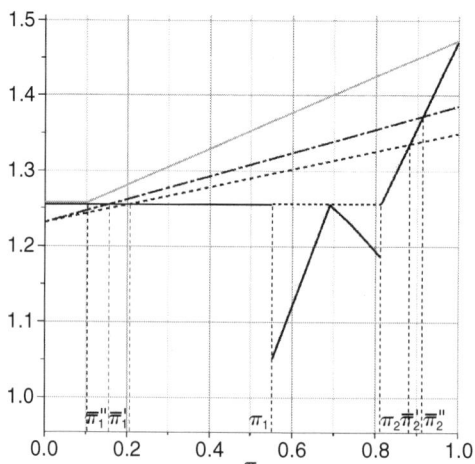

Figure 9.6 Investors' expected return in equilibrium: market economy (solid black line) versus economy with (1) conditional liquidity injection & procyclical taxation (solid grey line) (2) pure equity requirement (black dash line) (3) equity requirement & liquidity regulation (black chain line).

Note
Parameter values: $(p \cdot \eta)_H = 0.36$, $(p \cdot \eta)_L = 0.24$, $\gamma = 0.6$, $R_1 = 1.5$, $R_2 = 4$, $c = 0.3$, $\bar{\eta} = 0.8$, $\eta_H = 0.9$, $\eta_L = 0.6$, $\bar{p} = 0.4$, $p_H = 0.45$, $p_L = 0.3$, $\sigma = 0.5$, $\zeta = 0.5$. The outcome under equity requirement is superior to that of market economy for $\pi \in [\bar{\pi}'_1, \bar{\pi}'_2]$.

9.4 Is CoCo that sweet?

During the market stress, it is extremely difficult for a troubled bank to raise new capital; therefore, the bank in such situation usually ends up with asset fire sales and the following plummeting asset price sometimes leaves the entire financial system under threat. Because of this, the contingent convertible debt, or CoCo, enabling raising new capital in no time, is proposed as a promising regulatory tool. In the orderly time, such convertible debt is just the normal debt. But in some predefined contingencies, the debt can be converted into common stocks. For example, in the crisis when a bank's capital ratio falls below some predetermined value, the convertible debts in the bank's balance sheet are automatically converted into equity, and the bank gets immediately recapitalized. Instead of being bailed out by the taxpayers' money, the bank bails out itself by its own assets and avoids the stress from spilling over to the other financial institutions. The advantage of such "bail-in" mechanism, as claimed by *The Economist*, January 28, 2010, is

> A "bail-in" process for bank resolution is a potentially powerful "third option" that confronts this problem head-on. It would give officials the authority to force banks to recapitalize from within, using private capital, not public money. The concept builds on time-tested procedures that have been used to keep airlines flying and industrial firms going even as their capital structures were being reorganized. It accelerates those procedures to address the unique circumstances of financial firms operating in today's fast-moving markets. If done correctly it should strengthen market discipline on banks and reduce the potential for systemic risk.

Therefore, it is widely suggested (for example, Flannery, 2009; Turner *et al.*, 2010, pp. 181) that holding a certain fraction of CoCo in the banks' balance sheets should be made obligatory in the new banking regulation framework. As claimed by some optimists, "if a contingent-capital proposal is adopted, this could be the last major worldwide banking crisis – at least until some new source of instability emerges and sends financial technicians back to work to invent our way of it" (Robert Shiller, *Engineering Financial Stability*, January 18, 2010). However, there are still many designing issues to be worked out, since the details of the rule as well as its impact on the financial institutions' behavior are not yet fully clear. In the following, we briefly sketch the role of convertible debts in stabilizing the financial system, and raise several incentive problems on having CoCo in banking regulation.

9.4.1 Recapitalization through debt conversion

The design of convertible debt as a regulatory tool is pioneered by Flannery (2002) and Raviv (2004). As summarized in Flannery (2002), convertible debts have the following appealing features:

1   they are automatically converted into common equity if some trigger crite-
    rion is met – this usually means that the debt issuer's capital ratio falls
    below a predefined critical value, and "automatically" means that the debt
    contract doesn't contain any options for debt holders;
2   as long as the conversion doesn't happen, they have all the features of plain
    debts, i.e., the debt holders get tax deductible interest payments;
3   they are subordinated to all the plain debt obligations;
4   the critical value of the capital ratio is measured by the outstanding equity's
    market value, and the conversion price is the current share price.

The following example, based on Flannery (2002), shows how such convertible
debts work. Suppose that, as Table 9.1, one bank's investments on $100 securi-
ties are backed by $80 from debts, $10 from convertibles, and $10 from common
equity. There are ten outstanding shares, therefore, the share price is $1. The
adequate capital ratio defined by the banking regulation is 10 percent; the conversion thus automatically happens once the bank's capital ration falls below 10
percent.

Suppose that the asset prices falls, making the bank's security holding worth
only $97. Then the value of equity falls to $7, as Table 9.2 shows, and the share
price becomes $0.7. The bank's capital ratio is now below the adequacy require-
ment since

$$\frac{\$7}{\$97} \approx 7.22\% < 10\%,$$

triggering the conversion of the debts.

The convertibles are converted to common equity until the adequacy requirement is met again. This implies that $97 \times 10\% - \$7 = \$2.7$ has been raised. Since

Table 9.1 The balance sheet of an imaginary bank

Assets	Liabilities
$100 securities	$80 debts
	$10 convertibles
	$10 equity

Table 9.2 The balance sheet after asset price shock

Assets	Liabilities
$97 securities	$80 debts
	$10 convertibles
	$7 equity

the conversion price is the current share price, this means that the convertibles worth $2.7 have been converted to

$$\frac{\$2.7}{\$0.7} \approx 3.86$$

new outstanding shares for the convertible debt holders. Table 9.3 provides the summary.

Comparing with a bank without convertible debt financing, one can see how introducing the notion of convertible debt helps increase the resilience of banks in times of economic downturn. For the bank in reference, the investment on securities worth $100 is financed by $90 from debts and $10 from equity, as in Table 9.4.

Once there is a negative shock on the value of the bank's assets, the reference bank has to mop off its equity value and the capital ratio is regarded as inadequate as long as the bank doesn't issue new equity. Without issuing new equity, as the gray line in Figure 9.7 shows, the capital ratio gets lower when the shock becomes larger, and the bank is insolvent once the value of assets falls below $90.

In contrast, the negative shock triggers debt conversion for the bank holding convertible debts, and the capital ratio can remain adequate without the need to issue new equity unless all the convertibles have been converted, as the black line in Figure 9.7 shows. The bank's capital ratio is adequate as long as the value of assets is above $88.88. Without issuing new equity, the bank has to shed off the value of equity when the value of assets goes below $88.88, but it still remains solvent whenever the value of assets is above $80. As a contrast to the reference bank, the holding of convertible debts allows the bank to stay adequately capitalized when the value of risky assets falls between $100 and $88.88, and to stay solvent when the value of risky assets falls between $90 and $80.

Table 9.3 Recapitalization through debt conversion

Assets	Liabilities
$97 securities	$80 debts $7.3 convertibles $9.7 equity

Table 9.4 The balance sheet without convertible debts

Assets	Liabilities
$100 securities	$90 debts $10 equity

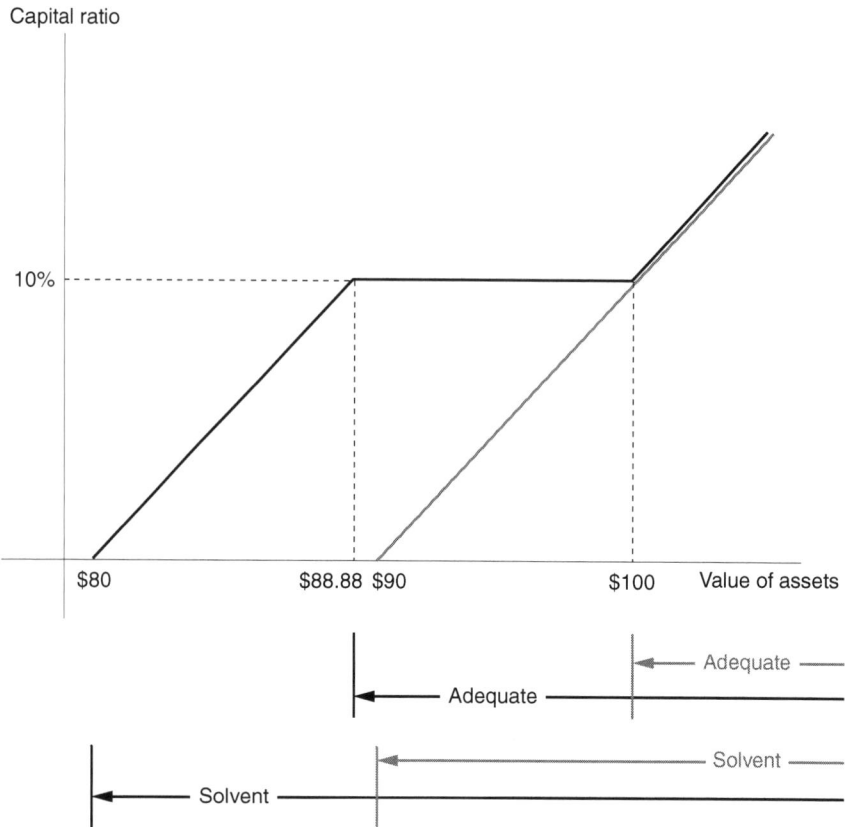

Figure 9.7 The bank recapitalization through convertible debts.

To better understand how the convertible debts provide additional protection for the banks against shocks, Figure 9.8 depicts the value dynamics of the convertible debts. The black line tracks how much the debts are converted along with varying asset value: the conversion starts when asset value falls below $100 and ends up when the debts are completely converted. The gray line shows the value of the convertibles: although the conversion starts once the asset value falls below $100, the holders of convertibles will still get fully repaid with a mixture of cash and shares because the conversion price is the current share price. The payment to the convertibles shrinks at a time the asset value falls below $90, when the old share holders are gone and part of the converted starts to be wiped out, too.

Another interesting feature is the dynamic of the initial equity holders' payoff. As Figure 9.9 shows, when the value of risky assets falls below $100, for both the bank with convertible debts and the reference bank, the initial equity holders' share value has to decline to the same extent as the incurred loss. The

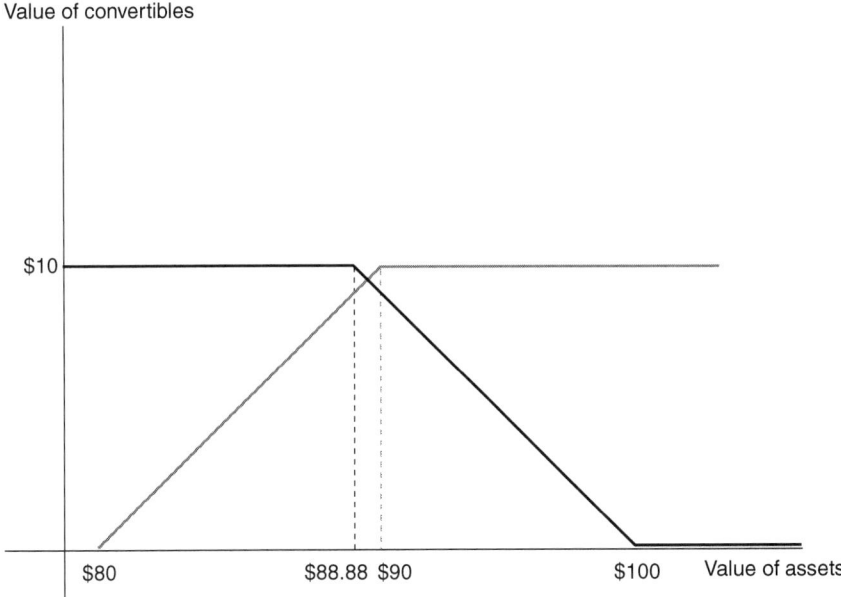

Figure 9.8 The value dynamics of the convertible debts.

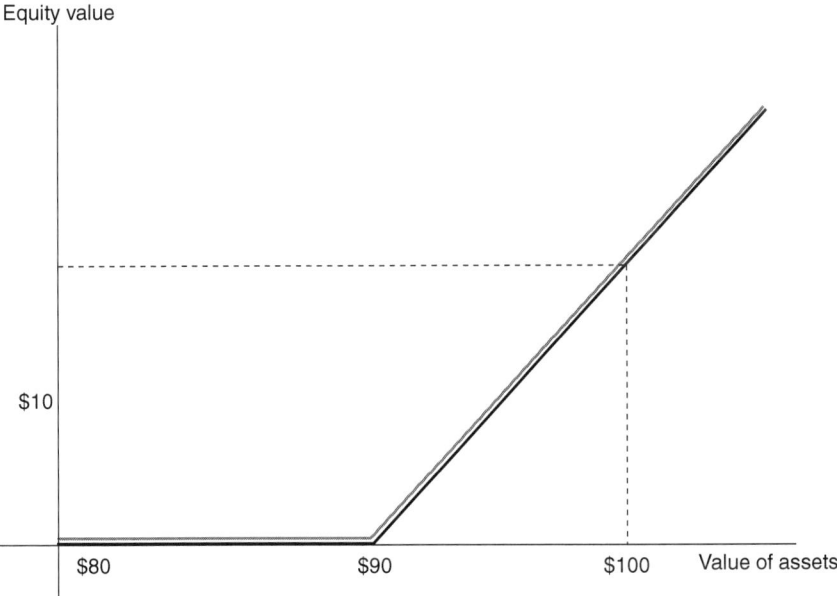

Figure 9.9 The payoff to the initial equity holders.

only difference is the bank in our model can convert its debts into common equity and restore its capital ratio, but this does not make any difference in the initial equity holders' payoff. Therefore, the dynamic of the initial equity holders' payoffs for both banks (the solid black line for the bank with convertible debts in Figure 9.9, and the gray line for the reference bank) coincide. Such features imply that introducing convertible debts at least does not add extra incentive problems for the initial shareholders. If in the reference bank there are incentive problems coming from the initial shareholders' payoff structure, such as debt overhang problem, adding convertible debts to the bank's balance sheet does not make the problems worse.

So far the convertible debts seem to have many appealing features as a candidate for banking regulation. However, the regulator should understand how the banks are likely to respond to the rule to make sure that the regulation indeed provides the right incentive and is incentive compatible. As of the time when this chapter is written, there is rarely any research on this issue, to my best knowledge.

One of the potential problems is that the convertible debts may increase the banks' risk taking, hence raise the systemic risk, if there is no further complementary rule to deter such incentive. By making the debts convertible, the payoff of the debts is actually made contingent and the bank failure is fully eliminated if such CoCo buffer is large enough. However, as demonstrated in Section 1.3, the potential bank failure is also a credible tool to discipline the banks' behavior. The banks thus take more risks if the discipline is assumed away by regulation.

9.4.2 A banking model with CoCo financing

Such incentive problem can be seen in the following model, extending the banking framework in Section 3.1. The settings are quite similar as those in Section 3.1, except that the banks are now financed by the convertible debts and there is no intermediate date $t=0.5$.

Model setup

Here we briefly summarize the setups:

1 The economy lives for three periods, $t=0, 1, 2$. There are three groups of risk-neutral agents: a continuum of investors who want to consume at $t=1$ after they invest their endowment at $t=0$, a continuum of entrepreneurs with either safe or risky projects, a limited number of banks as intermediaries between investors, and entrepreneurs competing in the deposit market *à la* Bertrand. Both entrepreneurs and banks do not have preferences on the timing of consumption.

2 Each entrepreneur owns either a safe or a risky project, which is financed at $t=0$ by the borrowing from the banks. The safe project returns $R_1 > 1$ at at

$t=1$ with certainty, while the risky project returns $R_2 > R_1$ either at $t=1$ with probability p or is delayed to $t=2$ with probability $1-p$. Two values can be taken by p: p_H with probability π, or $p_L < p_H$ with probability $1-\pi$. At $t=0$, p is unknown to all, but becomes public information when it gets revealed at $t=1$.

3 The banks have the expertise to collect a share γ from the entrepreneurs' return and get the investors repaid. This justifies the banks' role as intermediaries. The deposit contracts between banks and investors are convertible: when a bank is not able to fulfill its promise in the deposit contract, part of the debt is converted to equity and erased from the bank's balance sheet to cover the loss.

The potential liquidity problem again comes from the fact that investors are impatient such that they want to consume early. In contrast, both entrepreneurs and bank managers are indifferent between consuming early or late. Such mismatch of time preferences leads to the typical funding structure as observed in the financial market in which long-term but high yield projects are financed by the short-term funding.

In contrast to the banking system purely financed by the demand deposit contract such as that in Section 3.1, the costly bank run is assumed away here by the contract of convertible debts – the banks' losses will be completely absorbed by converting the debts to common equity. Although a banking system fully financed by convertible debt contracts sounds unrealistic, any other alternative setting assuming that the banks' holding of convertible debts is large enough to stabilize the economy, is sufficient to eliminate the bank runs. Therefore, our assumption that the banks are financed by pure convertible debts is a reasonable abstract.

The timing of the model is summarized in Table 9.5.

1 At date $t=0$, banks competing for investors offer deposit contracts with payment d_0 for $t=1$, which maximize expected return of investors. Banks compete with each other by choosing the share of deposits invested in the safe projects, α, taking their competitors' choice as given. Investors have

Table 9.5 Timing of the model

$t=0$	$t=1$ *p gets revealed*	$t=2$
Investors Contract with banks	Withdraw	
Banks Offer convertible debt contract d_0 Choose liquid asset holding level α	Get returns from short assets Get deposits from early entrepreneurs Debt conversion if needed Repay early investors	Get returns from long assets Repay the early entrepreneurs

rational expectations about each bank's probability of converting the debts; they are able to monitor all banks' investments. Remember that, at this stage, the share p of risky projects that will be realized early is not yet known.

2   At date $t=1$, the value of p is revealed, so is the expected return of the banks at $t=1$. Since the bank runs are eliminated by assumption, in contrast to the model of Section 3.1, it is no longer necessary to include the intermediate date: a bank will convert part of its debt to equity if it cannot meet the promised d_0. In order to maximize expected return of investors, banks can trade with early entrepreneurs in a perfectly competitive market for liquidity at $t=1$, clearing at interest rate r. Note that entrepreneurs retain a rent $(1-\gamma)R_i$, $i=1, 2$. Since early entrepreneurs are indifferent between consuming at $t=1$ or $t=2$, they are willing to provide liquidity (using their rent to deposit at banks at $t=1$ at the market rate $r\geq1$). Banks use the liquidity provided to pay out investors. In this way, impatient investors can profit indirectly from the investment in high yielding long-term projects. So banking allows the transformation between liquid claims and illiquid projects.

3   At date $t=2$, the banks collect the return from the late projects and pay back the early entrepreneurs at the predetermined interest rate r.

The market equilibrium

Let us now characterize the market equilibrium with banks as financial intermediaries. Note that the aggregate liquidity available at date $t=1$ depends on the total share of funds, α, invested in liquid safe projects at date $t=0$. The bank's problem is simply to choose an optimal α that minimizes its funding cost at $t=1$, hence maximizes the expected return.

If there is no aggregate uncertainty, i.e., if the value of p is already known at $t=0$, the market equilibrium coincides with that in Section 3.3.1. The reason is simple: if there is neither boom nor bust, the bank will simply choose the optimal strategy and return all the intermediate yields to the investors. The way of funding is irrelevant. Therefore, the market outcome is the same as Proposition 3.2, Section 3.3.1:

Proposition 9.3 If there is no aggregate uncertainty, the allocation in the market equilibrium is characterized by

1   all the banks set

$$\alpha = \frac{\gamma - p}{\gamma - p + (1-\gamma)\dfrac{R_1}{R_2}};$$

2   the market interest rate at $t=1$ is $r=1$.

If the value of p is unknown at $t=0$ and revealed at either p_H or p_L, by the Law of Large Numbers, the share of risky projects returning early becomes either p_H or p_L for all the banks, i.e., such shock from p leads to aggregate uncertainty. The market equilibrium can be characterized by the following proposition:

Proposition 9.4 When there is aggregate uncertainty

1 There is a symmetric pure strategy equilibrium such that all banks set $\alpha=\alpha_H$ for all $\bar{\pi}_2 \leq \pi \leq 1$ with

$$\bar{\pi}_2 = \frac{\gamma E[R_L] - \kappa}{\gamma E[R_H] - \kappa},$$

$E[R_s] = \alpha_s R_1 + (1-\alpha_s)R_2$, $s \in \{H, L\}$, $\kappa = \alpha_H R_1 + (1-\alpha_H)p_L R_2$, and

$$\alpha_s = \frac{\gamma - p_s}{\gamma - p_s + (1-\gamma)\dfrac{R_1}{R_2}}.$$

2 There is a symmetric pure strategy equilibrium such that all banks set $\alpha=\alpha_L$ for all $0 \leq \pi < \bar{\pi}_1$ with

$$\bar{\pi}_1 = \frac{\gamma E[R_L] - \kappa}{\gamma R_2 - \kappa}.$$

3 there exists no symmetric pure strategy equilibrium for all $\bar{\pi}_1 \leq \pi \leq \bar{\pi}_2$. However, there exists a unique equilibrium in mixed strategies such that

   a at $t=0$, with probability θ a bank chooses to be a free-riding bank which sets $\alpha=0$ and with probability $1-\theta$ a bank chooses to be a prudent bank who sets $0 < \alpha_s^* < \alpha_L$;
   b in the mixed strategy equilibrium, investors are worse off than if all banks would coordinate on the prudent (non-equilibrium) strategy α_L.

The proposition suggests that the banks' maximizing investors' expected return coordinate on riskier strategy (since $\alpha_H < \alpha_L$) when the probability of the good state π is high. If the bad state is revealed, part of the debt will be converted to equity and get erased to cover the loss. But when π is very low, the banks coordinate on the safe strategy by choosing α_L instead. This makes the banks able to meet the deposit contract in both states without debt–equity conversion. In addition, the excess liquidity supply in the good state makes free-riding attractive for the intermediate value of π. In the prevailing mixed strategy equilibrium, the banks are endogenously separated into two groups:

1 prudent banks holding liquid assets between $t=0$ and $t=1$, and meet the deposit contracts in both states without converting the debt;

2　free-riding banks holding no liquid assets between $t=0$ and $t=1$ free-ride on the cheap liquidity in the good state. The investors get higher return in the good state, but have to suffer from a loss from debt conversion in the bad state.

In terms of social welfare, the gain and loss from introducing convertible debts can be inferred that

1　The convertible debt contract in this model implies that the contracts are implicitly renegotiatable and the payoffs are made state contingent. By agreeing to convert the debt to equity, the investors actually give up bank runs as a commitment device. In the range of high πs, the elimination of costly bank runs replicates the constrained efficient solution.

2　However, without the discipline from bank runs, the free-riding problem that plagued the market equilibrium gets aggravated in the current setup. By eliminating bank runs using debt–equity conversion, the banks' loss gets lowered in the downturn, which makes free-riding even more attractive in the good time.

Figure 9.10 compares the investors' expected return with the market outcome under pure demand deposit contract (depicted in the gray line) which has been studied in Section 3.3.2. The investors' expected return is now improved because the convertible debt contract eliminated the costly bank runs and replicates the constraint efficient solution. However, without the high bankruptcy cost caused by the bank runs, the banks have higher incentive for free-riding in the good state. Therefore, the investors get even worse off in the mixed strategy equilibrium under intermediate πs.

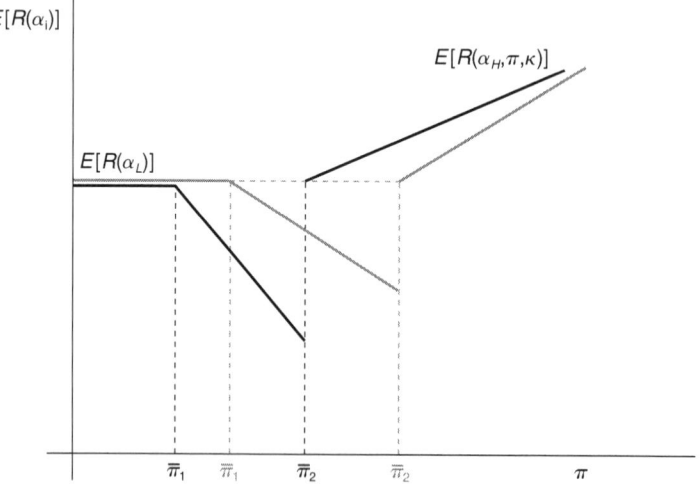

Figure 9.10 Investors' expected return with/without convertible debts.

Comparing the investors' expected return under various regulatory rules, it can be seen that even in this simplest setting, convertible debt financing is not strictly superior to deposit financing with minimum capital requirements, as depicted in Figure 9.11 where the gray line shows the outcome under pure minimum capital requirements as studied in Section 9.2.1. The appealing feature seems to be the fact that by immediate conversion, convertible debt eliminates the costly bank runs and achieves constrained efficiency under high πs. However, this comes from the typical setting in banking models that holding equity is costly in the sense that the bank managers pocket some rents for themselves. But it is also shown in Cao and Illing (2010) that by redesigning the bank managers' compensation structure, one can reduce this cost and replicate the first best allocation, too.

9.4.3 Some pitfalls

Although in this simple model Bertrand competition in the deposit market still ensures that the banks return all the yields to the investors, in the downturn the cost of the banks' risk taking is completely shouldered by the investors through debt conversion, making the free-riding problem even worse. One may still argue, that although systemic risks are reduced because any loss can be easily covered without triggering costly liquidation, this doesn't give convertible debt an advantage over pure equity financing – under which costly liquidation is eliminated as well – not to mention the other by-products convertible capital may bring out in more complicated settings.

The advantage of convertible debts in stabilizing financial market, is that it provides an immediate airbag to avoid the financial crash while still offers all the appealing features of debt financing (such as monitoring the banks' behavior, tax advantage) in the normal times, has been fairly well understood. However, there

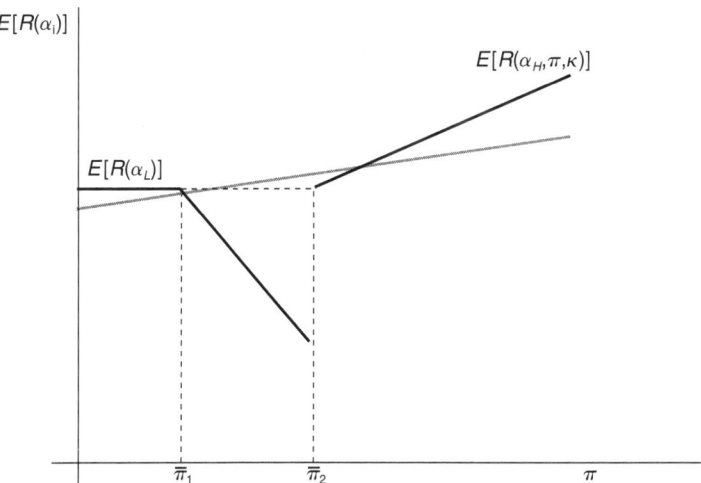

Figure 9.11 Investors' expected return under convertible debts/pure equity requirements.

is still a long way to go before it is finally adopted as a regulatory tool. Much research needs to be done to fully understand its impact on the market participants' incentives, and the details of the regulatory rules implementing the convertible debt instrument.

For example, it is unclear why convertible debt is superior to the other existing regulatory tools that are used to offer the similar buffer, such as pure capital requirement which is much easier to be defined and implemented (and is obviously much simpler and better understood). Just as our simple model shows, via equity conversion the costly bank run can be fully eliminated and this improves social welfare. However, without the cost of bank runs, the banks are encouraged to take more risks and increase their investment on illiquid assets, which aggravated the liquidity shortages in the downturn. In the other words, since the investors are converted to equity holders and get wiped out, the banks intrinsically get rid of the discipline from bank runs.

One may argue that in this simple model – although 100 percent convertible debt financing is an unrealistic assumption – it is still appealing to hold convertible debts instead of pure equity when π is high since holding pure equity is costly. It is true that in our model the investors are worse off with pure equity requirement since the bank managers are designed to capture some private rent. However, such cost goes away when the bank managers' share in the dividend becomes zero. In Admati *et al.* (2010), the authors examined various arguments on the cost of equity holding and claimed that none of them are convincing. The most likely (opportunity) cost associated with pure equity holding is the tax disadvantage, comparing with debt financing. However, the policy makers should fix the distortion coming from the institutions, instead of taking it as an argument against raising capital requirements.

There are more incentive problems associated with convertible debts. The regulators need to define explicitly the types of eligible convertible bonds that can be taken into regulatory requirements, and probably even the rules regarding the eligible bond holders and the market for such convertibles, just to eliminate the potential regulatory arbitrage that attempts to undo the regulation. The big banks may strategically get more interconnected by cross holding each other's convertible debts, which makes it harder for the regulator to start the conversion – for fear of contagion – and forces the regulator to bail them out altogether instead: a typical "too-big-to-fail" or "too-interconnected-to-fail" problem.

Another potential problem associated with convertible debts is the "death spiral" problem. The holder of convertible debts can short sell the debt issuer's common stock, lowering its stock price until the conversion is triggered. Since the debts are converted at current price, the short seller can cover its position by the converted stocks. At the same time, the steady falling price induces the shareholders to sell, making the price falling even further like a vicious cycle. Therefore it is suggested (for example, French *et al.*, 2010, p. 91) that the conversion is only allowed under the "systemic event" which is announced by the regulator. The conversion is forbidden when the shock is only idiosyncratic.

However, a systemic event can be triggered by some idiosyncratic shock, especially the shock on a systemically important financial institution. It would be too late to create the buffer via starting the conversion in the failing financial institution when the initial shock has rippled into a systemic tsunami. But again, if the equity conversion has been opened for idiosyncratic shocks on a systemically important institution, the potential of speculative attack raises the systemic risk.

9.5 Appendix

9.5.1 Proof of Proposition 9.1

The investors' expected return with equity requirements

$$\Pi_e(\pi) = d_0 + \frac{\Pi}{2}\pi$$

is a linear increasing function of π, starting from $d_0 < \gamma E[R_L]$ when $\pi = 0$ and ending with

$$d_0 + \frac{\Pi}{2} < \gamma E[R_H]$$

when $\pi = 1$. Whether imposing equity requirements improves investors' expected return (such "improved" region is denoted by the interval $(\tilde{\pi}_1', \tilde{\pi}_2')$ in Figure 9.1) depends on the intersection between

$$d_0 + \frac{\Pi}{2}\pi$$

and $\gamma E[R_L]$, denoted by A as in Figure 9.1. Generically, there are three cases concerning the relative positions of $\Pi(\pi)$ and $\Pi_e(\pi)$:

1 As Figure 9.1a shows, when $A \in (0, \bar{\pi}_1]$, $\Pi_e(\pi)$ is higher than $\Pi(\pi)$ for $\pi \in [\bar{\pi}_1, \bar{\pi}_2]$.
2 As Figure 9.1b shows, when $A \in (\bar{\pi}_1, \bar{\pi}_2)$, $\Pi_e(\pi)$ is only higher than $\Pi(\pi)$ for part of $\pi \in [\bar{\pi}_1, \bar{\pi}_2]$. In addition, $\Pi_e(\pi)$ is higher for part of $\pi \in (\bar{\pi}_2, 1]$.
3 As Figure 9.1c shows, when $A \geq \bar{\pi}_2$, $\Pi_e(\pi)$ is only higher than $\Pi(\pi)$ for part of $\pi \in [\bar{\pi}_1, \bar{\pi}_2]$. In addition, $\Pi_e(\pi)$ is no higher for all $\pi \in (\bar{\pi}_2, 1]$.

To be more precise, note there are two intersections which separate these three generic cases. One is the intersection between

$$\Pi_e(\pi) = d_0 + \frac{\Pi}{2}\pi$$

and $\gamma E[R_L]$, denoted by A in Figure 9.1 which is equal to

$$A = \frac{2(R_1 - p_L R_2)}{(1-\gamma)R_1 + (\gamma - p_L)R_2}.$$

The other is intersection between

$$\Pi_e(\pi) = d_0 + \frac{\Pi}{2}\pi$$

and $\gamma E[R_H]\pi + (1-\pi)c$, denoted by B in Figure 9.1 which is equal to

$$B = \frac{2[(1-\gamma)(cR_1 - p_L R_1 R_2) + (\gamma - p_H)(cR_2 - R_1 R_2)]}{2(1-\gamma)cR_1 + 2(\gamma - p_H)cR_2 + [\gamma(p_H - 1) - (\gamma - p_H) - (1-\gamma)p_L]R_1 R_2}.$$

Those three cases quantitatively correspond to

1    $A \in (0, \bar{\pi}_1]$, or $(2\gamma R_2 - \gamma E[R_H] - d_0)(\gamma E[R_L] - d_0) + (2\gamma E[R_L] - \gamma E[R_H] - d_0)(d_0 - c) \leq 0$, then $(A, B) = (\bar{\pi}_1', \bar{\pi}_2')$ is where the equity regulation regime dominates the market equilibrium.
2    $A \in [\bar{\pi}_1, \bar{\pi}_2]$ or $(2\gamma R_2 - \gamma E[R_H] - d_0)(\gamma E[R_L] - d_0) + (2\gamma E[R_L] - \gamma E[R_H] - d_0)(d_0 - c) > 0$ and $\gamma E[R_H] - E[R_L])(d_0 - c) \geq (\gamma E[R_H] - c)(\gamma E[R_L] - d_0)$, then $\Pi_e(\pi)$ intersects the market equilibrium in the range for mixed strategy equilibrium $(\bar{\pi}_1, \bar{\pi}_2)$, call the intersection $\tilde{\pi}$. $(\tilde{\pi}, B)$ is where the equity regulation regime dominates the market equilibrium.
3    $A \in (\bar{\pi}_2, 1]$, or $2(\gamma E[R_L] - d_0)(\gamma E[R_H] - c) \geq (\gamma E[R_H] - d_0)(\gamma E[R_L] - c)$, or, then $(\tilde{\pi}, \bar{\pi}_2)$ is where the equity regulation regime dominates the market equilibrium.

9.5.2 Proof of Proposition 9.2

Equation (9.4) implies that the investors get the same nominal deposits returns in both states, therefore, there will be no bank runs. The investors' expected real return

$$\pi\gamma = \frac{E[R_H] + E[R_{H|L}]}{2} + (1-\pi)\kappa,$$

linear in π, becomes κ when $\pi = 0$ and

$$\gamma \frac{E[R_H] + E[R_{H|L}]}{2}$$

when $\pi = 1$. Since

$$\gamma \frac{E[R_H] + E[R_{H|L}]}{2} < \gamma E[R_H],$$

such real return is below $E[R(\alpha_H)]$ for all $\pi \in (0, 1]$.

Compare the investors' expected real return here with that under pure equity requirements, as in equation (9.3). It is easily seen that equation (9.3) becomes κ when $\pi = 0$ and

$$\frac{\gamma E[R_H] + \kappa}{2}$$

when $\pi = 1$. Since $\kappa < \gamma E[R_{H|L}]$, the investors' expected real return under pure equity requirements is lower for all $\pi \in (0, 1]$.

References

Acharya, V. V. (2009) "A theory of systemic risk and design of prudential bank regulation," *Journal of Financial Stability*, 5: 224–55.

Acharya, V. V. and M. Richardson (eds.) (2009) *Restoring Financial Stability: How to Repair a Failed System*, New York: John Wiley & Sons.

Acharya, V. V. and T. Yorulmazer (2008) "Cash-in-the-market pricing and optimal resolution of bank failures," *Review of Financial Studies*, 21: 2705–42.

Acharya, V. V., T. F. Cooley, M. P. Richardson and I. Walter (2010) *Regulating Wall Street: The Dodd-Frank Act and the New Architecture of Global Finance*, New York: John Wiley & Sons.

Acharya, V. V., L. H. Pedersen, T. Philippon, and M. Richardson (2010) "Measuring systemic risk." Unpublished working paper.

Acharya, V. V., S. van Nieuwerburgh, M. Richardson and L. White (2011) *Guaranteed to Fail: Fannie Mae, Freddie Mac and the Debacle of Mortgage Finance*, Princeton, NJ: Princeton University Press.

Admati, A. R., P. M. DeMarzo, M. F. Hellwig, and P. Pfleiderer (2010) "Fallacies, irrelevant facts, and myths in the discussion of capital regulation: Why bank equity is not expensive," *Stanford GSB Research Paper* No. 2063.

Adrian, T. and M. K. Brunnermeier (2010) "CoVar." Unpublished working paper.

Adrian, T. and H. Shin (2009) "Money, liquidity and monetary policy," *American Economic Review*, 99: 600–5.

Adrian, T. and H. Shin (2010) "Liquidity and leverage," *Journal of Financial Intermediation*, 19: 418–37.

Adrian, T. and H. Shin (2011) "Procyclical leverage and value-at-risk," *Federal Reserve Bank of New York Staff Reports* No. 338.

Agion, P. and A. Benerjee (2005) *Volatility and Growth*, Clarendon Lectures, New York: Oxford University Press.

Akerlof, G. A. and R. J. Shiller (2009) *Animal Spirits: How Human Psychology Drives the Economy, and Why It Matters for Global Capitalism*, Princeton, NJ: Princeton University Press.

Albertazzi, U., G. Eramo, L. Gambacorta, and C. Salleo (2011) "Securitization is not that evil after all," *Bank of International Settlements Working Papers* No. 341.

Alessandri, P., P. Gai, S. Kapadia, N. Mora, and C. Puhr (2009) "Towards a framework for quantifying systemic stability," *International Journal of Central Banking*, 5: 47–81.

Allen, F. and E. Carletti (2008a) "Mark-to-market accounting and cash-in-the-market pricing," *Journal of Accounting and Economics*, 45: 358–78.

Allen, F. and E. Carletti (2008b) "Should financial institutions mark to market?" *Banque de France Financial Stability Review*, 12: 1–6.

Allen, F. and E. Carletti (2011) "What should central banks do about real estate prices?" *Wharton Financial Institutions Center Working Paper* 11–29.

Allen, F. and D. Gale (1998) "Optimal financial crises," *Journal of Finance*, 53: 1245–84.

Allen, F. and D. Gale (1999) "Innovations in financial services, relationships, and risk sharing," *Management Science*, 45: 1239–53.

Allen, F. and D. Gale (2000) "Financial contagion," *Journal of Political Economy*, 108: 1–33.

Allen, F. and D. Gale (2004) "Financial intermediaries and markets," *Econometrica*, 72: 1023–61.

Allen, F. and D. Gale (2005) "From cash-in-the-market pricing to financial fragility," *Journal of the European Economic Association*, 3: 535–46.

Allen, F. and D. Gale (2007) *Understanding Financial Crisis*, Clarendon Lectures, New York: Oxford University Press.

Allen, F., E. Carletti, and D. Gale (2009) "Interbank market liquidity and central bank intervention," *Journal of Monetary Economics*, 56: 639–52.

Allen, F., E. Carletti, and D. Gale (2011a) "Money, financial stability and efficiency." Unpublished working paper.

Allen, F., E. Carletti, and R. Marquez (2011b) "Credit market competition and capital regulation," *Review of Financial Studies*, 24: 983–1018.

Altunbas, Y., L. Gambacorta, and D. Marques-Ibanez (2010) "Does monetary policy affect bank risk-taking?" *Bank for International Settlements Working Papers* No. 298.

Bagehot, W. (1873) "A general view of Lombard Street." Reprinted in C. Goodhart and G. Illing (eds.) (2002) *Financial Crises, Contagion, and the Lender of Last Resort: A Reader*, New York: Oxford University Press.

Bank of England (2009) *The Role of Macroprudential Policy: A Discussion Paper*, London: Bank of England.

Bernanke, B. and M. Gertler (1989) "Agency costs, net worth, and business fluctuations," *American Economic Review*, 79: 14–31.

Bernanke, B., M. Gertler, and S. Gilchrist (1999) "The financial accelerator in a quantitative business cycle framework," in J. B. Taylor and M. Woodford (eds.) *Handbook of Macroeconomics* (vol. 1: 1341–93), Amsterdam: Elsevier.

Blinder, A. S. (2010) "It's broke, let's fix it: Rethinking financial regulation," *International Journal of Central Banking*, 6: 277–330.

Bolton, P., T. Santos, and J. Scheinkman (2009) "Market and public liquidity," *American Economic Review*, 99: 594–9.

Bolton, P., T. Santos, and J. A. Scheinkman (2011) "Outside and inside liquidity," *Quarterly Journal of Economics*, 126: 259–321.

Borio, C. and H. Zhu (2008) "Capital regulation, risk-taking and monetary policy: A missing link in the transmission mechanism?" *Bank of International Settlements Working Papers* No. 268.

Brunnermeier, M. K. (2001) *Asset Pricing under Asymmetric Information: Bubbles, Crashes, Technical Analysis and Herding*, Oxford: Oxford University Press.

Brunnermeier, M. K. (2008) "Bubbles," in S.N. Durlauf and L. Blume (eds.) *The New Palgrave Dictionary of Economics* (2nd Ed.), New York: Palgrave Macmillan.

Brunnermeier, M. K. (2009) "Deciphering the liquidity and credit crunch 2007–08," *Journal of Economic Perspectives*, 23: 77–100.

Brunnermeier, M. K. and M. Oehmke (2009) "Complexity in financial markets." Unpublished working paper.

Brunnermeier, M. K. and Y. Sannikov (2011) "A macroeconomic model with a financial sector." Unpublished working paper.

Brunnermeier, M. K., A. Crockett, C. Goodhart, A. Persaud, and H. Shin (2009) "The Fundamental Principles of Financial Regulation," 11th Geneva Report on the World Economy, International Center for Monetary and Banking Studies (ICMB) and Centre for Economic Policy Research (CEPR).

Buiter, W. H. (2007) "What did you do in the open market today, Daddy?" Blog entry. Online, available at http://blogs.ft.com/maverecon/2007/12/.

Buiter, W. H. and A. C. Sibert (2007) "The central bank as market maker of last resort." Blog entry. Online, available at http://blogs.ft.com/maverecon/2007/08/the-central-banhtml/.

Cao, J. (2010) "Illiquidity, insolvency, and banking regulation." Unpublished working paper.

Cao, J. and G. Illing (2008) "Liquidity shortages and monetary policy," *CESifo Working Paper* No. 2210. Online, available at SSRN: http://ssrn.com/abstract=1090825.

Cao, J. and G. Illing (2010) "Regulation of systemic liquidity risk," *Financial Markets and Portfolio Management*, 24: 31–48.

Cao, J. and G. Illing (2011) "Endogenous exposure to systemic liquidity risk," *International Journal of Central Banking*, 7: 173–216.

Carlin, B. I. (2009) "Strategic price complexity in retail financial markets," *Journal of Financial Economics*, 91: 278–87.

Carlin, B. I. and G. Manso (2011) "Obfuscation, learning, and the evolution of investor sophistication," *Review of Financial Studies*, 24: 754–85.

Chen, Y. (1999) "Banking panics: The role of the first-come, first-served rule and information externalities," *Journal of Political Economy*, 107: 946–68.

Clement, P. (2010) "The term 'macroprudential': Origins and evolution," *BIS Quarterly Review*, March: 59–67.

Cooper, G. (2008) *Origin of Financial Crises: Central Banks, Credit Bubbles and the Efficient Market Fallacy*, Petersfield, UK: Harriman House Publishing.

d'Aspremont, C., J. J. Gabszewicz, and J. F. Thisse (1979) "On Hotelling's 'stability in competition,'" *Econometrica*, 47: 1145–50.

Dang, T. V., G. Gorton and B. Holmström (2009) "Ignorance and the optimality of debt for the provision of liquidity." Unpublished working paper.

Dasgupta, P. and E. Maskin (1986) "The existence of equilibrium in discontinuous games, I: Theory," *Review of Economic Studies*, 53: 1–26.

Diamond, D. W. and P. H. Dybvig (1983) "Bank runs, deposit insurance, and liquidity," *Journal of Political Economy*, 91: 401–19.

Diamond, D. W. and R. G. Rajan (2000) "A theory of bank capital," *Journal of Finance*, 55: 2431–65.

Diamond, D. W. and R. G. Rajan (2001) "Liquidity risk, liquidity creation, and financial fragility: A theory of banking," *Journal of Political Economy*, 109: 287–327.

Diamond, D. W. and R. G. Rajan (2005) "Liquidity shortage and banking crises," *Journal of Finance*, 60: 615–47.

Diamond, D. W. and R. G. Rajan (2006) "Money in a theory of banking," *American Economic Review*, 96: 30–53.

Drehmann, M. and N. Tarashev (2011) "Systemic importance: Some simple indicators," *BIS Quarterly Review*, March: 25–37.

Duffie, D. (2011) *How Big Banks Fail, and What to Do About It*, Princeton, NJ: Princeton University Press.

Dwyer (2009, November 6) "What is systemic risk, anyway?" Blog entry. Online, available at http://macroblog.typepad.com/macroblog/2009/11/what-is-systemic-risk-anyway.html.

Economist, The (2009, August 6) "In defense of the dismal science."

Economist, The (2010, January 28) "From bail-out to bail-in."

Eisenberg, L. and T. H. Noe (2001) "Systemic risk in financial systems," *Management Science*, 47: 236–49.

Ellison, G. and S. F. Ellison (2009) "Search, obfuscation, and price elasticities on the Internet," *Econometrica*, 77: 427–52.

Farhi, E. and J. Tirole (2011) "Collective moral hazard, maturity mismatch and systemic bailouts," *American Economic Review* (forthcoming).

Flannery, M. (2002) "No pain, no gain? Effecting market discipline via 'reverse convertible debentures.'" Unpublished working paper.

Flannery, M. (2009) "Contingent tools can fill capital gaps," *American Banker*, 174, Issue 117.

Flannery, M. and K. Rangan (2008) "Market forces at work in the banking industry: Evidence from the capital buildup from the 1990s," *Review of Finance*, 12: 391–429.

Freixas, X., B. M. Parigi, and J.-C. Rochet (2000) "Systemic risk, interbank relations, and liquidity provision by the central bank," *Journal of Money, Credit and Banking*, 32: 611–38.

Freixas, X., B. M. Parigi, and J.-C. Rochet (2004) "The lender of last resort: A twenty-first century approach," *Journal of the European Economic Association*, 2: 1085–115.

French, K. R., M. N. Baily, J. Y. Campbell, J. H. Cochrane, D. W. Diamond, D. Duffie, A. K. Kashyap, F. S. Mishkin, R. G. Rajan, D. S. Scharfstein, R. J. Shiller, H. Shin, M. J. Slaughter, J. C. Stein, and R. M. Stulz (2010) *The Squam Lake Report: Fixing the Financial System*, Princeton, NJ: Princeton University Press.

Gale, D. and M. Hellwig (1985) "Incentive-compatible debt contracts I: The one-period problem," *Review of Economic Studies*, 52: 647–64.

Geanakoplos, J. (2003) "Liquidity, default, and crashes: Endogenous contracts in general equilibrium," in Econometric Society Monographs, Eighth World Conference, 2, *Advances in Economics and Econometrics: Theory and Applications* (170–205), New York: Cambridge University Press.

Geanakoplos, J. (2010a) "The leverage cycle," in D. Acemoglu, K. Rogoff, and M. Woodford (eds.) *NBER Macroeconomic Annual 2009* (vol. 24: 1–65), Chicago, IL: University of Chicago Press.

Geanakoplos, J. (2010b) "Solving the present crisis and managing the leverage cycle," *Federal Reserve Bank of New York Economic Policy Review*, August: 101–131.

Gertler, M. and P. Karadi (2011) "A model of unconventional monetary policy," *Journal of Monetary Economics*, 58: 17–34.

Gertler, M. and N. Kiyotaki (2010) "Financial intermediation and credit policy in business cycle analysis," in B. Friedman and M. Woodford (eds.) *Handbook of Monetary Economics* (vol. 3A: 547–599), Amsterdam: Elsevier.

Gertler, M., N. Kiyotaki, and A. Queralto (2011) "Financial crises, bank risk exposure and government financial policy." Unpublished working paper.

Glaeser, E. L., J. Gyourko, and A. Saiz (2008) "Housing supply and housing bubbles," *Journal of Urban Economics*, 64: 198–217.

Goldstein, I. and A. Pauzner (2005) "Demand deposit contracts and the probability of bank runs," *Journal of Finance*, 60: 1293–328.

Goodfriend, M. and R. G. King (1988) "Financial deregulation, monetary policy, and central banking," *Economic Review*, Federal Reserve Bank of Richmond, May, 3–22.

Goodhart, C. and G. Illing (2002) *Financial Crises, Contagion, and the Lender of Last Resort: A Reader*, New York: Oxford University Press.

Gorton, G. (2008) "The panic of 2007," in *Maintaining Stability in a Changing Financial System*, Proceedings of the 2008 Jackson Hole Conference, Federal Reserve Bank of Kansas City, KS.

Gorton, G. B. (2009) "The subprime panic," *European Financial Management*, 15: 10–46.

Gorton, G. B. (2010) *Slapped by the Invisible Hand: The Panic of 2007*, New York: Oxford University Press.

Gorton, G. B. and A. Metrick (2010) "Regulating the shadow banking system," *Brookings Papers on Economic Activity*, Fall, 261–97.

Hart, O. and J. Moore (1994) "A theory of debt based on the inalienability of human capital," *Quarterly Journal of Economics*, 109: 841–79.

Himmelberg, C., C. Mayer, and T. Sinai (2005) "Assessing high house prices: Bubbles, fundamentals and misperceptions," *Journal of Economic Perspectives*, 19: 67–92.

Holmström, B. and J. Tirole (1997) "Financial intermediation, loanable funds, and the real sector," *Quarterly Journal of Economics*, 112: 663–91.

Holmström, B. and J. Tirole (1998) "Private and public supply of liquidity," *Journal of Political Economy*, 106: 1–40.

Huang, X., H. Zhou, and H. Zhu (2009) "A framework for assessing the systemic risk of major financial institutions," *Journal of Banking and Finance*, 33: 2036–49.

Jeanne, O. and A. Korinek (2010) "Excessive volatility in capital flows: A Pigouvian taxation approach," *American Economic Review*, 100: 403–7.

Jeanne, O. and A. Korinek (2011) "Managing credit booms and busts: A Pigouvian taxation approach." Unpublished working paper.

Jorion, P. (2007) *Value at Risk: The New Benchmark for Managing Financial Risk* (3rd Ed.), New York: McGraw-Hill.

Kashyap, A. K., R. G. Rajan, and J. C. Stein (2008) "Rethinking capital regulation," in *Maintaining Stability in a Changing Financial System*, Proceedings of the 2008 Jackson Hole Conference, Federal Reserve Bank of Kansas City, KS.

Kindleberger, C. P. and R. Z. Aliber (2005) *Manias, Panics, and Crashes: A History of Financial Crises* (5th Ed.), New York: John Wiley & Sons.

Korinek, A. (2011) "Systemic risk-taking: Amplification effects, externalities, and regulatory responses." Unpublished working paper.

Krugman, P. (2009) *The Return of Depression Economics and the Crisis of 2008*, New York: W. W. Norton & Company.

Lewis, M. (2010) *The Big Short: Inside the Doomsday Machine*, New York: W. W. Norton & Company.

Manchester, M. (1975) *The Glory and the Dream: A Narrative History of America, 1932–1972*, New York: Little, Brown and Company.

Martin, A., D. R. Skeie, and E.-L. von Thadden (2010) "Repo runs," *Federal Reserve Bank of New York Staff Report* No. 444.

Mas-Colell, A., M. D. Whinston, and J. Green (1995) *Microeconomic Theory*, New York: Oxford University Press.

Matsuyama, K. (2008) "Aggregate implications of credit market imperfections," in D. Acemoglu, K. Rogoff, and M. Woodford (eds.) *NBER Macroeconomics Annual 2007* (1–60). Cambridge: MIT Press.

Minsky, H. P. (1986) *Stabilizing an Unstable Economy*, New Haven, CT: Yale University Press.

Myers, S. (1977) "Determinants of corporate borrowing," *Journal of Financial Economics*, 5: 147–75.

Norden, L. and W. Wagner (2008) "Credit derivatives and loan pricing," *Journal of Banking and Finance*, 32: 2560–9.

Pearson, N. D. (2002) *Risk Budgeting: Portfolio Problem Solving with Value-at-Risk*, New York: John Wiley & Sons.

Posner, R. A. (2009) *A Failure of Capitalism: The Crisis of '08 and the Descent into Depression*, Cambridge, MA: Harvard University Press.

Rajan, R. G. (2010) *Fault Lines: How Hidden Fractures Still Threaten the World Economy*, Princeton, NJ: Princeton University Press.

Raviv, A. (2004) "Bank stability and market discipline: Debt-for-equity swap versus subordinated notes." Unpublished working paper.

Reinhart, C. M. and K. Rogoff (2009) *This Time is Different: Eight Centuries of Financial Folly*, Princeton, NJ: Princeton University Press.

Repullo, R. (2005) "Liquidity, risk-taking, and the lender of last resort," *International Journal of Central Banking*, 1: 47–80.

Repullo, R. and J. Saurina (2011) "The countercyclical capital buffer of Basel III: A critical assessment." Unpublished working paper.

Repullo, R. and J. Suarez (2009) "The procyclical effects of bank capital regulation." Unpublished working paper.

Rochet, J.-C. (2004) "Macroeconomic shocks and banking supervision," *Journal of Financial Stability*, 1: 93–110.

Rochet, J.-C. (2008) *Why Are There So Many Banking Crises? The Politics and Policy of Bank Regulation*, Princeton, NJ: Princeton University Press.

Rochet, J.-C. (2010) "Systemic risk: Changing the regulatory perspective," *International Journal of Central Banking*, 6: 259–76.

Roubini, N. and S. Mihm (2010) *Crisis Economics: A Crash Course in the Future of Finance*, London: Penguin.

Rubinstein, A. (1998) *Modeling Bounded Rationality*, Cambridge, MA: MIT Press.

Saita, F. (2007) *Value at Risk and Bank Capital Management*, Burlington, VT: Academic Press.

Segoviano, M. and C. Goodhart (2009) "Banking stability measures," *IMF Working Paper* 09/4.

Shin, H. (2008) "Risk and liquidity in a system context," *Journal of Financial Intermediation*, 17: 315–29.

Shin, H. (2009) "Reflections on Northern Rock: The bank run that heralded the global financial crisis," *Journal of Economic Perspectives*, 23: 101–19.

Shin, H. (2010a) *Risk and Liquidity*, Clarendon Lectures, New York: Oxford University Press.

Shin, H. (2010b) "Discussion of 'the leverage cycle' by John Geanakopolos," in D. Acemoglu, K. Rogoff, and M. Woodford (eds.) *NBER Macroeconomic Annual 2009* (vol. 24: 1–65), Chicago, IL: University of Chicago Press.

Shin, H. and S. Morris (2008) "Financial regulation in a system context," *Brookings Papers on Economic Activity*, Fall: 229–74.

Shleifer, A. and R. Vishny (1997) "The limits of arbitrage," *Journal of Finance*, 52: 35–55.

Shleifer, A. and R. W. Vishny (2010) "Unstable banking," *Journal of Financial Economics*, 97: 306–18.

Sinn, H.-W. (2010) *Casino Capitalism: How the Financial Crisis Came about and What Needs to Be Done Now*, New York: Oxford University Press.

Stahl, D. (1989) "Oligopolistic pricing with sequential investor search," *American Economic Review*, 79: 700–12.

Stein, J. C. (2011) "Monetary policy as financial-stability regulation," *NBER Working Paper* No. 16883.

Stiglitz, J. (2010) *Freefall: Free Markets and the Sinking of the Global Economy*, London: Allen Lane.

Taleb, N. N. (2004) *Fooled by Randomness: The Hidden Role of Chance in Life and in the Markets*, New York: Random House.

Taleb, N. N. (2007) *The Black Swan: The Impact of the Highly Improbable*, New York: Random House.

Tirole, J. (2009) "Illiquidity and all its friends." Unpublished working paper.

Tirole, J., M. Dewatripont, J.-C. Rochet, and K. Tribe (2010) *Balancing the Banks: Global Lessons from the Financial Crisis*, Princeton, NJ: Princeton University Press.

Topkis, D. M. (1998) *Supermodularity and Complementarity*, Princeton, NJ: Princeton University Press.

Townsend, R. (1979) "Optimal contracts and competitive markets with costly state verification," *Journal of Economic Theory*, 21: 265–93.

Turner, A., A. Haldane, P. Woolley, S. Wadhwani, C. Goodhart, A. Smithers, A. Large, J. Kay, M. Wolf, P. Boone, S. Johnson, and R. Layard (2010) *The Future of Finance: The LSE Report*, London: London School of Economics and Political Science.

Varian, H. (1980) "A model of sales," *American Economic Review*, 70: 651–9.

Wagner, W. (2009) "Efficient asset allocations in the banking sector and financial regulation," *International Journal of Central Banking*, 5: 75–95.

Wagner, W. (2011) "Systemic liquidation risk and the diversity-diversification trade-off," *Journal of Finance*, 66: 1141–75.

Wickens, M. R. (2010) "What's wrong with modern macroeconomics? Why its critics have missed the point," *CESifo Economic Studies*, 56: 536–53.

Wolf, M. (2008) *Fixing Global Finance*, Baltimore, MD: Johns Hopkins University Press.

Index

Page numbers in *italics* denote tables, those in **bold** denote figures.